CW01160465

Developing Social Science and Religion for Liberation and Growth

By

Chris Adam-Bagley, Mahmoud Abubaker and Alice A. A. Sawyerr

Developing Social Science and Religion for Liberation and Growth

By Chris Adam-Bagley, Mahmoud Abubaker and Alice A. A. Sawyerr

This book first published 2023

Ethics International Press Ltd, UK

British Library Cataloguing in Publication Data

A catalogue record for this book is available from the British Library

Copyright © 2023 by Chris Adam-Bagley, Mahmoud Abubaker and Alice A. A. Sawyerr

All rights for this book reserved. No part of this book may be reproduced, stored in a retrieval system, or transmitted, in any form or by any means, electronic, mechanical photocopying, recording or otherwise, without the prior permission of the copyright owner.

Print Book ISBN: 978-1-80441-123-0

eBook ISBN: 978-1-80441-124-7

Acknowledgements

Parts of Chapter 2 have some textual overlap with an article on critical realism by Chris Adam-Bagley, Alice Sawyerr and Mahmoud Abubaker published in *Advances in Applied Sociology*, in 2017. About a half of Chapter 3 draws directly from Chris Adam-Bagley's pamphlet *Islam Today: A Muslim Quaker's View*, published by the Quaker Universalist Group, in 2015. We hold the copyright to these works, Chris Bagley adopted the Muslim name *Adam* after his conversion to Islam in 2010, becoming "Chris Adam-Bagley". In the references below his publications before 2010 have all adopted the changed appellation of "Adam-Bagley".

Dedication

We dedicate this book and its ideas to our children and grandchildren: Michael, Daniel, Abigail, Jessica, Richard, Khalid, Mohammed, Yousef, Zain, Logan, Falan and Devon; to the many hundreds of children who are our nieces and nephews in England, Jamaica, Sierra Leone, Ghana, Gaza, Palestine, Jordan, Canada, Germany and America: and to children, everywhere, past, present and future.

Contents

Introduction and Overview of Chapters ix

Chapter 1
Humanism, Religious and Secular: Charting Childhood and Humanistic Psychology, Chris Adam-Bagley, Alice Sawyerr and Mahmoud Abubaker 1

Chapter 2
Critical Realism and Autoethnography: A Review, Chris Adam-Bagley, Alice Sawyerr and Mahmoud Abubaker 33

Chapter 3
A Social Scientist's Journey from Quaker to Muslim: Developing A Theology for Social Action, Chris Adam-Bagley 71

Chapter 4
Explaining Evil in a World Where Humans are Motivated by a Spirit of Inward Goodness, Chris Adam-Bagley 134

Chapter 5
The Retelling of Our Stories - Abraham Maslow, Religion and Human Transcendence, Chris Adam-Bagley 164

General References and Bibliography 196

Index 232

Introduction and Overview of Chapters

Chapter 1 establishes the intellectual grounding of this book in the discipline and approach of *humanism* (both secular and religious), as the compass for a set of beliefs (derived from different branches of philosophy, social science, and religion) for understanding a humanity which is born 'without sin'. Given the loving care of parents, we grow into adults who seek the companionship and welfare of others, through our social contract with the whole of society.

In describing these goals we are inspired by the research and writing of Gordon Allport, Abraham Maslow, Karl Rogers, Erik Erikson, Rollo May and others, in creating a methodology and focus on humans as unique individuals, with stories to tell which enable us to learn from one another in the crucial tasks of improving society in ways which serve the needs of children, in our doctrine of *Child-Centred Humanism*. Margaret Archer too in her critical realist model of morphogenesis shows how we can develop the sharing of ideas, stories and experiences in ways which may engineer such positive change.

We are impressed by Martin Seligman's adoption of humanist ideals in developing, through classical learning models, the ideals of promoting happiness in all children and adults. The social connexions which result are built into the human psyche, in which positive social relations become functional for civilization's growth. We emphasize the importance of the *Social Contract* as the implicit but crucial way in which democratic societies share values, and respect each other's needs and rights, in the making of the good society. We draw on the philosophical ideas of Descartes, Hobbes, Hume, Rousseau and Green in developing this social democratic model.

The evidence from many studies shows that love and stability in childhood is crucial for adult adjustment, happiness, prosocial behaviour, and the ability to engage creatively and synergistically in 'the social contract', which knits us together in a powerful bond.

Chapter 2 explains the philosophical grounding of *dialectical critical realism* and its guiding principle *Child-Centred Humanism* which is passionately concerned with the unmasking of the alienation which clouds the consciousness of alienated or oppressed families and their children (who in England temporarily contain ethnic and religious minorities, and refugees; but with a solid phalanx of 'poor whites'). As Graham Scambler writes of Margaret Archer's view of Marxian theory: "To introduce the concept of ideology is necessarily to introduce that of false-consciousness." And dialectic critical materialism's reflexive model can in its reflexive, morphogenesis help those with "fractured reflexivities" to grasp "true consciousness", sharing with similarly oppressed people, a fuller realisation of their position.

Everyone, in Thomas Green's and Margaret Archer's models of social action may achieve upward mobility, to the life of the gentleman or gentlewoman. In Matthew Wilkinson's Islamic Critical Realist model, it is the journey on the Straight Path that ensures that the faithful may imitate Prophet Muhammad's peaceful example of social behaviour. For Muslims, the soul given by God resides in each human being, not merely in Muslims. The Muslim's task is to seek out and serve (as do Quakers) the soul of everyone. Again Child-Centred Humanism's model of reciprocal love, and Critical Realism's reflexive morphogenesis seem to converge in this social contract.

In *Chapter 3* Chris Adam-Bagley describes his intellectual, moral and spiritual journey from Judaism, through Anglicanism, into Quakerism and then into Islam, inspired by a pacifist ideology.

Adam-Bagley makes the case for Islam as a peace-making movement, based on the idea that humans are born "without sin". These themes are illustrated by accounts of research with colleagues in Gaza, Bangladesh and Pakistan. But critical conclusions are also reached, arguing that neither Bangladesh nor Pakistan have properly applied Islam in ways which fulfil Qur'anic principles. For Gaza, we reach to the pacifist core of Judaism and Islam in seeking both justice and rapprochement. Thus Adam-Bagley's most recent challenge has been the engagement with Palestinian brothers and sisters, which has significantly modified the way he thinks about himself as an ethnic Jew, and about Israel in general, but has certainly reinforced his pacifist confidence in Islam.

> "God is the Light of the heavens and the earth; the likeness of His Light is a niche wherein is a lamp (the lamp in a glass, the glass as it were a glittering star) kindled from a Blessed Tree, an olive that is neither of the East nor of the West, whose oil well-nigh would shine, even if no fire touched it; Light upon Light." (The Qur'an, Surah 24 Light, verse 35).

The image and metaphor of this *light* is shared by both Muslims and Quakers. Adam-Bagley's goal, as a religiously-motivated social scientist has been to understand and assist oppressed populations, including abused children, exploited girls and women, victims of racism and Islamophobia – and to understand and perhaps counter the negative social forces which initiate such oppressions. As a value-based social scientist he follows ethical and moral principles derived from (and shared by) Islam, Judaism and Christianity.

A value-based approach to humanism and social science has led the authors of this book to receive with enthusiasm new directions in the epistemology of social science, pioneered by Roy Bhaskar. This value-based ontology has been used fruitfully by Muslim scholars, by Catholic educationists and social scientists, and by a Quaker child welfare advocate. Critical realism has also enabled us to begin to understand the complex layers of value-based social structure embedded in the Arabic society of Gaza, as this nation endures chronic siege and warfare.

Chapter 4 addresses the paradox of explaining the nature and prevalence of evil, which seems to contradict the idea that human beings are born without original sin, seeking for goodness in themselves, their families, and in society. Writing about evil is both easy and hard. It's everywhere, and its multiple forms in individuals, groups and occasionally in nations is easy to describe but hard to understand.

We offer redemption and change in society's evils through the humanist methodology of the "telling of stories". This is illustrated by the accounts of death camp survivors (Viktor Frankel, Eugene Heimler, Elie Wiesel and others) who create optimist movements of narrating human goodness and creativity, themes carried forward by Art Frank, Rollo May and Ken Plummer.

Another theme in this chapter is that of eliciting goodness in humans through the nurture of children, treating these precious beings with love and tenderness, within safe environments, with an education which enables them to cope with life's challenge. We must also nurture them with systematic structures, offering affection, guidance and praise. We need also to emphasise a moral education which them to become good citizens, able to take part in a social contract which avers: *I am, because you are; I serve you, my fellow citizen, with respect and esteem, and I know that you will value me likewise.*

Chapter 5 turns to the spiritual power of humanism, religious and secular, impressed and inspired by scholars writing about a "post-holocaust" world in which both spiritual excellence and social harmony seem attainable. If we treat our children well, there is hope for all of humankind. Through stories, and humanist case studies of adversity, struggle, triumph and transcendence, we share values and critical rationality, a form of morphogenesis, the remaking of ourselves and the world around us.

Evil still lurks in the telling of false and malicious stories that beget hatred and violence. It is therefore essential that *our* stories must focus on "the moral beauty of others". The stories of holocaust victims and survivors are the most moving. As Vincent de Paul has taught us, the experience of extreme poverty, slavery and genocide does not defeat us, nor eliminate our goodness of spirit.

"Religious experience" enervates humankind, giving us awe and transcendence. Being religious brings many unexpected benefits in physical and emotional health. Evidence shows that the sharing of religious bonds and rituals helps rather than hinders the survival of humankind, in constructive ways. We honour the great scholar Abraham Maslow, ostensibly a secular Jew, but whose psychology nevertheless has much spiritual healing power for those of all religions, and for secular humanists. This humanism, of treasuring the worth in each other regardless of ethnic or religious origin, is the only way forward for the social contract of a civilized world.

Abraham Maslow's model of development has much overlap with and support from the developmental models offered by other humanist psychologists. This synergy which is central to these models engenders a universal social contract, in which the two of us relating creates a third force, a metaphysical goodness in which goodwill begets goodwill, with a growing synergy. Martin Seligman's positive psychology movement is an excellent example of how humanist psychology increasingly informs mainstream psychological research and practice.

We experience with delight Scott Barry Kaufman's taking forward Maslow's models of fulfilment through self-other relationship. Maslow tossed his ideas forward in 1968 like a 'Hail Mary' throw. Kaufman caught the ideas and has enlarged them in forging towards the touch-down. Abraham Maslow began his humanist journey with the Blackfoot people, and the synergy and transcendence of this people inspired him (and us) in careers in nursing, social work, clinical psychology, and management.

Evil lurks everywhere, but so does goodness which shines through and transcends in all human institutions and religions, including secular humanism. What matters on the final day is that God believes in you, not that you believe in God. But loving and listening to the divine is an excellent way to go forward.

Chapter 1

Humanism, Religious and Secular: Charting Childhood and Humanistic Psychology

Chris Adam-Bagley, Alice Sawyerr and Mahmoud Abubaker

> The final and unavoidable conclusion is that education-like, all our social institutions must be concerned with final values, and this in turn is just about the same as speaking of what have been called 'spiritual values' or 'higher values'. These are principles of choice which help us to answer the age-old 'spiritual' (philosophical? humanistic? ethical?) questions: What is the good life? What is the good man? The good woman? What is best for children? What is justice? Truth? Virtue? What is my relation to nature, to death, to ageing, to pain, to illness? How can I live a zestful, enjoyable, meaningful life? What is my responsibility to my brothers? Who are my brothers? What shall I be loyal to? What must I be ready to die for?
>
> Abraham Maslow (2021).
> *Religions, Values and Peak Experiences*, p. 64.

What is humanism?

We follow, with joy and inspiration, the questions posed by Abraham Maslow who in his short life laid down further principles of humanism (religious and secular) which relate to and inspire management studies and ethical economic enterprise, as well as providing the groundwork for a social psychology of human growth. Maslow was Jewish, a secular humanist, and also an inspirational writer for modern humanism (Maslow et al., 1937 to 2022; Kaufman, 2020).

Today, *Humanism* is often claimed as the worldview of secularists (particularly non-theists) who wish to position themselves in an ethical relationship with a world which they do not see as divinely inspired or created. These people (for example, some of our children) lead excellent lives, committed to family and community in a deeply moral way. This is important. You do not need to have any religious belief in order to be a good citizen, and a morally committed and fulfilled person. God, like the dutiful parent, still loves you!

Critical humanism for secular humanists such as Ken Plummer (2020)

> " ... engages with (and tells the stories of) the perpetual narrative reconstructions and conflicts over what it means to be human. Ultimately it does this with the goal of building on these contested understandings to find pathways into better futures and worlds. Critical humanism is an emerging project to remake sense of all this. Even as it will raise many problems, it enables us to ask questions about what kind of human world we want to live in, what kind of person we want to be in that world, and how it needs to be transformed." (Plummer, 2020, p. 7)

There is often a peacefulness and a calm in the lives of these secular humanists, and we (two Muslims and a Christian) admire them. Humanism is the philosophy of social action adopted by the radical Christian political scientist, Palestinian Edward Said, who averred that: "…humanism is the only – I would go so far as saying the final – resistance we have against the inhuman practices and injustices that disfigure human history…". (Said, 2016, p. 417)

For Jerome Bruner (1990), humanism was the starting point for a leap forward from the mechanistic discipline that psychology had become, trying too hard to imitate the methods of natural science, and missing "the whole picture", the very humanity of psychology's human subjects. He addressed "… the failure of the cognitive revolution to unravel the mysteries of the workings of the human mind, as the creator of meanings", as the beginning point for his book *Acts of Meaning*. Bruner argues that psychology's new, human face must become a cultural psychology, absorbing folk cultures and "the autobiography of the self."

We elaborate some of these themes in this book, drawing on Abraham Maslow's experience of the Blackfoot Nation's psychology in his accounts of synergy and self-actualization; and the telling and recording of stories to reframe our human(ist) identities, advocated with elegant force by Ken Plummer (2000).

Another leading advocate of humanism whom we commend as a scholar and political advocate, the valuing of all people as being of equal worth (and therefore "equally grievable") is the Jewish feminist writer Judith Butler (2020), who advocates pacifism through seeing all human beings as equally valuable – and has applied her generous intellect and profound scholarship to advocating for Palestinian women's pacifist struggle against occupying forces.

Humanism, religious and secular, is the intellectual, moral and emotional thread which allows us to weave together a cross-disciplinary understanding of how seemingly diverse religious and ethnic groups may knit together a cloak which encompasses a *social contract*, in which we love our neighbours as ourselves, doing good by small acts of humility and kindness which are at the core of all world religions. This is the message, for example, of the Muslim scholar Faysal Maulawi (2012) on *The Muslim as a European Citizen*.

When people ask one of us (CAB) why he believes in God, he may reply: "It's not that I believe in God: rather, I know that God believes in me." From his earliest Christian childhood (and later, as a Muslim) CAB had the powerful intuition that an immanent God watches, with loving understanding, his every move. Muslims believe that late in the second trimester of the foetus, Angel Gibreel breathes a spirit of light into *every* human. Thus if one becomes a Muslim one becomes a "revert", not a "convert", in beginning a journey of self-discovery. Secular humanists also have the light of a divine spirit within them, and it is this innate goodness (of which they may not be aware) which is the quiet engine of being for all humanists, secular and religious.

'Innate goodness': the crucial link between positive humanism, religious humanism, and positive social science

The chapters in this book have an underlying thread: describing, intuiting and understanding the potential for goodness (based on innate personal and social drives) of human beings, and how this goodness may be evoked in programmes of research and social action (such as Critical Realism, discussed below).

The journeys we describe are those of ourselves in understanding the journeys of inspiring scholars, from Descartes to Maslow and Bhaskar, as well as the journeys of intellectual movements such as humanist psychology into positive psychology; and of critical realism, into dialectical critical realism and morphogenesis (Archer, 2017). We continually try to make links between these intellectual, social and moral journeys both in parallel, and in their intellectual contact and buffering. We are concerned too with the ways in which children can be nurtured and educated so that their innate tendencies towards 'goodness' may flourish. We acknowledge too that this growth may be corrupted or negated by adult forces of greed and hatred.

Much of Christian theology focuses on how humans may be redeemed from the sin of Adam. Wrapped up in this ideology is blame attributed to the "murderers" of God's son, the Jews who (allegedly) shouted in favour of the murder of Jesus – perhaps meaning according to Matthew's Gospel, that Jews should bear responsibility for this murder "forever", an ideology which justified even modern holocausts and pogroms (Sandmel, 1978) – a false theology carefully deconstructed by Wilson (2022).

A minority of Christians (e.g. Quakers) are not motivated to seek an extirpation of the sin of "Old Adam" and Eve's surrender to the will of Satan which caused the subsequent suffering of humankind – a sin that could only be redeemed by the "New Adam", Jesus himself. An alternative Christian view is that the incarnation has involved the unfolding of God's loving kindness (and its manifestation in humans) throughout history – a view expressed by some Catholics such as Duns Scotus and Teilhard de Chardin, and a number of Protestants, who advocate peace-making and pacifism in human conflict, as a way of energising the innate goodness of humans.

Muslims in particular have a different view of Adam, whose initial sin of gaining knowledge was readily forgiven, the penitent Adam and Hawwa being rewarded as stewards of a green earth. This, for us, is the crucial difference between Islam and Christianity: in Islam a loving and merciful God is ever-ready to forgive any wrong-doers. In Islam there is no 'original sin'.

Positive, non-religious humanism believes in reform rather than in the punishment of wrong-doers; *positive religious humanism* (e.g., that inherent in Islam, Quakerism and some other Christian groups) has a similar approach. And both groups frequently have similarities in their approaches to social action, social reform, and social science methodologies. That is the theme of this book.

Humanism's history: Our personal review

René Descartes

Our first figure in modern humanism is the polymath scholar and former Jesuit, René Descartes. Descartes is dismissed by some scholars as the author of a "mistake", that of Cartesian Dualism in which the mind is conceptualized as separate from, and in command of the body. We do not see this as a problem. Of course, "I" am separate from, and not determined by my physicality: this separation is the basis of freedom of choice, or free will.

Descartes was a mathematician (founder of modern algebra), and also a humanist educator whose focus on individual learning and a personalised curriculum for each pupil, is still the foundation of European educational systems: we may paraphrase Descartes "You think, therefore you are free, a self-directing, moral individual." (Gibson, 2016). Freedom is a central theme in Descartes's philosophy, where it is linked to the idea of the infinite: "It is through the freedom of the will, experienced as unlimited, that the human understands itself to bear the 'image and likeness' of the infinite God." (Xyst, 2016, p. 11) Having the freedom to make choices for good or ill, is according to Descartes a sign of God in human nature, and human beings can be praised or blamed according to their use of this power of choice. (Berman, 2004).

There is an interesting link between the Islamic philosopher Abu Hamla al-Ghazali and René Descartes, established by Catherine Wilson in her *History of Islamic Philosophy* (1996). Descartes knew al-Ghazali's work on 'spiritual dualism', in which the soul is separate from the body: it is 'the mind' or soul which is the driver of the body's actions, the engine of free will (Zamir, 2010). Parvizian (2020) in comparing the concordance between the models of rationality offered by al-Ghazali and Descartes argues that there is a striking concordance between the approaches of these two philosophers: but al-Ghazali uses "divine light" as the metaphysical driver of his logic, while Descartes uses the "natural light" of reason. Between religions, there is a shimmering light of concordance in understanding the world.

In terms of modern sociology (Giddens, 1992) offers the view that: "A person's identity is not to be found in behaviour ... but in the capacity to keep a narrative of life going ... Taking charge of one's life involves risk, because it means confronting a diversity of open possibilities." (p. 78) In this he echoes Jackson (1984) on "elaborating the self through personal stories." This idea of "the narrative self" we develop in Chapters 4 and 5. Creating your own story as a willful, forward-moving action in "being your own hero", is the essence of David Robson's (2022) idea of personal, self-willed emancipation when faced with a variety of choices.

Carl Rogers and Abraham Maslow: Founders of modern humanistic psychology

Mark Kelland's excellent textbook (building on Perrin's 2013 account of positive psychology addressing racism), on *Personality Theory: A Multicultural Perspective* (2017) offers a valuable perspective on these two key scholars:

> Carl Rogers is the psychologist many people associate first with humanistic psychology, but he did not establish the field in the way that Freud established psychoanalysis ... Rogers felt a need to develop a new theoretical perspective that fitted with his clinical observations and personal beliefs. Thus, he was proposing a humanistic approach to psychology and, more specifically, psychotherapy before Maslow. It was Maslow, however, who used the term humanistic psychology as a direct contrast to behaviorism and psychoanalysis ... and it was Maslow who ... led to the creation of the American Association for Humanistic Psychology. Rogers was included in that group, but so were Erich Fromm and Karen Horney, both of whom had distinctly humanistic elements in their own theories, elements that shared a common connection to Alfred Adler's Individual Psychology. In addition, the spiritual aspects of humanistic psychology, such as peak experiences and transcendence, have roots in the work of Carl Jung and William James ..." (Kelly, 2017, p. 5)

Alfred Adler (on successful engagement with relationships in the world as a social individual: Carl Jung on the spiritual depth and potential of humans; and Sigmund Freud, on individual struggles to find ego-balance) all have some validity in mapping the ways in which humans strive to succeed in the world, and provide intellectual guidance and challenge for the newly developing discipline of humanist psychology (Adler, 1940; Jung, 1958; Kelly, 2017; Obuchowski, 1988; Schott & Maslow, 1992; Ewen, 2014; Sedikides & Brewer, 2015).

Rollo May

We add to the cadre of humanist psychologists and social philosophers Rollo May (2007 & 2015), with a perspective on humanistic psychology in his book *Love and Will*:

> "Will without love becomes manipulation ... I feel again the everlasting going and coming, the eternal return. The growing and maturing of dying and growing again. And I know that human beings are part of this eternal going and returning, part of its sadness as well its song." (May, 2007, p. 1).

This *Will* is both the ability and the ambition to wish for a better life for oneself and others. This idea links too with Matthew Ridley's "rational optimism", for all human transactions. Thus on economic exchanges Ridley observes that: "We only trade productively when we trust one another." (Ridley, 2010, p. 4). This trust and a spirit of openness and honesty is exemplified, for example, in the success of Quaker business enterprises.

"Free will" and the natural choosing of the pathways wrong or right, turning, making amends, loving and growing as May puts it, is at the heart of every form of interaction between adults, and between adults and children: our freedom to love one another means that *I* acknowledge *your* spiritual essence, and this act of interchange is mutual. It is, in the Catholic sociologist Margaret Archer's (2017) analysis, *morphogenetic*, always leading to something new, each light created by human interchange creating a new flux in the process of social change.

This is part of what the pioneer of humanist psychology, Gordon Allport and colleagues (1954 to 1978) described as *becoming*, transcending the mundane account of personhood offered by behaviourist psychology (DeCarvalho, 1989 to 1992). Thus "The humanist is concerned with the fullest growth of the individual on areas of love, fulfilment, self-worth, and autonomy." (Allport, 1954, p. 6). Allport's emphasis on autonomous selfhood as the basis for loving, growing, and being an excellent citizen was grounded in his Christian theology of selfhood (Allport, 1978). And William James, another pioneer of the social psychology of religious belief, remains a stalwart intellectual guide for humanistic psychology (Taylor, 2010).

Rollo May's essay of 2015, in taking forward the humanist concepts of Maslow, Rogers and others, offers an elegant analysis of the influence of humanism on personality theory: "Humanist personality theory offers the realization of the human spirit in intentionality, care, love, will and ultimately in 'stories' (the narratives we live our life by)." (p.20) This is similar to the approach to humanist psychology charted by Jerome Bruner (1995): "There are two forms of thinking which inform 'the science of psychology': the first is based on classification, categorization, manipulation and measurement. The alternative approach to psychology is based on the 'narrative organization' of the world in storied form." (p.162).

To this opinion we add Kenneth Gergen (2016) who lauds the approach of humanist psychology in his essay "towards a visionary psychology": we should tell our stories to others not as pessimist ruminations about the past, but as stories not only retelling our past, but also about what the future for ourselves and others might be. In this remaking of the future through optimism "humanistic psychology should be at the core of interdisciplinary research." Rollo May's use of life-stories is also used with effect by Dan McAdams (2001 & 2011) in research on "narrative identity". We add to this approach Andrew Bland's (2019) humanistic model of creating stories based on hero figures. An excellent example of this is the retelling of part of Homer's *Odyssey* by the feminist writer Madelene Miller in *Circe* (2019).

Child-Centred Humanism

We add to our catalogue of humanists both Thomas Hobbes and David Hume, whose common-sense reasoning liberates humans from "original sin", and also establishes ways in which freedom of the will (being 'determined' by the matrix of choices which previous interactions have crafted) may be a central issue in social science research, in ways which are compatible with Islam's idea of freedom of choice. As Hobbes said, pragmatically it is not "the will" that is free: the issue rather, is whether human beings are free to act. The issue is one of human liberty, not the metaphysical clutter of clerical (non-Cartesian) notions of 'free will' (Seligman, 2012).

Hobbes is for us an important philosopher because of his common sense "under-labouring" which is like the cobbler sticking to his last, crucial in the application of critical realism, outlined in detail in the next chapter. This *under-labouring* involves evaluating every human action and institution to the extent that these meet the ethical goals of our chosen research model (Wilkinson, 2015a). The grounded value which we choose is that of *Child-Centred Humanism* (CCH), in serving the basic needs and rights of children. *Children* first is the principle that serves and guides our approach to both secular and religious humanism.

This idea of CCH grew out of Adam-Bagley's (1973) review of literature on legal decisions surrounding childcare and adoption, in which it became clear that the higher courts in Britain were increasingly likely to put the child's interests first, when the rights (or demands) of adults for possession and control of the child conflicted with what judges thought were the child's best needs and interests. Adam-Bagley translated this idea of "children first" into a more general philosophy of child welfare and child care (e.g. Adam-Bagley, Young & Scully, 1993; Adam-Bagley, 1997), termed "total child welfare" meaning that all human institutions and actions should be designed and operated on the principle of "children first".

Inspirational here was Chris Adam-Bagley's mentor Colin Ward, and Ward's 1990 book of joyful anarchy on *The Child in the City*, which showed how children adapted to, and then took over, city spaces. Adam-Bagley expressed outrage at the violation of children's space and movement, involving (in critical realist terms) an "absent" army of victims, by the power given to an adult-centred, materialist world in which the motor vehicle and its right to move speedily through children's spaces, had primacy. Adam-Bagley showed that in Canadian and in British cities (1992 & 1993) that many thousands of children were killed or severely injured each year by these steel assassins as the children ran, played, or crossed roads to reach play spaces or schools, or cycled on city streets. Moreover, it was children of the economically poor who were most likely to be killed in this way, since they perforce lived in areas most cut through by traffic.

In introducing the idea of child-centred humanism in the understanding and treatment of children who had been victims of sexual abuse (Adam-Bagley, 1997), we quoted the American poet, Walt Whitman. We reproduce that quote here, since it sums up both religious and secular humanist ideas - we are, like Whitman: *A novice beginning yet experient of myriads of seasons; Of every hue and caste am I, of every rank and religion; A farmer, mechanic, artist, gentleman, sailor, quaker; Prisoner, fancy-man, rowdy, lawyer, physician, priest.* (Walt Whitman, *Song of Myself*, lines 346-349).

Carl Rogers

Child-Centred Humanism (CCH) has strong psychological roots in Carl Rogers' humanist psychology, the "third way" (the middle ground of integration between Skinner's behaviourism, and Freud's psychodynamics), work which is elaborated, explored and applied by Gordon Allport, Erik Erikson and other 'fathers' of humanistic psychology (DeCarvalho, 1989 to 1992). From Rogers (1951 to 1995) and his school CCH draws pedagogic ideals of knowing each *individual* child in a group, and (following Descartes) caring deeply about his or her needs, strengths and aspirations.

Abraham Maslow's humanistic idea of positive psychology (which we elaborate in a later chapter) fits well within this CCH philosophy of serving the developing needs of the child, adolescent and adult for nurturing, physical care, safety, love, esteem, and stimulation, to reach the fullest fulfilment for both the child and the adult. This *Psychology of Being* (1968) is embedded in religious ideals and values which enables the individual through positive supports in childhood and adulthood, to achieve "peak experiences" of actualization and self-transcendence (Maslow, 2021).

CCH has a *theological underpinning*, assuming (with Quakers and Muslims) that all children are born, not sinful, but are joyfully seeking from birth with their inmost spirit a search that must inevitably flower as the spirit of playfulness, love and joy which exists in all children, as they "play cheerfully in the world" (to paraphrase George Fox). CCH treats each child as a unique human being, with a special combination of needs, abilities, strengths, and aspirations. This the parent, the teacher and the counsellor need to understand, in the

Thomas-Chess account of the uniqueness of child in the developmental matrix – and the principle that adult actions and interactions regarding the child must be modelled on the "goodness of fit" between the unique combination of each child's biological, personal and social gifts, and the adult nurturing of those gifts (Chess & Thomas, 1976 & 2013; Adam-Bagley & Mallick, 2000). Humanist psychology has identified ways in which we can enable "the authentic happiness" of children to develop (Wellik & Hoover, 2004).

Children's rights

Children's rights are central in the Child-Centred Humanism (CCH) model (CRAE, 2007). For children there are three kinds of rights: *transcendental or absolute welfare rights* (e.g. the right to have basic needs for nutrition, safety and love to be fulfilled); *contractual* (e.g. those mutual rights and obligations as the child grows older, and becomes of age); and *social* (e.g. the developing citizen's right to freedom, and their obligation to respect the freedom of others, in the social contract on which society is crucially founded.)

Children have a special set of rights, and for further definition of these we turn to the developmental psychology of Abraham Maslow (1987). Maslow's pyramidal diagram of human needs is well-known, and we revise and restate it in Chapter 5: at its base are the child's physiological needs for good prenatal care, safe birthing, food, water, warmth, safety and security in the first three years of life. In the CCH model the child has an *absolute right* to have those needs met by surrounding adults. As the child grows older, she or he is socialized and educated, within a growing body of reciprocal relationships. "I help you" is implicit in the relationship in which "you help me."

These reciprocal relationships grow into a set of interactions which make up *the universal social contract*. Society has a duty to enable young people to maximise their talents, and to esteem themselves (and others) psychologically. Near the apex of Maslow's developmental pyramid is *self-actualization*, which involves making the most of the talents and the psychological, social and material wealth which society has given us, for the benefit of our own spiritual growth, in ways which maximise the welfare of our fellow citizens: and of course, the welfare of the most precious citizens, who are our children.

Even beyond this is the idea of *self-transcendence*, in which individuals achieve their final, spiritual goals through successful interactions. The parallel with Roy Bhaskar's stage of final fulfilment of self-other relationships in *ubuntu*, is striking: in this principle (discussed in detail in the next chapter): *We are no longer ... subjects opposed to an object world, which includes other subjects. Rather we approach the thought embodied in some southern African languages by the notion of 'ubuntu' which means roughly 'I am because you are'.* (Bhaskar, 2015, p.211). Now self-transcendence becomes cultural self-transcendence (Wong, 2016). D'Souza & Gurin (2016) characterise Maslow's psychological thinking as " ... embodying humanist ideals and philosophy ... Maslow's theory of self-actualization is synonymous with seminal psychological, philosophical, and religious theories that support the noble human transition from self-indulgence to selflessness and altruism." (p. 210).

In defence of Descartes, we offer the idea that the "loving ego" can only achieve transcendence through first loving oneself, and then loving others. The final destination is Maslow's transcendent self. As another teacher put it: "Love your neighbour as yourself."

Abraham Maslow

The ethical thrust of humanism in modern psychological thought is well illustrated in this quotation from Abraham Maslow (1971) on a pinnacle of human development, that of self-actualization, a theme we expand on in the final chapter:

> A[n] assumption of self-actualization theory is that it very strongly requires a pluralism of individual differences .... Such a true acceptance of individual differences has several key implications that should be stated briefly ... it means that we try to make a rose into a good rose, rather than seek to change roses into lilies. It implies a kind of Taoism, an acceptance of what people really are; it necessitates a pleasure in the self-actualization of a person who may be quite different from yourself. It even implies an ultimate respect and acknowledgment of the sacredness and uniqueness of each kind of person. In short, humanistic psychology involves an acceptance of people as they are at their intrinsic core and regards their therapists as simply Taoist helpers for them. We strive to enable to become healthy and effective in their own style. (Maslow, 1971, p. 100)

Maslow has also made important contributions to developmental psychology, making the humanist case for child-centred education and emotional support which parallels the work of Carl Rogers (Bland & DeRobartis, 2021). In the humanist tradition, cognitive achievements are not enough for the child: creativity and quality of relationships are crucial too (Sternberg, 2003; Seligman et al., 2009). For humanists too, the educational study of science and human nature, in school and college, is "awe-some" (Valdeslo et al., 2017).

The Social Contract

For us, the idea of humanist society, describing a community with shared values within a mutually supportive social structure must draw on John Locke, and his influence on Rousseau's development of the idea of the social contract (Rousseau, 1979). In this model every person (man and woman alike) is truly free because they have surrendered part of that freedom to every other citizen, by mutual consent: you have a right, and I have a mutual obligation to fulfil that right This mutual exchange of liberty and obligation is the essence of humanism, both religious and secular. What remains then is to define who is human, and what are the best social systems and cultures in which this network of rights and duties may develop most fruitfully. The essence of this liberal ideal is that these principles apply to *all* humans (regardless of say, age, ethnicity, gender or sexual orientation), and to *all* human societies.

The social economist Ove Jakobsen (2017) draws on Maslow's writing on synergy, in developing an idea of the social contract which marks social health and economic well-being in the wider society: "The society with high synergy is one in which virtue pays." Doing good and being good, in Jakobsen's thesis is rewarded by reciprocal goodness from one's neighbour, and a kind of "loving your neighbour as yourself".

Thomas Hill Green, 1836 to 1882

Thomas Green was a remarkable thinker, a religious humanist who in his brief life laid (or under-laboured) the intellectual and moral ground for the development of the British welfare state by Beveridge and his followers (Beveridge, 1968; Greengarten, 1981). Green argued that the twin goals of human activity should be to maximise the citizen's welfare and to maximise that citizen's freedom. Green argued that being economically poor, being poorly educated, enduring degraded housing, physical environments and working conditions, undermined the citizen's freedom, including that citizen's ability to contribute interactively in any kind of metaphysical social contract, to the welfare of others (Wempe, 2004; Porter, 2011). Green stated: "An interest in the common good is the ground of political society, in the sense that without it no body of people would recognise any authority as having a claim on their common obedience." (Green, 1986, 45-46).

Green's ethical socialism had a metaphysical ground, which he took from Hegel's *Propaedeutik*: that in self-reflection the individual citizen *recreates himself or herself* in daily reflection in acknowledging their duty (maximising concern for others, and the freedom in oneself). In this practice the citizen elicits such actions in fellow citizens, in a dialectical system of interchange with oneself and with one's compatriots seeking as Quakers would say, that of the divine light in everyone. In elaborating this ideal Green was a committed religious socialist - Boucher & Vincent, 2006.

It should be noted that Green took on board Hegel's "naïve idealism", which is criticised and reformulated by Roy Bhaskar (2008) in his marriage of critical realism and the dialectical method (Norrie, 2010). But it should also be said that for all its challenging complexity, Roy Bhaskar's *The Philosophy of Metareality: Creativity, Love and Freedom* (2012a) also has much to commend itself to Child-Centred Humanism (CCH). We are also glad to sign up T.H. Green as a patron of CCH, since his heir, the British welfare state, is a crucially important element in fostering "total child welfare" (just as dismantling the welfare state is an attack on children and their welfare).

In Green's personal self-development in supporting a benevolent social contract (Leland, 2011; Brooks, 2014), there is an interesting parallel in Margaret Archer's (2003) idea of *morphogenesis*, part of the critical realist model. Indeed, Green's model of metaphysical introspection and recreation of the self-other bond of mutual generosity in daily thought and interaction, seems to us to fit well with Archer's idea of a morphogenesis - social structure grounded in a process of continuous reflexivity in which social actors understand themselves, in entering dialogue with others in "unmasking alienation".

Margaret Scotford Archer

Archer's ideas (Archer, 1995 to 2017) on reflexivity fit well within the Child-Centred Humanism (CCH) model outlined here, and also with the ideas of the loving interchange between human beings advocated by Carl Rogers (1995). The critical realism that Archer proposes is a revolutionary model (following Bhaskar, 2008) of how humans conduct themselves in everyday life, achieving high levels of "ethical autonomy" in which one appraises oneself in relation to other agents in the wider social system. This reflexive self-other system is a "morphogenetic" one of continuous change, based on social dialogue. Everyone, in this reflexive process, engages in "internal conversations" which are shared with the reflexivity of others who are also reflecting on and communicating their own internal conversations about novel situations. Each day these collaborating individuals in their networks of support and friendship, both negotiate, and create the matrix of change (Power 1, *liberation* versus Power 2, *oppression*, in Bhaskar's model).

But of course evil remains in the world, including existing power systems of rich over poor, and the subsystems of controlling or ignoring children remain too (Sawyerr & Adam-Bagley, 2017; Adam-Bagley, 2022), Archer's emphasis on liberation and 'upward mobility' through an increasing self-consciousness in all of our actions is clearly an optimistic one. One is struck by similarities between Thomas Green's Hegelian dialectic in recreating selfhood on a daily basis (in Green's case, through daily prayer and contemplation), and Margaret Archer's perpetual reflexivity in finding ethical pathways for oneself in relation to one's fellow citizens with the Muslim's daily dialogue with the divine, through the five daily prayers. For both Green (an Oxford don) and Archer (advisor to The Pope on women's issues), the goals seem to be freedom, choice, and autonomy in reaching goals of social justice.[1] Likewise, Muslims review their actions each day, asking Allah for further spiritual guidance which accords with the Qur'anic interpretation (the Sunnah) of Prophet Muhammad.

Maslow, Kelly and Rogers

Abraham Maslow, George Kelly and Carl Rogers have been categorized as "phenomenological personality theorists" (Chamorro-Premuzi & Furnham, 2014) who are ideologically grounded in notions of personal freedom and personal development (the essence of Child-Centred Humanism). Carl Rogers' humanistic psychology which focuses on individual uniqueness and the possibilities for "harmonic growth" - that is, achieving fulfilment through meeting ethical goals involving other people - is important in CCH *provided that* self-development is intimately linked to social development, in that it serves the community. Rogers teaches the psychology of human development not by statistical materials, but by a series of individual case studies of adults reflecting on how they have experienced challenge in childhood and young adulthood (Rogers, 1995).

We learn, says Rogers "to be free" firstly through our parents' care and the kindliness of our teachers - the reciprocal rewards that being a good (child/adolescent/adult) citizen brings. "Trust" and "empathy" are the markers of the progress of the adult. "Being free" has to be learned, through self-discipline. It is a reflexive process, in which learning to love ourselves, we love others: we love "our" child, we love children, we love "your" child.

---

[1] Wilkinson (2015) uses an Islamic model of critical realism in a similar way: the five daily prayers and reflection on The Qur'an and Sunnah (life and teaching of the Prophet Muhammad) are models by which human reflection can be liberating, enabling the ideal society created by the Prophet Adam, to roll out across the earth.

In this reflexive social contract we seek the equality of all citizens (Kirschenbaum, 1990; Rogers, 1995). In the Rogerian model of social exchange each person "opens the spirit" to others in a trusting and creative manner, absorbing the goodness and goodwill of the other person. In this process the individual acts freely (including making freely willed choices, and in doing this, uses self-discipline or 'discernment' as Quakers would say). 'Free will' in the Critical Realistic dialectical model which we are applying here, is not merely an abstract decision or choice: it is based on dialogue, communication and questioning, making sense of oneself in relation to one's past, one's current interactions, and fresh information on the meaning and effect of one's potential choices. Alderson (2013) illustrates this beautifully in her accounts of children making choices concerning life-changing surgery for conditions such as scoliosis.

Five levels of "The Social Contract" involving reciprocal obligations and social relationships

We try and synthesize the concepts of contrasted scholars (humanist psychologists, critical realists, political scientists) in the Table below, which offers five levels of the Social Contract between citizens, and between government and citizens. In the highest orders of society, leaders and people have mutual respect in a social contract which leads to the development of social government for the welfare of all citizens. At the lowest level are authoritarian and corrupt cultures, in which the social contract between government and citizens is often debased and distorted.

This five-level model is one grounded in the ideologies of democratic socialism (Olssen & Mace, 2021). For humanists and positive psychologists, the development and strengthening of the mutuality of good will which binds together citizens in a 'good' society, is both possible and desirable.

Character & Source of Proposition	Characteristics of The Social Contract
Self-Actualizing Synergy Maslow's (1943) *Eu-Psychia* (the society of good minds); Archer's (2015 & 2017) *Morphogenesis* (successful social exchanges for achieving political & economic change)	All in this social organisation are moving towards self-actualizing & care for each other in a process of *synergy* (gladly giving support and praise, to others; receiving this support & praise with joyful humility.)
Reciprocal Honour Maslow (2022); Archer (2000); Bhaskar (2008)	We mutually address the need for self-esteem, pride in ourselves & our work, & feelings of personal honour. There are social forces which work against the achievement of this ideal
Bureaucratic & Legal Social Contract Tawney (1964); Beveridge (Timmins, 2017); T. H. Green (Muirhead, 1908; Boucher & Vincent, 2006)	State ordered government, police & judicial systems socialise us in respect for law, accepting the reciprocal rights & freedoms of all citizens. Welfare state ensures that basic needs (for health, security & education) are met, so that "envy" does not undermine social contracts
Alienated or Extrinsic Reciprocity Weber (Kemple, 2014)	Obeying the law on respect for others through fear of punishment, shame, or so as to appear 'good in public'
Debased Reciprocity Marx (Adam-Bagley, 2022)	Pretending to obey the law requiring tolerance of and safety of others, while corruptly bending or breaking laws and conventions for personal gain

Table 1.1 *Characteristics of the Social Contract*

Education and humanism

Child-Centred Humanism (CCH) as applied to education follows Rogers & Freiberg (1994) in insisting that teachers should know their children as *individuals* and be focused on the child's individual development within the classroom's group. This is only possible if the class of children is small enough for the teacher to know each child (and their family) well, and engage in an individual teaching plan for *each* individual child in the classroom. In this model, a school class should not contain more than 15 children, large enough for children to play creatively with others, and to learn co-operation within the larger group. 'The fifteen' may also contain children with challenging psychological and physical needs. This idea of 'the good school' which focuses on the individual needs of each child (White & Waters, 2015), also owes a debt to the educational philosophy of Descartes (Boyce, 2016).

Some critics of Carl Rogers argue that his humanistic model of psychology is a bourgeois, individualistic concept of self-realisation, unavailable to "ordinary" working people and their families. It is true that being a pupil in a class of 15 students or less is usually the privilege of those whose parents have been able to purchase a private education. But it does not deny T. H. Green's social democratic principle that *every* child should be enabled to enjoy the privileges enjoyed by the most privileged (Boucher & Vincent, 2006; Boucher, 2014; Olssen & Mace, 2021) – the principle that democratic socialism (or social democracy) should ensure *equality* of privilege. The same socialist ideal emerges in G. H. Mead's social psychology of human interaction (Shalin, 1988).

Carl Rogers' person-centred therapy survives as a viable model which can foster the equality of privilege for all children. (Kirschenbaum, 1990; Kirschenbaum & Jourdan, 2005; Joseph, 2015). Joseph (2015) lauds Rogers' approach as one antidote for the dehumanising effects of neoliberal capitalism upon humankind - a strong antidote to the idea of some critics of Rogers' model as "bourgeois". Margolin (2020) further extends the application of the Rogerian approach in melding it with Bourdieu's concept of enriching the 'social capital' of all citizens, young and old. There is an intriguing junction of these ideas with those of British psychiatrists who draw on the concept of 'social capital' to explain adult maladjustment, drawing on both the ideas of Bourdieu and Maslow (McKenzie at al., 2002; Healy, 2016). The poverty of selfhood in adult life, in this model, stems from the abuse and deprivation in childhood.

Quakers and the humanist education movement

John Lampen, an advocate of schools founded on Quaker educational principles argues that we must look not to the schools themselves for an understanding of their success, but at:

> " ... the environmental therapy movement which Friends and others developed to meet the needs of 'difficult' children, evacuated during 1939-45 War. Their practice recognised each child's innate worth and capacity for good by creating systems of governance and discipline which embodied Quaker testimonies to peace and equality ... this is one of the great Quaker contributions to education in the last 200 years." (Lampen, 2015, p. 295)

Within Quakers there is currently a vigorous debate about what exactly Quaker values in education are, or should be, and the organisation and practise of the seven Quaker secondary schools in Britain and Ireland has been examined in detail (Newton, 2016). What is common in these schools is that classes are small, and teachers focus on "the inner worth and capacity for good" of each child[2].

---

[2] www.qvine.org.uk

The dialectical critical realist model's perspective on moral realism (Bhaskar, 2008; Archer, 2016) seeks "to avoid the *anthropic fallacy* that places humans at the centre of the purpose and meaning of the universe." (Bhaskar, 2008 p. 26). Following this principle, CCH is not an individualist goal, even though it adopts Rogerian principles of phenomenology in child and adult development: it has a universalistic purpose, applying not merely to individuals, your children and my children, but to all of humanity's children, past, present and future.

Thus Child-Centred Humanism (CCH) has a view of the history of childhood which western society has only recently come to accept as a fundamental area of concern (Mayall, 2013). This suppression of childhood's history is a form of alienation - in Priscilla Alderson's (2016) words:

> "The present estranged, destructive relations between humans and nature suggest that many people are alienated from their physical human nature in different ways that need to be researched separately and together ... The effects of alienation were evident in the severe ill-health of children and adults in Victorian slums and factories ... and are replicated today in many majority world cities." (Alderson, 2016 (p.27)

Erik Erikson and the humanist journey

Erik Erikson (1902-1994) is an outstanding scholar and advocate for humanist psychology, who reacted against the pessimism of Freud, and the scientific yet brutal rigours of behaviourist psychology (Nye, 2000). Erikson is for us a key figure in humanistic scholarship, which includes other leading researchers, theorists and activists, including Carl Rogers (1902-1987) and Gordon Allport (1897-1967). These were American scholars who knew and influenced one another and contributed to the same academic journals. But they remained a minority influence on American psychology and social science until the advent of Martin Seligman's important work on positive psychology, discussed in detail below.

Behavioral psychology's translation to a humanist model

There has been a quiet but remarkable conversion of the behavioural psychology approach to understanding and changing human behaviour, towards a merging with humanist psychology's model of how 'clients' and 'pupils' should be regarded (with optimism, love and hope as self-directing humans). We owe this development mainly to a charismatic American psychologist, Martin Seligman colleagues (2002 to 2018). The title of Seligman's leading book on his new paradigm gives the tenor of this approach: Flourish: *A Visionary New Understanding of Happiness and Well-Being*.

Dillon (2020) in his historical review of the humanistic psychology movement credits Seligman with absorbing, translating and applying frames of understanding from Rogers, Maslow, Erikson and Allport in focussing on *individual* development within those occupying various roles within social institutions, in achieving both harmony and change. Employees, in Maslow's model, are enabled to self-actualize and Seligman's positive psychology techniques gives them ways of doing this.

In autoethnographic introductions concerning his transition from pessimistic behaviourism, to an optimistic (humanist) psychological approach, Seligman describes his earlier career in employing behavioural management models to the learning capacity of dogs: the animals received electric shocks when searching for food; but when the non-shock sources of food diminished, instead of learning correctly, most lapsed into a state of "learned helplessness", accepting that painful shocks were part of their life. Seligman generalised these findings to humans, and his concept of learned helplessness gained wide use in clinical psychology: chronically depressed people entered states of helplessness, enduring trauma, stigma, and social pain (Seligman, 1975 & 2018; Seligman & Garber, 1980).

In his epiphany, a "conversion" to humanist principles in psychology, Seligman was nevertheless critical of the Rogerian school because of what seemed to be its over-optimism: it was not enough to love and accept yourself, your family, your child, your students, your clients, your patients as unique individuals with enormous potential for growth and achievement. There had to be a grounding of this model of the potential for positive development in principles of behaviourist psychology. Seligman had earlier applied these learning models in trying to explain continuations of despair and "learned helplessness" in individuals. In his eureka moments, Seligman realised that these learning principles could equally well apply to "learned optimism", in ways which could enhance and operationalise Rogerian principles of psychotherapy, so as to foster unique individual development, based on the freedom of will and action promoted by mastery of the learning process (Seligman, 2002).

This led Seligman, clearly a man of dynamic energy to apply his brilliant intellect in pioneering the "positive psychology" movement, and to founding of the influential Authentic Happiness Centre (www.authentichappiness.org). Seligman (2018), now in his ninth decade of life, observed in his autobiographical memoir *The Hope Circuit: A Psychologist's Journey from Helplessness to Optimism* that: "We continually imagine different futures, we evaluate them, we choose among them." (p. 66). Seligman offers us ways to improve our intellectual (and moral) strengths, in ways which enable us (hopefully) to choose the best outcomes, for ourselves and others. An excellent example of this application comes from Fowler & Christakis (2008) study of "the dynamic spread of happiness in a large social network."

Seligman and his colleagues (Dahlsgaard et al., 2005) sought to establish an ethical or moral dimension for their new and powerful techniques of using learning theory models for advocating and engineering change, not only in distressed individuals but also in whole populations, for whom self-directed techniques of 'learned optimism' are now increasingly available. In order to move the positive psychology model to "the moral high ground ... with an agreed-upon way of classifying positive traits", Seligman and his team studied scholarly commentaries and texts from eight different traditions: Greek philosophers; Confucianism; Daoism; Buddhism; Hinduism; Judaism; Christianity; and Islam. From this intensive inquiry and textual analysis, the authors established six traits salient in all of the eight religious or philosophical traditions, which could describe the highest goals and achievements for humans and their institutions. These are:

Courage and integrity when faced with stress, violence and attack (including the choices between angry resistance, and non-violence);

Justice and equity for individuals in all institutions;

Humanism – the fundamental value of honouring and nurturing all human beings, and their choices;

Temperance – moderation in all human endeavours;

Wisdom and its development through educational institutions, and individual study;

Transcendence – rising beyond the self and one's temporal existence, in achieving higher levels of self-understanding (also, perhaps involving the soul's further journey).

Seligman, a secular Jew with a generous spirit, applauds these "universalist" principles of achieving the best life through the honouring and promotion of principles in both education, and in therapy. The self-completion scales and learning materials offered by the Authentic Happiness centre clearly reflect these principles.

Seligman (2006) summarises the major themes of his new optimism, based on the remarkable marriage of behaviourism's cognitive psychology with models of humanist psychology, as follows:

1. Whether you are a pessimist or an optimist depends on how you explain bad events to yourself.
2. Your parent-figures and teachers had the most influence on your "explanatory style."
3. Pessimists often personalise bad life events, attributing them to permanent, pervasive causes. But they ascribe temporary, impersonal, specific causes to good events.
4. The projection of present despair into the future causes a kind of chronic hopelessness.
5. By contrast, optimists externalize adversity's causes and see them as fleeting and specific. They credit good events to personal, permanent, pervasive causes, and to events within their span of control.
6. Optimists are much quicker than pessimists to get over a setback and try again.
7. Pessimism is a consistent predictor of depression's onset, under conditions of stress.
8. Through cognitive therapy, it's possible to change one's "explanatory style" to become more optimistic.
9. Pessimists have one advantage over optimists - they are better at realistically assessing their current situation.
10. Optimists sometimes exaggerate the control they have over challenging events.
11. The goal of life is to achieve "realistic optimism", for yourself and for others, in practised and mutual exchange: achieving this is the goal of positive psychology in achieving "authentic happiness".

The purpose of learned happiness techniques is to sponsor optimism in individuals who had often been depressed, pessimistic, or expected the worst in others/ Seligman's goals connect with our focus on the importance of the "implicit social contract", which binds citizens together in an invisible but crucially important way. This is Roy Bhaskar's *ubuntu* principle: *I am, because you are.*

The traditional discipline of humanist psychology acknowledges the contribution which Seligman and his colleagues have made in enlivening and optimising the discipline of psychology (DeRobartis & Bland, 2018 to 2021). While humanist psychology is grounded, methodologically in qualitative accounts of personality and personal development (Friedman, 2008), many from this school of psychology accept the marriage of qualitative and quantitative methodologies which positive psychology offers (Franko et al., 2008; Edwards, 2017).

Humanist psychologists express the hope that Seligman's "post-industrial psychological science" (which is now strongly supported by clinical and managerial psychologists - Linley at al., 2004 to 2012) may yet move towards "the humanistic revolution" which humanist psychology anticipates, including Gergen's (2016) "visionary psychology", which challenges the biases (or ignorance) that traditional psychology had shown towards minority or oppressed groups such as women, abused children, and ethnic minorities (Sawyerr & Adam-Bagley, 2023). Humanistic psychology continues to make important contributions to business ethics and practice: respecting the dignity and welfare of workers, customers, and the environment is the basis for this business model (Mea & Sims, 2019).

Certainly, psychological and counselling research has made many strides since Gordon Allport (1968) criticized "nomothetic" researchers for their systematic ignorance of the individual needs and capacities of their "subjects". An excellent example of humanist principles at work in scientific research comes from the project led by Robert Waldinger and his colleagues (2015 & 2023) which followed up a cohort (and their descendants) born in Boston, US in 1938 until the present time, focussing on interviewees from all ethnicities, genders and social classes, from childhood to life's end. They identified factors contributing to well-being and happiness. Happiness fell into two types: *hedonic*, a kind of pure pleasure in one's activities; and *eudaimonic* "… which is a sense of life having meaning, and being worthwhile" (Flood, 2023). This latter stage bears a strong resemblance to Maslow's (2021) life stages of achieving self-actualization, and then self-transcendence.

Another research-based approach to promoting personal happiness as the basis for a healthy and successful life, comes from the work of the economist David Layard and his colleagues (2009 to 2014). Bowlby (1982) had found that secure attachments in childhood led to the development of warm and friendly social and emotional relationships in later life. This "social bond" led to good health, prosocial behaviour, and healthy ageing. Using UK longitudinal data from a national cohort, Layard and colleagues supports these ideas, showing that the basis for "success", broadly conceived in both economic and psychological ways, was most powerfully linked to the stability and warmth of care experienced in childhood. In adulthood both psychological distress, and economic dependency and failure were linked to miserable and unstable childhoods. These findings are confirmed by the US longitudinal studies of Waldinger & Schultz (2015 & 2016).

Waldinger (2023) cites the work of Sonia Lyubomirsky and colleagues (2005, 2008 & 2016) which shows that around 40 percent of the ability to achieve lifelong, self-actualizing happiness is inherited; another 40 percent reflects our caring family and community which builds on that genetic potential; but the remaining proportion is due to impacts of current life stressors (which diminish the capacity to achieve one's full 'happiness potential'). These findings have led this research team to focus on eliciting "the urge to prosocial happiness" in abused or economically depressed youth (Layous et al., 2012). The links to Seligman's (1995) idea of creating the "the optimistic child" are clear.

Dovidio et al. (2017) support these ideas using case histories to illustrate "the social psychology of helping behaviour", in establishing the 'prosocial' core of everyday human behaviours. These and other findings have led Waldinger to conclude:

> " … the fundamentals of becoming happy are biologically ingrained. We evolved as social animals. That's a very important evolutionary concept. As we evolved as a species, the people who are more social were more likely to survive and reproduce, and, because of that, more likely to pass on their genes … that's why, I think … generation after generation, we continue to need social contact." (Waldinger, interviewed by Flood, 2023).

Put another way, we are born seeking social bonds, acting creatively in love and co-operation throughout our lives. And we are born without original sin.

Conclusions

We define humanism (secular and religious) as the compass for a set of beliefs (derived from different branches of philosophy, social science and religion) for humans who are all born 'without sin'. Given the loving care of parents, we grow into adults who seek both the companionship and welfare of others, through our social contract with the whole of society.

In reaching these goals we are inspired by the research and scholarship of the discipline of humanist psychology, exemplified in the work of Allport, Maslow, Rogers, Erikson, May and others, in creating a methodology and focus on humans as unique individuals, with stories to tell which enable us to learn from one another in the crucial tasks of improving society in ways which serve the needs of children, in our doctrine of *Child-Centred Humanism*. Archer too in her model of morphogenesis shows how we can develop the sharing of ideas, stories and experiences in ways which can engineer such positive change.

We are impressed by Seligman's adoption of humanist ideas in developing through classical learning models, the ideals of developing human happiness. The social connexions which result are built into the human psyche, in which positive social relations become functional for civilization's growth. We emphasize the importance of the *Social Contract* as the implicit but crucial way in which democratic societies share values, and respect each other's needs and rights, in the making of a good society. We draw on the philosophical ideas of Descartes, Hobbes, Hume, Rousseau and Green in developing this model.

The evidence from many studies shows that love and stability in childhood is crucial for adult adjustment, happiness, prosocial behaviour, and the ability to engage creatively and synergistically in 'the social contract', which knits us together in a powerful bond. This is a theme we take up again in Chapter 4, in discussing the nature of evil in society, and how healthy childhoods can counter the development of antisocial personalities.

Chapter 2

Critical Realism and Autoethnography: A Review

Chris Adam-Bagley, Alice Sawyerr and
Mahmoud Abubaker

Introduction: Autoethnography and self-other relationships

In 2016 the anthropologist Francis Huxley reached the age of 93 and began a new journey, to a place unknown. He was and remains for us the epitome of the intellectual adventurer, the scholar and anthropologist: a reflexive-anthropologist who devoted his life to scholarly research, and to social activism. His anthropology began with the study of indigenous peoples of South America which rapidly grew into social activism on behalf of these indigenous peoples who were experiencing genocidal decimation of their lives and culture. He was a founder of *Survival International*, an advocacy group on behalf of indigenous peoples: he continued this combination of research and advocacy throughout his life, and for us he is the epitome of the politically-grounded scholar and activist.

One of his emergent concepts was that of *The Mutual Self*: "We swim in a sea of mutualities … and mutuality changes as we change each other." This idea, developed in his 1974 book *The Way of the Sacred*, is for us close to the dualism of research and social activism developed by Roy Bhaskar (2015), whom we laud as a pioneer of scholarship linked to social action. The implicit mutually of obligations is the hidden but powerful *social contract* which makes civilization possible. The purpose of living is to enact this universal social contract through research, theology and the generation of values through Bhaskar's dialectical critical realism which results in *the pulse of freedom* (Bhaskar, 2008).

Huxley developed the research approach of *reflexive anthropology* in which the ethnographer shares his initial intellectual models, with those he or she is researching, offering tentative models of social system, values and interactions. Following these conversations, the ethnographer will develop and change these models, according to the reactions of people's reactions. The ethnographer becomes both researcher and the researched, and this mutuality of intellectual modelling becomes a duality which coheres within a dialectic of action and change.

This exchange with about others about what is "real" and "important" in their self and social system, creates fresh forms of identity and a new form of "the moral good", according to Christian Smith's (2011) enquiry into "what is a person". This dialectic of mutual interest is according to Bhaskar (2012b) a profoundly useful way of transcending the alienation of human aspiration which still powerfully pervades so many human institutions (Scambler, 2013; Adam-Bagley, 2022).

Autoethnography (the researcher as part of the community he or she researches, with a mutual dialogue with those studied, leading to increased understanding of shared interests, and dialogue for change) is increasingly influential, and has been used by the three authors of this book, including the Chapter below by Chris Adam-Bagley offering an autoethnographic account of an academic, religious and ethical journey through Christianity into Islam. Alice Sawyerr (in Sawyerr & Adam-Bagley, 2017) describes her ethnographic journey from the roots of slavery (from her Yoruba ancestors transported to St. Lucia; and following 'emancipation', to Nova Scotia) and then into the 'land of free slaves' of Sierra Leone; and then finally into Ghana. Her 'return' journey involved graduate study in Canada, and professional and doctoral studies in England.

Mahmoud Abubaker's autoethnography has informed his research on women and work in Gaza, Palestine: he (and his wife Wesam) offer accounts of a value-changing experience of sheltering for ten days during continued rocket fire upon their partially-collapsed, bombed house, in which he, his wife and older son, and their newborn son were trapped (W. Abubaker, 2019; M. Abubaker et al., 2022).

Our shared *consciousness of being* has been informed by different life experiences which have united us (as Muslims and Christians) with a shared identity of research values and procedures; values of pacifism within Christianity and Islam; values in social practice and teaching, with a focus on students' individuality; and in the energy for pressing the dialectical model of achieving social change. Critical Realism (elaborated below) fits well with our autoethnographic research model.

Roy Bhaskar's Critical Realism: A model for social action and social change

> Critical Realism is one of the main theoretical orientations of the social sciences in the twentieth and twenty-first centuries. Critical realism aims to study the transcendental conditions of cognition, and it assumes that reality exists independently of our perceptive abilities ... it assumes that reality is ontologically stratified wherein one can distinguish three ontological domains: empirical, actual, and real. In terms of social science, critical realism, therefore, posits that social structures have a real ontological basis independent of researchers' empirical observations .... This model is not a solution developed within the social sciences, but a philosophical approach that proposes how knowledge about people and social structures can be developed, interpreted and described. (Bukowska, 2021, p. 441)

The concept of Critical Realism (and its later development using concepts from Hegel and Marx) known as dialectical critical realism (DCR), comes from philosophy, and not from social science. It uses philosophical language and reasoning, which is often challenging for the social scientist who has had no grounding in formal logic, or in the discipline of philosophical analysis. DCR is not an account of social science, but rather a philosophy of how knowledge about people and their social structures may be construed, interpreted, described and fitted together. DCR assumes that although the ground of knowledge is real, it also has a value base with which the researcher must interact: there is no such thing as value-free social science.

Critical Realism (CR) emerged from the writings of the philosopher Roy Bhaskar who was seeking an alternative to what he saw as ambiguous and often confusing models of scientific methodology, particularly, the Popperian doctrine of "falsifying hypotheses" (Popper, 2005). He extended his critique to the methodologies of social science (Bhaskar, 1986), attempting to find a way forward from what he saw as the stultification and confusion of "positivism", "phenomenology", "post-modernism", and "social constructionism". Critical realism has been attractive to social researchers, and theorists who are committed to a firm ideological basis for viewing human action (e.g. Marxists, Muslims, Catholics) in asserting that *structures* within society are real and although their influence may be debated, their *being* or ontology (e.g. class exploitation, alienation, the nature of spiritual being) is not in doubt.

It is of course possible that Marxists and Catholics will disagree profoundly on what is or should be salient (Creaven, 2007) but CR nevertheless also lays the way open for dialogue and compromise between seemingly incompatible systems through the process of dialectical critical realism (Bhaskar, 1986). Bhaskar adapts the Hegelian model of dialectical debate (traditionally: thesis, antithesis, synthesis) but goes beyond this model in positing a fourth level in the dialectical process which leads to action for advocacy of change. Moreover, this process of dialectical critical realism (DCR) is a continuous process in the lives of social systems, dyads and individuals, and there is continuous feedback between the 'agents' (the actors or individuals in DCR), or between various individuals: through these reflexive dialogues, organisations are in a process of continuous change and adjustment to new feedbacks, with the potential for changing social structures.

At this stage, a challenge in reading CR theoretical texts and research emerging from that theory should be mentioned: Critical Realism has developed its own vocabulary, and has coined new words ('neologisms') which the student may have difficulty in learning, or retaining. Furthermore, common English words are used in a way which attributes a rather different meaning to that of everyday language. The use of the word *absence* is a case in point. The difficulty of grasping CR concepts may be illustrated by this quotation from Anderson (2016):

> "Absence as a noun or verb is central to the DCR process of absenting absences, constraints, ills, contradictions, oppressive power, relations or inequities. Absence is the crucial empty physical, social and mental space that enables movement, imagined alternatives, processes and change." (Anderson, 2016, p. 166)

Thus "absence" actually means (in some, but not in all situations) the presence or existence of some positive force for social change.[3]

---

[3] "At its philosophical core lies a theory of *absence*, which Bhaskar combines with his pre-existing arguments from critical realism for the significance of ontology. This is a basis for the realist understanding of human *being* in society and in nature which, through the account of absence, is aligned to a theory of *becoming* and change in a spatio-temporal world. The alignment of being and becoming is achieved in a manner that displays both a uniqueness of individual philosophical voice and boldness of intellectual

Despite the complexities of her CR model, Anderson in her two volumes on *The Politics of Childhood Real and Imagined* (2013 & 2016) offers many valuable observations on how DCR can be employed as a model for understanding oppressions, and of advocating and engineering change (Alderson, 2021).

What one finds in CR writing is an absence of dogma, and a willingness to engage in debate (the essence of DCR) to reach compromise. Thus Collier (1994) offers a useful synthesis of Weber's "individualism" and Durkheim's "collectivism" showing (pp 144-145) that these are not alternative models of individuals within social systems, but in the DCR mode, interactive ones, which coexist and offer simultaneously, ways of promoting social action for change: individuals co-operate collectively, but remain individuals, is the message.

Thus, in Collier's (1994) analysis of Marx's writing on *Capital*, most wage earners are mystified by the nature of capitalism that exploits them: their alienation remains unmasked. But in the Dialectical Critical Realist model they are capable of understanding and changing both their modes of thought and their social actions, their necessary "underlabouring" (using a term borrowed from Locke) in addressing capitalist exploitation. The worker who fails to grasp the nature of his or her exploitation remains in a state of "non-realism", asserts Collier (1994, p. 12).

In response to critics of this Marxian approach, Collier (1994) says: " ... modern non-realists often accuse realists of dogmatism because of our defence of objectivity. They accuse us of arrogance in claiming truth for our theories ...[but] ... To claim objective truth for one's statements is to lay one's cards on the table, to expose oneself to the possibility of refutation." (p. 13)

---

vision, and these gave Bhaskar a fair claim to stand ... in the first rank of western philosophy today." (Norrie, 2010, p. 3).

This bold claim to recognise "reality" (which is, of course, initially an intuitional process) rejects postmodern ideas of the relativity of knowledge and the impossibility of constructing linear models of basic cause; and the rejection of social constructivist ideas that knowledge and values are relative, and are generated through unique sets of social interactions. One understands why CR has proved attractive to the Muslim scholar Matthew Wilkinson (2015). In "making sense" of his experience of teaching in a Muslim school he says:

> " ... this book draws upon the tradition of dialectical European philosophy, epitomised by Hegel ... Most recently, this tradition has been brought with great energy and conceptual sophistication into the contemporary academy by the founding figure of the philosophy of critical realism, Roy Bhaskar, as well as others following his lead, such as Alan Norrie, Andrew Wright and Margaret Archer. Critical realism is exceptional in its coherent articulation of a contemporary philosophy of being, of knowing and real personal, ethical and social change, and its refusal to reduce being of all types, including spiritual being, to socially constructed epistemology or merely psychological or semantic meaning. This makes the philosophy of critical realism at its original, dialectical and spiritual moments an ideal vehicle for the development of a systematic rationale to interpret Islam and Islam-in-education in a multi-faith world." (Wilkinson, 2015, p. 10)

Wilkinson draws on both Islamic and critical realist thinking in arguing that Muslim education should be "a philosophy for success", or empowerment (as Marxists would put it, the unmasking of alienation). *Success* is seen by Wilkinson as embedded in the multidimensional development and self-realisation of human social interaction within and between the four planes of social being defined by Critical Realist (CR) theorists. These planes are:

The Real: material transactions with nature (e.g. "the ground of being", "the essence of humans", "the uniqueness of each human being" counterpoised with forces of nature, polity and economy which impose themselves on humans; and the divine revelations of various world religions);

The Actual: Inter-subjective (interpersonal) transactions between individuals or 'human agents' in different settings, including socialization and social control, the imposition of racialized identities; economic deprivation; forced migration et alia: and the understandings which humans have of these controlling forces, in dialogue, in writing, in protest, in political movements;

The Empirical: Social relations at the *non-reducible* level of structures, institutions and forms;

The Transcendent: The embodied personality's liberation through mutual tolerance, the shedding of false consciousness, spiritual fulfilment; awareness of self-potential, self-actualization. (Adapted from Bhaskar 2008 – this is also the basis of Alderson's MELD model, explained below).

Wilkinson focuses his analysis on "the embodied personality" and his or her spiritual, intellectual, affective-cultural, civic, and instrumental dimensions. Each of these dimensions has distinct and interrelated or "articulated" ontologies. "Ontological realism" concerns the philosophical study of being (the first level of being in CR theory), and is a central concept within DCR:

> "A basic understanding of critical realist ontology, the philosophical study of being is ... that being exists independently of our knowledge of it and in particular, our ability to describe it, so that it cannot be reduced to discourse, nor is it merely contained or constructed in the semiotics of our speech." (Wilkinson, 2015, p. 50)

Alderson (2016) in construing "the politics of childhood" offers the following explanations of DCR's 4-levels of analysis, which, following Bhaskar, she terms **MELD**. The first level is **1M** - DCR concepts of basic reality e.g. moral realism, which consists (in social science) of ethical naturalism. The 'moral realism' inherent at this basic level of DCR:

> "... accepts that harm and benefit are universal, causal, moral realities, which are defined and experienced in varied local and personal ways. To deny moral realism would set up theory/practice inconsistency ... Because humans are vulnerable, sensitive, social beings, able to flourish and to suffer, moral realism is part of human nature and daily life, and is not artificially introduced (Archer, 2003; Bhaskar, 1986; Collier, 1999) ... **1M** seeks to avoid the anthropic fallacy that places humans at the centre of the purpose and meaning of the universe (Bhaskar, 2000, 26). Instead, **1M** sees that we are part of nature ... A related problem is the adultist fallacy. This sets rational adults at the apex of morality, and regards childhood as a slow climb up from lower, natural, pre-social, pre-moral babyhood to higher, socialised, moral adulthood." Alderson, 2016 pp 28-29)

Priscilla Alderson in her two volumes on 'the politics of childhood' offers a vigorous and often moving account of the children she has been involved with in her research over a 30-year-period, but admits that she is a recent 'convert' to DCR: "The challenge of rethinking my past research in relation to DCR, and of writing this book, has helped me, and I hope it will help readers, to see how DCR enlarges research theory and analysis. Since learning about DCR, I have revised some of my former ideas and discarded others, on the continuing journey of learning and changing." (Alderson, 2013, p. 8).

Alderson terms the second level in her DCR analysis **2E** (second edge) " ... which concerns the transition into intervention and *process in product*. **2E** concerns actively negating problems that were identified at 1M (Bhaskar, 2008, 97-8). This involves absenting *aporia* (contradictions and constraints, ills and untruths) ..." (Alderson, 2016. p. 34). Exactly how this is done is problematic however, and often one is challenged to know where to "fit" one's research findings within the four levels of analysis, and how to interpret findings (and undertake further research) in terms of absence, dialogue, dialectic or change – for example, the research studies on children which Alderson presents us with. She continues (p. 36): "A seven-scale DCR framework for interdisciplinary analysis (Bhaskar & Danemark, 2006) helps to connect many themes ..."

We move to Alderson's third level called **3L**. She terms this level the *totality of change*, and comments:

> " ... **3L** recognizes that we all share the core universal human nature our common humanity, and we are all unique and ethically different ... We are interconnected and interdependent, dialectic replaces dichotomy, 'is' connects to 'ought', and 'ought' connects to 'can' (Bhaskar, 2008, 146-8) ... " (Alderson, 2016, p. 41).

It is at this level of understanding social structure that Margaret Archer's ideas (1995, 2000, 2003) of *morphogenesis* (personal change through dialectic interchange, and self-reflection) becomes increasingly important. And then at the level of the fourth dimension **4D**, there occurs the fullest realisation of *reflexive analysis*.

The transformative agency of **4D** aims for " ...emancipation ... in the free society where each individual's flourishing depends on everyone flourishing. **4D** works to overcome the false sense of self as separate and isolated. We relate to the world and to other people through recognising what we share in common (Bhaskar, 2002, 305). The key questions concern identity (who am I?) and agency (what am I to do?)." (Alderson, 2016, p. 46). At this stage then, false consciousness is shed, and alienation is unmasked.

The combined model is thus called **MELD** – in summary:

1M: Basic values, which are often unseen or unrecognized, but which inform or control action (e.g., covert power systems and alienation)

2E: Seeds of hope, and the dawning of understanding and dialectics. The realisation of *absence,* of lack of fulfilment, and yearning for change.

3L: Understanding of how social structures constrain us.

4D: Critical reflection and social change.

Clearly, this is an ideal (and idealistic) model, and Bhaskar (2000, pp 8-9) warns us of the possibility of "malign MELD", in which negative, coercive powers subvert consciousness, control debates (e.g. through online misinformation), and ensure that the powers of capital are unassailed, however much information we have (e.g. on health inequalities, on educational underachievement, or on poor quality schools – Scambler, 2018). The 'seeds of hope' of 2E are often dashed.

Alderson devotes her two volumes to accounts of how, effectively, to liberate children so that their rights are fully realised. She uses the 1E assumptions about the "real" world and its state in nature (what Wilkinson in his Islamic formulation would call the original garden of paradise in which, following the acquisition of knowledge, Adam and Eve are charged with "naming all things").

> "Childhood and nature overlap in symbol and in practice ... ways in which children are treated reflect activities towards nature. These range from neglect and abuse to violence that wastes potential and ends the lives of millions of children." (Alderson, 2016, p. 46)

Alderson then devotes her two volumes to analysing children's lives (especially those in contact with health care systems) in detail, explaining how their condition is perceived and classified, and how they are treated - fit into the MELD hierarchy.

> "The DCR aim of promoting utopias is to negate alienation ... schools are particularly good places for transformation, having the

time, space and long-term relations to nurture utopian work ... DCR concepts can assist teachers in being reflective, self-critical, and collegial ... DCR's concrete utopian imagination is not a prescription for the future, but for an open society where individuals decide what to do with their freedom. It is an inner urge that flows universally from the lack of elemental absence (lack, need, want desire)." (Alderson, 2013, pp 157-158)

Considering alienation's ending, Alderson speculates about the 'natural communism' that would follow – what Quakers (like Alderson) would call it the Kingdom of Heaven existing on earth now, through the process of constructive relationships. In Alderson's formulation this communism goes beyond Marx (who merely wanted 'from each according to his ability, to each according to his need'): "Marx's ... generous giving and taking is not possible if everything is already shared."[4] (p. 159) In this model, the needs, rights and interests of children are not separate, but shared, in the utopia which Alderson anticipates.

Alderson's (2013) chapter on "Inner Being: Alienation and Flourishing" sums up, for us what is most inspirational in Alderson's critical realist theory of social science. She comprehensively demolishes the myth of "value free social science". Research with children, she argues, is not only value-informed: its entire goal in showing how children can "flourish" at the highest level of the MELD model and is, as Bhaskar put it "value saturated" at each step in the MELD framework:

"Having reviewed support for value-informed social research, I now summarise MELD 4D, fourth dimension, where values are central ... the traditional Hegelian dialectic is taken towards logical, consistent

---

[4] There is an intriguing parallel with Flaschel's (2009) idea that Marx's "reserve army of labour" will disappear if the social democratic state gives all citizens, whether working or not a generous living allowance, in his model of 'flexisecurity'.

completeness ... To include real being (ontology) and real transformation, MELD 1M first moment begins with non-identity and absence; 2E second edge involves negativity and oppressive power; 3L, third level, concerns open, dynamic totalities [of social structure] which move on to 4D, fourth dimension, of praxis, transformative agency in ethical practice and liberating power, the dialectic that is 'the pulse of freedom'. I hope that this chapter, by showing all the MELD moments, will help to clarify the meaning and relevance of some earlier parts of this book. They all relate to the DCR logic that human beings inevitably desire and move towards freedom and justice, and that this is or should be the central concern of social science ... When individuals are out of touch and alienated from their body and nature (plane 1), from other people (plane 2), and from structures and institutions (plane 3) they can become unable to act in order to absent the absences and power2 [of oppressive forces], and they are denied the capacity for transformation at MELD 4D." (Alderson, 2013, p. 138)

Although DCR is a complex philosophy for social science research, Alderson's reconstruction of her previous research with children using the DCR framework, which she elucidates in the passage quoted above, is both enlightening and enervating. The reader's journey in following this difficult intellectual model seems justified. According to Bhaskar (2008):

"Practical, concrete utopianism stands in contrast to abstract, intellectual utopianism ... being practical involves absenting constraining absences, as each in their own way, human beings try to overcome power2 and 'master-slave' relations' in society and nature ... the dialectic is an inner urge that flows universally from the logic of elemental absence (lack, need, want, desire) ... against power relations towards freedom as flourishing." (Bhaskar, 2008, p. 20)

Priscilla Alderson's (2013) reflections on the religious origins of "theories of the self" in critical realist theory is fascinating too: she writes that: "Ideas about the self-illumination of the fourth plane of social being, the inner self, and MELD **4D** on *flourishing*, and its converse, *misery*." (p. 140)

Consideration of the soul, the inner or spiritual self, may be outside of the bounds of conventional sociology, but for the Quaker Alderson:

> "DCR explores unseen deeper realities, and shows the problems in social research that ignores them ... Without some explicit theories of human nature and the young self ... [research] ignores concepts of harm and benefit to children ... ideas from religion and philosophy seep into common imaginings of the self ... they [Jesus, Muhammad, Buddha] exemplified 'childlike' humility, poverty, humility, vulnerability, willingness to admit ignorance and to learn, with obedience to a transcendent goodness and an innocent detachment from worldly power." (Alderson, 2013, pp 141-142)

Alderson then turns to her mentor, Roy Bhaskar (2008, 2012 & 2016) who "theorised an embodied personality, a psychic being or soul or anima, and a ground state, all three striving for humanity."

Brad Shipway (2013) writing about critical realism's contribution to the discipline of education comments on Critical Realism as a philosophical and a transcendental (spiritual) model that "encompasses educational administrators and policy makers, teacher educators, and philosophers of education in what they do and think." CR uncouples itself from postmodernism, enabling researchers to describe the 'real' world through a grounded, value ontology. Shipway quotes Collier (1994):

> "... critical realism is an ongoing research programme within the human sciences, and in particular in their theoretically and politically contentious border areas. It is certainly not a completed system which can be applied in these fields to solve all problems: on the contrary, by treating scientific projects as explorations of realities with inexhaustible depths, it helps to keep these projects open for self-criticism and development." (Collier, 1994, p. 236).

According to Shipway (2013) CR has "an emancipatory mission" for research and practice in education. "Critical realism supports a stratified, democratic use of homology[5], and the exercise of power is a vital condition for the possibility of emancipation of students and those who work with them." (p. 5)[6]

Matthew Wilkinson: Dialectical Critical Realism and Islam

The generosity of the shared dialectical process also flows from Wilkinson's (2015a) analysis of Islam. He too uses the MELD hierarchy, and concludes his **1E** analysis:

> "The Islamic Critical Realism (ICR) fulcrum offers the philosophical possibility that God may have granted genuine spiritual insight to those who fall outside one's own religious tradition and this can enrich rather than threaten one's own commitment to faith and facilitate a genuinely respectful engagement with the 'other'." (p. 64)

Moving to **2E**, Wilkinson observes how Bhaskar (1993/2008) adapted Hegel:

> "He radically alters the phases of dialectic into non-identity, to absence, to totality to transformative praxis in an extension of the 'revindication' of ontology and the positing of a new ontology of original critical realism." (p. 66)

Further, on *absence*, Wilkinson observes:

---

[5] "Homology" is a term borrowed from biology which explains the link between "the transcendental realist world view", and Roy Bhaskar's political model of socialism (Collier, 1994, p. 469).

[6] It would be interesting to have a critical realist account of "emancipation" in the world of children's friendships described by George & Clay (2013) and their idea of "challenging pedagogy".

"According to critical realist thinkers, absence, negativity and change are essential parts of the duality of presence and absence in being (Norrie, 2010). For example, silence is the precondition of speech, rests are indispensable to musical sound, and as we know from natural science, empty space is a necessary condition of solid objects. In the experience of selfhood, a sense/knowledge/belief that 'I am this' necessarily entails a sense/knowledge/belief that 'I am not that.'" (Wilkinson, 2015a, p. 66)

In DCR absence is, crucially, transformative. "Indeed, dialectical change is understood by critical realists as the process ... of remedying or removing absence" (Bhaskar, 1993/2008). For Bhaskar, positive change is often the removal of, or progression from, something negative. The archetype of this movement is the process of abolishing (i.e. absenting) the conditions of slavery – and on the meaning of the "master-slave" relationship Bhaskar has much to say.

In Wilkinson's (2015a) account of the journey towards combining British and Islamic citizenship in Muslim adolescents, he first paints the **2E** picture of absence, and the 'absence' of seriousness' in the UK National Curriculum goals concerning citizenship education. As his research progressed, Wilkinson moved to **3L**, the level of 'seriousness'. As an example, he cites Lovelock's (2016) idea of *Gaia*, the self-regulating, self-healing universe, which he relates to the Qur'anic idea of *kalifa* or stewardship of the earth, the first stewards being Adam and Hawwa, in their divinely-instructed project of "naming all things in nature". At this level, Critical Realist concepts allowed Wilkinson to focus on transformative ideas, on the notion of the primacy of structure over individual agency. At the **4D** level, the meaning (and pedagogy) of citizenship education was taken outside of the classroom into 'the world', so that

" ... unity-in-diversity is the bedrock of society, in which institutional structure both predominates over individual agency and can be transformed by it. This task of linking agency with structure means that more than any other subject at the level of **4D** (Fourth Dimension – transformative praxis), citizenship education needs to be carried outside of the classroom into the community." (Wilkinson, 2015a, p. 246).

Margaret Scotford Archer

Archer is in our reading, the most impressive of the sociologists who have been inspired by Bhaskar's critical realism, and its unfolding from and through Marxism and Hegel into dialectical critical realism, and then into realms of theology. We learn too how in critical realist theory we may understand and apprehend notions of the divine (Archer et al., 2004).

Bhaskar's (1986 & 2008) earlier consideration of (and modification of) Marxian theory had led some American commentators to label him a Marxist (and hence the neglect of DCR by American sociologists – Gorski, 2013). Contrary to this stereotype, transcending the purely material concerns of Marxian ideolog, Bhaskar embarked on a spiritual journey, exploring Hindu and Buddhist concepts of self and soul (Bhaskar, 2015). Certainly, as Wilkinson (2013 & 2015a) saw in adapting DCR through an Islamic epistemology, there are profound possibilities of DCR transcendence in reconceptualising Islamic (and other theologies') approaches to designing citizenship.

Archer's fullest and most eloquent account of "the internal conversation" is her 2003 volume *Structure, Agency and the Internal Conversation*. Her arguments concern "structure" (which has variable meaning in philosophy and sociology, but is seen as an enduring form), and "agency" (with similar debates about its meaning, but intuitively, how individuals relate, subjectively, to structure). Both structure and agency exist independently (i.e. have ontological reality), and causal relations between them remain to be investigated. Structure and agency "are two distinctive and irreducible properties and powers, and ... human reflexive deliberations play a crucial role in mediating between them." (p. 14) Thus *reflexivity* is central in Margaret Archer's sociology:

> "Were we humans not reflexive beings there could be no such thing as society. This is because any form of social interaction, from the dyad to the global system, requires that subjects know themselves to be themselves. Otherwise they could not acknowledge that their words were their own, nor that their intentions, undertakings and reactions belonged to them ... not one social obligation, expectation or norm could be owned by a single 'member' of society." (Archer, 2003, p. 19)

Moreover, the reflexive, internal conversations and self-appraisals of individuals in their interactions with others have, in Archer's model, causal power in modifying structures: these "extrinsic effects ... mediating cultural and social properties of their societies ... and the private lives of social subjects, are indispensable to the very existence and working of society." (2003 p. 52)

Archer draws ideas and insights on the social psychology of the self, described in the writings of the forerunners of humanist psychology, William James (1983) and George H. Mead (1964), whose ideas of self-other, and I-myself she analyses in detail. She is critical of their ideas of "personal reflexivity": their idea of the "inner world" lacks autonomy in relation to the individual's "outer world" – a crucial shortcoming, in Archer's goal to "reclaim the internal conversation" as talking "to" society, not merely "about" society.

Only then, Archer proposes " ... we are in a position from which properly to consider the potentialities of our reflexive deliberations as the process which mediates between 'structure and agency'." (p. 129) Archer illustrates her thesis by analysing the "internal conversations" of twenty adults, making each a unique case study, in showing inter alia, "How the different *individual* modes of reflexivity, which mediate constraints and enablements in quite distinctive ways, are also related to *collective* action." (Archer, 2003, 166)

Reflexivity does not usually lead to structural change, of course, and Archer illustrates why this is so in her analysis of types of reflexivity. But, reflections upon reflections, refined, shared and polished reflexivities:

> "... 'meta-reflexives'... are such because they pursue cultural ideals that cannot be accommodated by the current social structure and the array of contexts it defines ... By personifying their ideals of truth and goodness, the meta-reflexives awaken them and re-present them to society. In so doing they re-stock the pool of societal values, by displaying alternatives to the aridity of third-way thinking – and its repressive consensus ... " (Archer, 2003, p. 361).

A useful critique of Archer's "reflexivity and conduct of the self" has been offered by Akram & Hogan (2015), who examine how Archer's idea of self-reflexion may challenge ideas of the "taken-for-granted" everyday events in the lives of individuals which form part of Bourdieu's (1989) account of *habitus*. Bourdieu downplays ideas of freely willed choice in making decisions, focussing instead on how powerful social and economic classes create reserves of social capital, through socialising those below them into "unconscious acceptance" of everyday lifestyles.

It's almost as if some wealthy elite had devised a newspaper called *The Sun*, which the workers may enjoy as their daily intellectual succour: this same cabal would have been responsible for creating 'sink estates' and poor quality comprehensives. This habitus of the labouring classes, and of the reserve army of labour is deeply entrenched, difficult to change (Scambler, 2018). The proletariat's only mode of upward mobility, like that of the proles in Orwell's *1984*, is to win the lottery. Yet despite this gloomy continuity of class,

Bourdieu allows that 'misrecognition' (akin to Marx's 'false consciousness') can change over quite lengthy periods of time, or change in response to sudden upheavals, such as war. Bourdieu has appeal for some radical sociologists in that he seems to have identified how socio-economic classes perpetuate themselves through symbolic rituals which can be enduring across generations: but these rituals may also be identified, and changed (e.g., Savage, 2015).

Archer's idea of morphogenesis, as part of a self-reflexive change in self-concept, a path to "social mobility" seems a light year away (or perhaps a "second edge" away in CR terms) from the rather depressing portraits of everyday social life which come from detailed ethnographic portraits of working class life which students of Bourdieu paint. For Akram & Hogan (2015) Archer proposes " ... a seismic shift [from Bourdieu's account] in how people form and conduct themselves in everyday life, a process that would result in the realization of extremely high levels of *ethical autonomy* ... she goes beyond Giddens' and Bourdieu's notions of everyday, routinized taken-for-granted actions ... offering an entirely new view of how people form, manage and understand themselves in everyday life." (p. 610).

Archer (like Alderson, 2013, p. 80) does not reject Bourdieu's account of "everyday habitus", but offers instead a novel form of the social psychology of everyday life. What is novel (among other things) is Archer's idea of *agency*, which is developed within the framework of Bhaskar's dialectical critical realism. Personal reflexivity (renewing one's own thoughts, feelings and actions in relation to those of others) is likely to be shared according to Archer, by all people who find themselves in similar social situations.

Akram & Hogan (2015) sum up their understanding of Archer's position:

"Reflexivity is the regular ability, shared by all normal people, to consider themselves in relation to their social contexts and vice versa ... Reflexivity in modern society means a transition from a morphostatic to a morphogenetic society of constant change. Reflexivity is also linked to our emotional commitments and our moral concerns ... all of which help to maintain 'the internal conversation' which reflects ongoing conversations in agents about who they are, and how they see their lives progressing ... Archer's work raises the idea that individuals think about who they are (in the sense of personal and social identity) and modify their identity in the course of everyday being ... Central to such a practice of the self is a deep sense of awareness of who one is, how one became who they are, and the benefits of pursuing such new performative aspects of identity." (Akram & Hogan, p. 620)

In this new world (for it seems to be too exciting to be like the old world which we all remember):

"Reflexivity emerges from a new social and cultural order, which creates novel situational contexts, and which they must negotiate ... In such a scenario, agents draw upon their socially dependent, but nevertheless personal powers of reflexivity to define their courses of action ... Reflexivity is not necessarily positive, because it can also have negative outcomes ... some will be taking the best course, but may make mistakes ... not all reflexion is successful, but all are crucially trying to be reflexive." (Archer, 1995, p 110).

In *Making our Way through the World* (1995) Archer argues that there is movement between modes of reflexivity, taking the agent through the various levels of the MELD model. But at each level the individual's "internal conversation" is crucial. Archer defines four types of reflexivity, which can occur at any of the MELD levels:

"Communicative Reflexivity (conversations with others, before they can lead to action); Autonomous Reflexivity (internal conversations that are self-contained, leading directly to action); Meta-Reflexivity (internal conversations about critical actions within society);

Fractured Reflexivity (broken or negative conversations). And reflexivity can assume crucial importance in times of stress and change. Progress and change are not inevitable." (Archer, 2013, p. 15)

Akram & Hogan (2015) are impressed by Archer's thesis, and comment:

> "Archer's work raises the idea that individuals think about the way they are (in the sense of personal social identity) modifying their identity in the course of everyday being ... But what does it mean when she says that agents regularly rethink and evaluate their everyday being? ... Central to such a practice of self-reflexion is a deep sense of awareness of who one is, how one became who they are, and the benefits of pursuing such new performative aspects of identity." Akram & Hogan, 2015, p. 621)

Akram & Hogan raise important questions of how different Archer's idea of self-reflexion is from Bourdieu's notion of habitus. This is clearly a fascinating area for qualitative research, for eliciting extended accounts of how people in specific communities, or with shared pasts (e.g., ethnicities, childhood experiences) construe themselves through their intellectual, moral and emotional histories, their reactions to others, how they share thoughts, feelings and opinions.

Margaret Archer (2014) replaces the idea of postmodernism with that of "late modernity", enabling a "trajectory towards a morphogenetic society". That, in Marxist terms, would be a society liberated from the oppression forces of alienation.[7] There is lyrical

---

[7] In an interview conducted with Archer by Jamie Morgan (Archer & Morgan, 2020), Margaret Archer observed that: "I have just finished my five-year term of office as President of PASS [Pontifical Academy of Social Sciences]. Pope Francis, who appointed me in 2014, pursues a humanitarian social agenda, ecumenical in outreach, which I have no problem at all in promoting. I often say that he has turned the Church into a social movement; despite internal opposition and external indifference. For

parallel to the morphogenetic insights which Archer writes about, in the model of "wonder" which Ahmed (2004) derives from the writing of Descartes (on the body's first passionate response to 'cognitive surprise'), and the "sensuous certainty" which Marx describes in his first dawning of consciousness concerning the unmasking of alienation:

> "The body opens as the world opens up before it; the body unfolds into the unfolding of a world that becomes approached as another body. This opening is not without its risks: wonder can be closed down if what we approach is unwelcome ... But wonder is a passion that motivates the desire to keep looking; it keeps alive the possibility of freshness, and vitality of living that can live as if for the first time ... wonder involves the radicalisation of our relation to the past, which is transformed into that which lives and breathes in the present." (Ahmed, 2004, p. 180).

This sense of *wonder* was also evoked by Abubaker et al. (2022) in which Mahmoud Abubaker describes following his post-Gazan warfare experience, an intellectual and emotional awakening. This is illustrated too, in the writing of Izeldin Abuelaish in his 2011 book *I Shall Not Hate: A Gaza Doctor's Journey on the Road to Peace and Human Dignity* in which he describes how an Israeli tank fired at close quarters into the first floor of his house, killing his teenaged daughters and their cousin, and severely injuring his son. His

---

example, his first initiative was to move against human trafficking and this was infectious. Thus, I edited books, wrote chapters – no different from what you are all used to – and ended up starting a small charity in my home town for trafficked women and their children (Archer, 2019) ... I was present at COP21 in Paris, 2015 ... My role was to field questions on social implications. Take advantage of our publications – they are free to download, and not pious. As one Cardinal advised me, 'Write about global social problems, but don't tangle with theology'. As for my more recent work on CSO [RC funded] projects, these too broadly align with a lifetime interest in emancipatory and explanatory social science, and my curiosity remains unabated in regard of a world that continues to 'intrigue'."

reaction was that of Islamic peace-making, and a campaign for the education of orphaned children. The sense of awe, of awakening awareness of possibilities of doing good deeds, of enhancing the social contract between individuals, groups, institutions and religions is a central part of the humanistic endeavour (Schneider et al., 2014). Indeed, Schneider (2017) writes of "the spirituality of awe" in how human experience can transcend base materialism..

This 'awe' implies too that critical realism should also like Marxism, be concerned with alienation, the separation of the individual from the 'natural' status implied by their relationship to the social equity required by 'labour'. This alienation, a form of habitus, is an "enslaving ideology" transmitted between generations: Dialectic Critical Realism's task is to 'unmask' this alienation, and replace 'false consciousness' with reflexive knowledge which enables social structures, and individuals interacting within those structures morphogenetically, to achieve freedom within the commonwealth of humanity.

Critical Realism's Marxist dimension

Throughout Critical Realist writing there is mention of Marx, much of it critical, although Roy Bhaskar (2008) clearly draws inspiration from Marx and Hegel, even when he is moulding their ideas creatively into an entirely new way of understanding "society and nature." Bhaskar, writing about critical realism before he developed influential ideas concerning dialectical critical realism, observed:

> On the basis of the critical realist solutions to these questions (e.g., how to reconcile structural causality with effective human agency) I suggest that Marxian social science is about constraints on the reproduction and transformation of social structures. The knowledge of these constraints is the ground for a liberated understanding. (Bhaskar, 2008, p. 29)

Yet the forces of capitalism in the post 1970s neoliberal mode have found new ways to mask alienation through the exploitation of despair, and control of electronic media (Case & Deaton, 2020; Adam-Bagley, 2022).

Critical Realism, in Daniel Little's (2012a & b) analyses sees critical thinking as "emancipatory". In both Marxist and DCR traditions the term "critical" has specific meaning. Bhaskar cites Marx's Feurbach thesis: "The philosophers have sought to understand the world: the point however is to change it." In this model, critical science is an engaged or committed scientific endeavour, aiming to construct knowledge that may be, according to CR's emancipatory paradigm, for humanity's long-term benefit. Like Marx's *Capital*, which was subtitled "a critique of political economy", DCR also attempts to expose the underlying ideologies of powerful interest groups, and to expose "false consciousness".

On the difficulties of research findings actually leading to change, Alderson (2013) observes:

> "Many childhood researchers are disappointed that their 'participative research' ends with the neat reported findings (words) seldom leading to real, messy, transformative change (deeds). DCR helps to identify and remedy this problem, in following Marx by identifying five types of practical contradictions to be resolved if real change is to occur." (Alderson, 2013, p. 91).

Alderson continues her analysis of DCR in Marxist mode in discussing Bhaskar's (2008) borrowing from Marx of the idea of "the master-slave relationship", which goes beyond the power of "masters" in older societies, to all kinds of power relationships:

> "'Master-slave' relationships involve Marx's understanding of concepts that are central to DCR [identifying] ... forms that have immanent contradictions that can suggest an ideal and misleading representation of the world; and also a real world that can be

described, classified and explained in various, changing and developing ways. Marx, as a scientific realist, believed that explanatory structures are essentially not only distinct from, but are often ... in opposition to the phenomena they generate. Examples include the way many schools fail many of their students ..." (Alderson, 2013, p. 111)

Marxist scholars who have identified "master-slave" relationships in schools are, for example Coard (2005) on the labelling of Black children in England as "subnormal"; Stahl (2015) and Willis (2017) on working class boys in England "learning to labour"; and Banfield's (2016) Marxist sociology of education. But the educational administrators of England often maintain that authority in schools must be preserved, if we are to produce workers for a functioning economy (Adam-Bagley & Pritchard, 2000).

"The ruling classes, according to Bhaskar, claim that their enduring power, far from being an abuse of the slave by his master, is, rather their right and duty (like the colonial 'white man's burden') and is also in everyone's best interests. This Marxist idea of false-consciousness, or mystifying of the reality, is propagated as a routine part of class power." (Alderson, 2013, p. 116)

Now "learning to labour" has evolved into "learning for precarity" (Dovemark & Beach, 2016), as disadvantaged young people move into precarious and low paid employment in a class-divided culture (Adam-Bagley, 2022).

Grant Banfield (2016) in his *Critical Realism for Marxist Sociology of Education* uses the terms "Marxist" and "Marxian" interchangeably. This, I infer, is a way of saying that although he is a Marxist, he is certainly not a Marxist-Leninist. He defers to Roy Bhaskar's 'spiritual socialism', quoting Bhaskar's early (1986) writing:

"I take it that whatever our politics ... socialists can agree that what we must be about today is the building of a movement for socialism

– in which socialism wins a cultural hegemony, so that it becomes the enlightened common-sense of our age." (Bhaskar, 1986, p. 1)

Banfield tells us that his 'starting premise', is that education should be, in Marx's words 'revolutionary practice.' According to Banfield:

"Education is part of what Gramsci has actually called 'the war of position' ... where the trenches of civil society are won in classrooms, workplaces, pubs and on street corners, that socialism becomes ... the enlightened common-sense of our age. According to Bhaskar, not only is there an elective affinity between critical realism and historical realism, but also the original intent of critical realism was to support the science of history that Marx had opened up ... it is in their differences that the real possibilities of a working relationship between critical realism and Marxism are established." (Banfield, 2016, p. 1)

This last point is important: DCR may draw on Marxist ideas, but it goes beyond Marx's interpretation, including his use of Hegel. Furthermore:

"A crucial defining feature of critical realism is the seriousness with which it takes ontology. This seriousness is an antidote to what we will see as tendencies in fields like the sociology of education (and Marxist sociology of education) to ontological shyness." (Banfield, 2016, p. 3)

An ontology based on the stratified, four-level MELD model permits

"... Bhaskar's stratified, differentiated ... real ontology indicating that what appears and is immediately experienced are only surface features of deeper realities ... Bhaskar's emergentist ontology allowed him to advance an emancipatory critique of human-harming social structures ... With understanding of the structural causal relations underlying them comes an ethical responsibility to negate and overturn them. Science is simultaneously a social and emancipatory practice: the underlying methodological content common to both the natural and social sciences is emancipation: Bhaskar's dialectic of 'the pulse to freedom.'" (Banfield, 2016, p. 4)

As Brad Shipway (2013) observes in his *Critical Realist Perspective of Education*, schools are particularly appropriate places for a (Marxian) critical realist analysis and reconstruction, in ways pioneered in the work of Margaret Archer (2014). They contain, and control (and often harm) our precious children; they are the state's agents of socialization; they control and discipline, preparing the young to be rulers, administrators, technicians, labourers, excluded minorities, or the reserve army of labour - according to the school's various rituals, values and social structures ranging from those of the 'public' schools to the 'crumbling comprehensive' servicing 'sink' housing estates (Sawyerr & Adam-Bagley, 2017).

Our conclusion is that critical realism enriches and humanises Marxism, and counters the development of reactionary themes such as "the dictatorship of the masses". DCR's spiritual aspirations concerning the soul and the self also enrich the insights of Marxism. Alderson's use (2013 to 2021) of Bhaskar's four level-analysis in writing about children and their emancipation, their flourishing, and their possibilities for fulfilled and non-alienated lives is profoundly creative, and inspirational. Collier (2002) argues that critical realism "can add to Marxism without taking anything away" - but he acknowledges that some of his fellow authors (in an edited volume on *Critical Realism and Marxism*), may disagree.

We note too the views of Creaven (2007), who is the most enthusiastic of the "Marxist critical realists". Examining how Marx and Engels worked together, he observed that Engel's was the "underlabourer", clearing away the underbrush of false ideas and philosophical nonsense that impeded the clarity of Marxian ontological analysis. (Wilkinson, 2015a, too uses this idea, taken from Thomas Hobbes, of underlabouring, which clarifies the road to emancipation in the critical realist model). Engels' survey of "the condition of the working class in England" was one of the underlabouring tasks for Marx's theory of *Capital*, for instance.

In Creaven's (2007) analysis "Marxism was already, implicitly a critical realist social theory." Thus Bhaskar's evaluative realism, " ... provides (in Marx's phrase) an ethical basis for championing the struggles of the oppressed' as a natural principle of justice." (p. 29) Creaven (2015) further uses Bhaskar's dialectical model to resolve the tensions between the "two Marxisms" – structuralism, and humanism - to show that there is a "coherent unity" between the two forms.

Application of Critical Realism models in contrasted fields of research

Critical realism and 'social ontology' models have become increasingly popular with researchers in several areas of social science research, although the bulk of research is still undertaken with children and adolescents in educational, health and social care settings (Alderson, 2021). One interesting development is the growth of CR research in the area of industrial sociology, and human relations management (Zacharialis et al, 2010), and a recent methodology textbook (Edwards et al., 2014) includes case examples of how to approach research settings in the CR mode, to collect relevant data, and interpret it using dialectical critical realism.

Easton (2010) offers a useful guide to case study research using critical realism, for use in organisational, business and human relations management. In Easton's Critical Realist model, the case study must be grounded on a firm ontological basis of "truth", of a description of the nature and implicit values of the organisation studied. He recites the "basic assumptions" of CR:

"Firstly, the world exists independently of our knowledge of it; secondly, our knowledge of the world is fallible, self-deceiving, cloaked in implicit or poorly-organised theories whose assumptions are not often explicit – thus our initial concepts of truth and falsity often fail to provide a coherent view of the relationship between knowledge and its object; thirdly, the realm we wish to research is differentiated and stratified ... by actions, texts and institutions, and they are all concept dependent." (Easton, 2010, p. 120)

Easton urges:

"Critical realism first of all makes the ontological assumption that there is a reality, but it is usually difficult to apprehend. I distinguish between the real world, the actual events that are created by the real world and the empirical events which we can actually capture and record. Thus we will always be surprised about the nature of the real ... The research process is one of continuous cycles of research and reflection. The final result is the identification of one or more mechanisms that can be regarded as having caused events." (Easton, 2010, p. 128)

The present writers have used Critical Realist approaches in studies of how women in an Islamic culture cope with oppression and change (Abubaker et al. 2022); and how nurses in England cope with stress in an era of COVID challenge (Adam-Bagley et. al, 2018 & 2021): CR is a way of researching, understanding and potentially changing many sub-systems in a complex social structure.

Reflections on Critical Realism

In reading Bhaskar, Alderson, Wilkinson, Archer and other critical realists, we have been struck by a new facet of communication and information which influences all of our lives: the electronic information system of the web from which we are constantly gleaning information; and as well as sending frequent e-mails and texts, the sharing of ideas and images with friends (and others) on sites such as

Face Book, Twitter etc. The youngsters among us are no longer truly part of themselves: we share ourselves, reflexively, with a much wider world than when Roy Bhaskar published his first book, in 1978. What is the meaning of this electronic world? Alderson (2013, p. 102) is worried about the covert collection of children's electronic data as a means of controlling them, an electronic version of Bhaskar's (2008) 'master-slave' relationship. But there is also a powerful anarchy in the data which is collected on all of us, and liberation when it is released through the integrity of 'whistle-blowing'. Adrian Smith (2023), who leads the Alan Turing Institute and is an expert on electronic intelligence argues that the massive amount of data shared on all of us requires a new form of "the social contract", in which we mutually agree not to use these data to manipulate or exploit one another. The best option is that of honesty, not concealing one's (evil) self behind an electronic firewall, but engaging frankly with honesty, love and respect with one's fellow citizens.

Critical realism gives to the student what Ahmed (2014) calls a sense of "wonder" in rediscovering and redesigning the social matrix of her world:

> "This critical wonder is about recognising that nothing in the world can be taken for granted, which includes the very political movements to which we are attached. It is this critical wonder about the forms of political struggle that makes Black feminism such an important intervention, by showing that categories of knowledge (such as patriarchy or 'women') have political effects, which can exclude others from the collective …" (Ahmed, 2014, p. 182).

Roy Bhaskar was intellectually active for 30 years of a brief life, but with each new book he continued to surprise us, adding to our intellectual awe. For the spiritually inclined, the development of his early Hinduism was startling, but pleasing, and increased our interfaith understanding and enterprise. In illustration we offer this quotation from one of his final writings:

Now, the principle of universal solidarity is grounded transcendentally in the fact that we could have been someone other than ourselves. But the philosophy of Meta Reality also grounds our capacity to empathize or transcendentally identify with the other more radically through the idea of co-presence. This involves the notion that the other is not just something I could have been, but rather that the other is indeed a part of oneself. This involves a radical displacement of the subject of the philosophical discourse of modernity ... we approach the thought embodied in some southern African languages by the notion of 'ubuntu' which means roughly 'I am because you are'. (Bhaskar, 2015, p.211).

Child-Centred Humanism (CCH): A guiding or underlabouring principal

Bhaskar (2008) advocates the idea of "underlabouring", derived from Hobbes, in clearing the intellectual debris which clutters the modern epistemology of social research. How such labour is construed and designed is a matter for the individual researcher: thus the Islamic scholar Matthew Wilkinson deploys the idea of fulfilment through performing "good deeds", an important principle of Islamic social action (Wilkinson et al 2012 to 2022). This involves too the principle of *zakah*, of giving to others according to their needs, an important principle of Islamic socialism (Hamid, 2003). While we commend these approaches, our own underlabouring guide stems from our definition of *humanism*, both religious and secular, as outlined in the first chapter of this book.

We advocate in particular the ideal of *child-centred humanism* as the principle through which all human actions (including social analysis, such as critical realism) should be judged. Within Critical Realism, what underlabouring is concerned with is a general ethical model, the working model through which ethical principles and practices are weighed and performed. The under-labourers are the everyday workers, of good-will who in Collier's (1994) script:

" ... aim to remove the idols (Bacon), obstacles (Locke) or ideologies (Marx) that stand in the way of, new knowledge to be produced by the [social] sciences." (Collier, 1994 p. 19)

Every person is their *own* philosopher in Critical Realism, not just the professor in her ivory tower. Alderson observed that critics of modern social research methods "... overlook how philosophy is integral to everyday and research thinking, and that a main task of philosophy is to be an under-labourer, clearing away rubbish, and laying foundations. The philosopher Mary Midgley (1996) in like manner, compares everyday philosophy with plumbing: "These can both be ignored and taken for granted until they are not working well ... [but then] plumbing's equivalent in clear logical thinking, has to be fixed. "

For the Muslim Critical Realist (Wilkinson, 2015a), underlabouring is both literally and figuratively, doing good deeds like clearing the highway of rubbish, effectively implementing the *Sunnah,* the life and teaching of Prophet Muhammad. In Hadith 26 of Imam Nawawi's collection of Muhammad's advice, for example: "Every joint of a person must perform a charity each day that the sun rises ... every good word is a charity ... and removing a harmful object from the road is a charity." Every step, every action, must serve others, and in our Child Centred Humanism (CCH) every action, thought, deed and intention must 'underlabour' the principle: *Children First.*

Margaret Archer, Critical Realism and morphogenesis

Margaret Archer's work grew out of her concerns with the struggles of working-class children to achieve upward social mobility through the comprehensive school system (the topic of her doctoral thesis), and her early publications were in the field of educational sociology (Archer, 2007 & 2013). Her work has now expanded its moral compass to possess a more complete ethical domain. Like other critical realists (e.g. Bhaskar, Collier, Wilkinson) she is both radical in a political sense (Scambler, 2012), but nevertheless, also appears to be strongly influenced (as was Green) by "the ontology of God".

Although Archer does not make explicit her theological position (except in one joint publication – Archer, Collier & Porpora. 2004, on "the divine ontology" replacing positivist agnosticism; and in her reflections on applied research – Archer & Morgan, 2020), we detect elements of the Vincentian *will* in her position: each human being, however wretched their situation (e.g. as a slave, or a prisoner) has moral challenges each day, possibilities of kindness and mercy to others which they may act upon, reflect upon, and recreate themselves in, despite their wretched situation: their spiritually at least, as Archer would put it, one of 'upward mobility' (St. Vincent de Paul, himself a slave for many years, argued that even the 'poorest' human is capable of daily acts of kindness – Pujo, 2003).

Reflecting on one's past, on the events of yesterday, and on the events of childhood are a core part of Roy Bhaskar's dialectical interchange in which the passive past ("the absence") is pondered and recreated in a new present. In this model we recreate in our new "story" not merely ourselves, but we also acknowledge the ethic that childhood is the primary social institution from which accounts of civilization are developed. This self-reflective pathway in seeking ethical behaviours is grounded psychologically, in Mead's (1964) idea of the reflexive self, modified and extended by Archer (2003), and carried forward in the ideas of stories for creative self-hood by Plummer (2020).

Conclusions

Finally, we add to Child-Centred Humanism (CCH), Marx's idea of alienation from the self. This alienation is imposed by an exploitive society in which making profit is the dominant motive, explicit or implicit, ordering how human values are *officially* framed, and how social institutions and public debates are moulded. In Marxian theory, the capitalist system has created an underclass, a 'reserve army of labour' who are chronically under-employed and under-skilled but who can be called on in times of economic boom or growth to become labourers and service workers, for the benefit of capital and the minimisation of wages (for the reserve army is constantly looking for work, at or below minimum wage). The children of the poor, in this model, must be segregated into 'sink' estates of public housing, in which they can be observed, ordered, schooled, contained and controlled. Some of these children would, as Engels (1845) observed, graduate into being career criminals and could then be safely contained in penal institutions. Others can be given a decent second class education which will enable them, when required, to be hewers of wood and drawers of water.

CCH is passionately concerned with the unmasking of the alienation which clouds the consciousness of these families and their children (who temporarily contain ethnic and religious minorities, and refugees; but with a solid phalanx of 'poor whites'). As Scambler (2013) writes of Margaret Archer's view of Marxian theory: "To introduce the concept of ideology is necessarily to introduce that of false-consciousness." And dialectic critical materialism's reflexive model can in its reflexive, morphogenetic mode, help those with "fractured reflexivities" to grasp "true-consciousness", sharing with those in the sink estate, a fuller realisation of their position.

Everyone, in Thomas Green's and Margaret Archer's models of social action, may achieve upward mobility, to the life of the gentle-person. In Wilkinson's Islamic Critical Realist (CR) model, it is the journey on the Straight Path (the focus on a self-disciplined journey, recited in each of the five daily prayers) that ensures that the faithful imitate Prophet Muhammad's peaceful example. For Muslims, the soul given by God resides in each human being, not merely in Muslims, and the Muslim's task is to seek out and serve (as do Quakers) the soul of everyone. Again, CCH's model of reciprocal love, and CR's reflexive morphogenesis seem to converge in this social contract.

Matthew Wilkinson and his fellow scholars in Cardiff and Manchester (Wilkinson et al, 2021 & 2022) in their work on Muslim prisoners in England and Wales are probably the most active scholars applying Critical Realism in addressing and solving crucial social issues, and it is clear that their influential work will be modelled and replicated by others. David Pilgrim (2019) in a textbook exploring and applying Critical Realism to the development of transdisciplinary psychological research concludes with a broad, but justified claim for DCR:

> " ... given the current existential threat to our species from ecocide and the remaining chance of nuclear annihilation, Bhaskar's teaching on seriousness has a wider pertinence. For psychology and other disciplines, the overarching question relates to the wider contribution it makes not only to human flourishing but now its very survival. Critical Realism provides a holistic philosophical framework to explore some answers. (Pilgrim, 2019, p. 179)

The Children's Charter of Development Rights

The following Children's Charter, which we reproduce here since it fits so well with CCH principles, comes from the Save Childhood Movement, reflecting Article 3 of the UN Convention of the Rights of the Child: "In all actions concerning children, whether undertaken by public or private social welfare institutions, courts or administrative bodies, the best interests of the child shall be of primary consideration." The Children's Charter advocates:

> '**Awareness**: Children have the right to live in societies that are fully informed about the evidence supporting healthy human learning

and development, societies which take action to protect children's rights and freedoms based on this awareness.

Health and Wellbeing: National and local decision makers have the duty to provide environments that maximise children's physical, mental, emotional and spiritual wellbeing. In doing so they should recognise the vital importance of parents, families and local communities and the intrinsic human need for belonging and contribution.

New Technology: Policy makers have the duty to ensure that young people's development is safeguarded from the unintended developmental consequences of living in a digital world.

Learning and development: Children have the right to be protected from any system that might inhibit their innate curiosity, creativity and love of learning ....

Adult Wellbeing is essential for child wellbeing. Adults have the right to expect the cultural and social systems within which they live to support their own learning and self-development. Children ... have the right to be protected from any relationships that are harmful to their health and well-being.

Pre-Birth: ... mothers and babies have the right to be protected from all factors that might compromise their prenatal health and their birth experiences.

Engagement and Encouragement: Children have the right to be in the company of informed and encouraging adults who help to enhance the ways in which they can relate to and understand the world.

Physical Activity: Children have the right to be provided with environments that enable them to develop all of their senses and physical capacities.

Body Image: Children have the right to be protected from negative media and commercial influences that might undermine their confidence and self-worth.

Play: Children have the right to be provided with the time and space to explore their environments in unstructured ways that nurture their creativity, independence, self-confidence, self-expression, cooperation and emotional resilience.

Risk-Taking: Children have the right to learn from challenge, to experience failure as learning, and to become confident and adventurous explorers of the environment.

Wonder and Awe: Children have the right to maintain a deep connection with the natural world that helps them feel part of something greater than themselves and fosters compassion and empathy ...

Stewardship: Children have the right to be protected from systems that endanger their own future. They need to learn about plants, animals and ecosystems so that they understand the importance of balance and sustainability and can grow up as stewards of the environment.'

For the full text see: www.savechildhood.net

Chapter 3
A Social Scientist's Journey from Quaker to Muslim: Developing A Theology for Social Action
Chris Adam-Bagley

"The humble, meek, merciful, just, pious, and devout souls are everywhere of one religion; and when death has taken off the mask they will know one another, though the divers liveries they wear here [on earth] makes them strangers."

William Penn, 1693 [1]

Introduction and purpose

My first purpose is to give a brief overview of Quaker Universalism, and of Quakers' sympathetic links to Islam. I then give an account of a personal intellectual, moral and spiritual journey from Jewish great grandparents escaping pogroms in Russia, who then recreating an "English" identity through Anglicanism; and following this, a theological journey through Quakerism into Islam, based on collaboration with Muslim social scientists in Britain, Palestine, Bangladesh and Pakistan. I give accounts of our research in Gaza, Pakistan and Bangladesh, describing the hard struggles to develop Islamically just and peaceful societies.

A particular focus has been on the emergence of powerful Muslim women, in Britain, Netherlands and Gaza as successful managers and professionals, in ways supported by the Qur'an (God's Message to humanity, delivered through Prophet Muhammad), and by Shari'a (Islamic moral and legal principles derived from the Qur'an, defining human morality and conduct).

I focus too on the pluralism of religious identities in Western countries, and how Islamic dignity may overcome the alienating trauma of Islamophobia, in peaceful ways. This theme is also explored in relation to Gazan women, whose pacifist identity may be a powerful tool in the struggles for national liberation; and through the co-operative and non-violent citizenship of Muslim youth in Britain through their endeavours to become good citizens, enlightened by the *Fiqh of minorities*.

In their citizenship struggles, aiming to forgive enemies through acts of kindness and graciousness, Muslims have a strong bond with the Quaker *jihad* of "wandering the earth, seeking the light of God in everyone" (Islam has many types of jihads, including the enduring patience of a woman in carrying and birthing a child). I offer the metaphysical idea that Quaker theologies and ethics may coexist, in loving tolerance, with Islam. In this Quaker-derived exegesis of Islam, I offer an application of classical Islam which may have relevance for Western societies (and for Israel): an Islam which may achieve the transcendent goals of peace-making, developing equitable welfare states, and supporting responsible youth through Islamically-inspired citizenship education.

Quakers were a "deviant" Christian group, which grew from the rebellion of George Fox against the brutalities of the English civil war of the 1600s. Quakers have continued to evolve in radical directions, both politically and theologically.

Probably a half of Quakers today are "humanists" or "universalists", not seeing Christ as divine, but they are still trying to act out Christ's radical message [2]. While conventionally drawing some theology from Lutheran traditions, Quakers are marked by rejecting the statuses and ranks of conventional society, and the building and veneration of shrines and cathedrals ("steeple worship", in which they have interesting parallels with Wahhabist teaching on rejecting tomb and minaret veneration). What marks Quakers above all is their pacifism and rejection of military order, seeking non-violent solutions in all human affairs. They seek the essential goodness ("the light of God") in all human beings, even the Hitlers, the Stalins, the Assads and the Putins.

Quakers in Europe are well known for the *kinder transport*, which (through friendship with Nazi officials) saved the lives of many thousands of Jewish children before the second world war. Excluded from conventional professions, Quakers from the 17th century onwards pioneered chocolate drinks and foods, and founded successful banks which thrived because of Quaker insistence on absolute honesty in all human dealings (Rowntree, Cadbury, Lloyd and Barclay are well-known Quaker names, and the nurture of these enterprises led to large-scale funding of social, charitable and educational enterprises in the UK and Ireland). In North America, William Penn pioneered the Quaker tradition following Fox's death, inspiring the foundation of the State of Pennsylvania [3].

Because of their non-credal status, their explicit assumptions concerning the innate goodness of human beings, and the ideas (of many, but not all) of Jesus as a non-divine preacher and prophet, Quakers have been attractive to Jews, to Humanists, and to various Christian individuals seeking non-dogmatic and largely silent worship. Within the silent meetings for worship some individuals who are "moved by the spirit" may speak, in a manner similar to some Pentecostal meetings. Quakers have been leaders in movements against slavery and social oppression; in the acceptance of same-sex marriage; and the humane treatment of those challenged by mental illness. A leading group within Quakers is that advocating *universalism*, which seeks to find unity and common purpose in all religions, and with non-theist humanists.

This chapter seeks to give an exposition of Quakerism using a Muslim lens in developing a "theology of social action" in the process. Many Christians still retain unfavourable stereotypes of Islam as a fiercely violent and militant, women-oppressing religion. I want to convey my experience (and the relevant research) which demonstrate the opposite: Islam may be a graceful, fun-loving religion, full of good deeds and gratefulness for Allah's creation, and guidance for each human individual. This essay is not simply "an Islamic perspective of Quakerism." It is the subjective reflection of one who was born a Jew, became a Christian, then a Quaker, and finally a devoted Muslim.

All of these statuses, given me at birth or from my later choosing, have led logically to one another, with the brilliant sensations of being created and loved by God, whose first level of paradise has already spilled upon the earth from the garden in which our first parents were created. We are all children of Adam and Hawwa, in becoming custodians of a beautiful earth.

From being a practising Christian (through an Anglican upbringing, through which our grand-parents sought to disguise our Jewish origins, in antisemitic England) I became a universalist Quaker, leaving behind the obfuscation and confusion of many Jewish and Christian texts.

No longer did I wish to believe that Jews/Christians should rejoice in killing infants by smashing their heads against the rocks (Psalms of David 137, v. 7-9). [4] But in criticizing "sacred texts" we should also remember, in humility, that there are elements of truth in these texts, and it is this truth that we should seek – to quote Karen Armstrong:

> " ... charity and loving kindness are essential to biblical interpretation. In our dangerously polarized world, a common hermeneutics among the religions should surely emphasize this tradition. Jews, Christians

and Muslims must first examine the flaws of their own scriptures and only then listen, with humility, generosity and charity to the exegesis of others." [5]

In relatively recent times, Christian leaders were caught up in a fugue of anti-Muslim hatred which exceeded in venom even the Christian diatribes associated with the Crusades [6] [7]. In contrast, remarkably throughout its history Islam has been faithful to Qur'anic principle in being tolerant of monotheistic groups in countries where several religious groups co-dwell. The Abrahamic religions of Judaism and Christianity have traditionally been tolerated (according to Qur'anic instruction) as minority groups within Muslim-majority cultures. All that has been required of these minority groups in Muslim states is that they should reciprocate this tolerance, follow their own religions faithfully, obey general laws, and if a working adult pay a basic tax (a traditional tithe of income).

Their rewards were protection and tolerance (including support from Islamic welfare systems) but without the obligation of military service. Jewish groups fleeing from religious oppression in Spain were offered sanctuary and protection in Muslim countries (including Palestine) for many centuries (Lapidus, 2002) [8]. This harmonious balance was undermined when Western colonialism suppressed the Muslim polity of North African and Middle Eastern countries (Lewis, 2013) [8], and more directly in 1948 with the founding of the State of Israel, which was imposed on Palestine without that nation's consultation, or any material assistance for relocation and social re-organisation of displaced people, from the major world powers.

Our reading of this history is that international powers, in horror at the revelation of the Nazi holocaust, washed their hands of the so-called "Jewish problem" by resettling Jews in a land long occupied by Arabs, to the profound disadvantage of the latter. As the American Muslim scholar Mehnaz Alfridi (2014) [8] puts it: "The

Holocaust was a crime inflicted by Europeans for which Palestinians paid the price." By this she meant, inter alia, that Christian ideas about Jewish responsibility for Christ-killing provided the ideological foundations of antisemitic values, culminating in National Socialism's holocaust of Jewish people. Mehnaz Alfridi has taken the bold step (as a Muslim) of teaching Jewish and Muslim history as an interwoven matrix, stressing that both Islam and Judaism have been historical victims of Christian imperialism.

Christianity in contrast, has been profoundly intolerant of other religions, particularly Islam and Judaism, providing the ideological underpinning of centuries of pogroms and ultimately, the value substrate of the holocaust itself [9].

Islam in Europe today: The life of the Mosque

My experience of Islam began in Britain, and extended to The Netherlands where I've long had research interest in religious pluralism and the treatment and acceptance of ethnic and religious minorities [10], so my account of everyday life in Mosques or Masjids is confined mainly to experience in these two countries. Central to Islam is the idea of surrendering oneself to the will of Allah, accepting God's final message to humanity in The Qur'an, and believing that Muhammad is the final Prophet in a long line of prophets.

Other obligations for the Muslim include prayer five times a day, from dawn until after sunset; giving *zakat*, a prescribed amount of personal wealth to charity each year; fasting during the month of Ramadan (the month in which The Prophet received the first of the Surahs of the Qur'an); and if health and means allow, making the pilgrimage to Makkah at least once in one's lifetime.

Besides the five daily prayers which are usually carried out with other family members, fellow workers, or in The Mosque, male Muslims are expected to attend for one of their daily prayers at The

Mosque each Friday, and hear a *khutbah* (sermon) from the local Imam or Sheikh . Mosques (in Britain, and across the world) are always busy places from dawn to late at night, with rich carpets upon which we pray towards Makkah. Scattered around the Mosque will be worshippers reading The Qur'an, saying private prayers, while gleeful young boys expend energy in racing along the carpet in their stockinged feet, in between bouts of learning the Qur'an by heart. Leaving one's shoes at the door is both a symbolic and practical way of leaving behind the sin and dirt of the outside world. Islam puts much emphasis on personal cleanliness, and cleansing oneself after toileting.

In the Mosque there are separate washing facilities for men and women, in which the ceremony of *wudu* (washing feet, hands, nose, ears, mouth and head) is performed as ritual purification before praying. Much food is served in anterooms, many study groups meet, brothers of the Ummah (the worldwide brotherhood and sisterhood of Muslims) greet one another, with young sons and daughters often accompanying their fathers in the main Mosque (women and girls pray separately).

Women enjoy their own sisterhood, or Ummah. Women pray in separate areas, or at the rear of the mosque, for dignity's sake. Puzzled Quakers have asked me why women pray separately – are they forced to do this? No, the nature of Muslim prayer justifies this. I stand in a prayer line shoulder to shoulder and foot to foot with my brothers on either side. In this physical unity we bend, kneel and pray with our foreheads upon the prayer mat, and in supplication to Allah as we recite the first chapter of the Qur'an. The physical closeness, and the balletic unison of our movement is an exquisite moment of bonding with one another, and with Allah. To be this close to a woman in the prayer line is physically and morally impossible: we would be utterly undone and distracted by having our Sisters in the same prayer line.

In the Masjid men greet affectionately, shaking hands, kissing and embracing. Worshippers are a mosaic of colours, ranging from the fair skin of the European converts and the Chechnya-heritage, through the medium brown of those of Arab, Iranian, Pakistani, Malaysian, Middle Eastern, Indonesian and Indian heritage, to the lovely richness of the dark skinned East and West African heritage groups.

In Islam the concept of 'race' is meaningless, although cultural differences often prevail so that a Mosque in a western country may reflect the language of the majority of Muslims in the local community, such as Urdu, Turkish or Arabic, and the *khutbah* will be delivered in an ethnic minority's language, but then will be translated into English or Dutch.

The Qur'an was received from Almighty God (through the agency of the Angel Gibreel) and was then relayed by the Prophet in classical Arabic; the Arabic language has remained largely unchanged since the first Qur'an's first revelation to Muhammad in 610 CE. Some of the five daily prayers are publicly recited in Arabic, although longer prayers may be silently uttered in translation: translations of The Qur'an are numerous, but sometimes controversial, since each translation is a form of exegesis. Arabic is not *the* language of God, and in receiving the message, Muhammed may have registered it within himself, but uttered it in Arabic. His companions learned by heart The Prophet's relayed message, and these learned versions were written down to form the whole Qur'an.

We are enjoined to learn Arabic in order to understand the Message fully: for those past childhood and without facility in language learning this is a major challenge, and we must often rely on translations into our local language [11].

During the month of Ramadan, no food or liquid is taken during daylight hours. This may be challenging for those living in countries of the far north or south. In Leeds in Northern England in 2022 the period of fasting was from about 4:00 in the morning until about 9:30 in the evening, so all food and liquid had to be eaten between late evening and early morning. The first special meal, *iftar*, involves a meeting of much social and spiritual significance, like the ritual meal which the Christian holy communion involves. Often the fast is broken in the late evening in the Mosque with a shared meal, followed by special prayers.

Ramadan (which begins on a different day each year, according to the moon's phase) is a time for specially nourishing and delicious food during the night hours. Ramadan too is a time for paying the *Zakat* contributions to charity (2.5% of one's material assets) since at this time the money is especially blessed. Islam is tolerant of those whose medical condition (e.g. diabetes, pregnancy) makes fasting inadvisable; children often fast for half of the fasting period, from about the age of 10.

Some foods in Islam are *haram* (forbidden) such as pork and alcohol, and other meat must be slaughtered by a humane method, and the animal's spirit blessed. Ramadan is a time of great bonding and shared discipline for Muslims worldwide, a remarkable event which endures in an atmosphere of mounting excitement until by the last 10 days the whole Qur'an will have been read and recited by the faithful, charitable offerings made, and sins privately confessed to, and forgiven, by Allah.

My fellow Muslims tolerate me as a vegetarian, and have friendly debates with me about my pacifist beliefs. Islam has a special role for the "stay at homes": the men who prefer to do 'women's work' rather than fight an external enemy, but who are nevertheless tolerated, just as 'quiet' gays are tolerated. "Allah will forgive him if he has deserted the army's ranks." (Hadith 2/85 recorded by Abu Dawud).

It interests me, as a (former) Quaker who had worked with a group working with lesbian and gay people, to offer an *Islamic ethic of gay conduct, and gay partnership*. A group of us argue, as Muslim men, that (a) homosexuality is not primarily about sex, it is about the enduring love and lifelong partnership of two people of the same gender being in love, caring and supporting one another; (b) such relationships can be celibate, but when sexual contact is engaged in, it must <u>not</u> involve anal intercourse, an unclean practice which is *haram*, forbidden by the Qur'an – a rule that applies to <u>both</u> homosexual and heterosexual couples; (c) Muslim gay couples should abide by rules which also apply to heterosexual couples, forbidding fornication (sexual coupling before lifelong partnership), and adultery; (d) rules of modesty mean that Muslim gay people should dress in a sober and well-covered fashion, appropriate to their gender; (e) flamboyant, sexual or quasi-sexual displays of gay affection in public by Muslims are not allowed; (f) lifelong, faithful gay couples should be respected and supported within Islam (as the 'left-handed people' whose homosexual being was created by Allah); and (g) the roles of faithful gay couples should not mimic those of 'husband' or 'wife' - each same-sexed male partner should be equal within the relationship.

The joyous "homo-sociality" of the male, Muslim ummah and the physical intimacy of the prayer line, are all metaphysical actions which bring joy and fulfilment to gay Muslim men [12].

The experience of becoming Muslim

When I began (under the guidance of my academic colleague Dr. Nader Al-Refai) researching Islam in order to compare Muslim and Quaker understandings of God and the moral behaviours that such beliefs imply, I had not anticipated that this intellectual journey would lead me to actually become a Muslim (although I should have been warned by Brett Miller-White's American experience, which led him both to convert to Islam, and also to remain if not a Quaker, at least someone understanding and respecting Quaker universalism). In the final phase of this spiritual development, I am wholly Muslim, devoted to the straight path of Islam, but sharing with Quakers a love of 'good deeds' and peace-making. [13].

Once I had embraced Islam my life changed in that a realisation of the nature of Allah, *the* God set my heart and mind spinning in a flux of wonder and joy. The moment my forehead rested on the prayer mat in submission to Allah, the whole Spirit of God renewed my soul, that soul which Almighty God implants in each of us early in our foetal life. This was a moment of awe, of religious ecstasy, a new flowering of the spirit within my body: a joy that is reached for five times each day as I repeat the *exordium*, the primary prayer of Islam on "the straight path" which we try and follow in the journey towards God, and Allah's final judgement.

Islam believes simultaneously in both free will and determinism, an interesting paradox that is resolved when we apprehend the Islamic understanding of Allah. First of all, Allah is the God, beyond and above, and different from the Christian idea of the friendly but ephemeral, shape-shifting being who is now god, now man, now father, now husband, now son, now ghost. The God of Islam is more similar in concept to the Jewish God of my early childhood.

The final message given by Allah makes it clear that this genderless God is simultaneously the creator of all things, including all universes, known and unknown; and miraculously also the knower of all thoughts, feelings and actions of each member of humankind from the beginning of creation, until the end of all human existence. For each of us Allah has ordained two angels who stand beside us recording both our good and our bad deeds.

At the final hour Almighty God will judge us: some will be found wanting, but some will achieve a life in paradise. I cannot know my fate in this regard: only Almighty God has knowledge of that final judgement. But Allah gives us numerous opportunities to earn forgiveness, in following the rules of conduct outlined in The Qur'an, through daily prayers, through fasting at the time of Ramadan, through pilgrimage, through giving to charity, through doing good deeds, and simply by asking the ever-merciful God for forgiveness.

The Blessed Prophet, in the collected Hadith (sayings of The Prophet Muhammad) has given us numerous guides to positive behaviours, the numerous good deeds which will redeem us. Islam enjoins a life of moral purpose, of joyful commitment and service to all of humanity, Muslim and Non-Muslim. Two main tasks for the Muslim are to pray to God daily, asking for guidance and forgiveness; and to undertake 'good deeds', in imitation of The Prophet's Qur'anically inspired thoughts and actions (known collectively as the *Sunnah*) [14].

Allah knows every detail of our lives (and this is true of all humans, believers and unbelievers alike), from the moment of birth to the moment of our death. God knows in advance all of the choices I will make in my life, for good or ill. The crucial point is that although God knows what my choice will be, I will only know what my choice is until the moment after I make that choice.

God has determined the choices my life course presents: but I have free will in making those choices, and God will not interfere with the manner of these choosings. Each choice I make directs my life path in a different direction, leading me to a fresh set of choices. It's as if, quantum-like, I am led by Almighty God into an endless series of fresh universes. In the words of Robert Frost's famous poem: "Two roads diverged in a wood, and I took the one less traveled by, and that has made all the difference." [15]

In Islam each individual is absolutely free in making choices, although there is an array of moral teaching to show each of us what the right choice might be on the journey to "the straight path". Like the Christian quantum physicist Don Page [16] who argues for the existence of free will, I intuit the infinite number of worlds in the quanta in which I have made (or could have made) different decisions: but in existential terms all I know is the now, my direct experience of the choices that Allah presents me with in the world in which I presently exist.

In the Islamic model, Allah is continuously giving us fresh choices, and sometimes will test our faith with severe challenges (as for example in the case of the Prophet Job). But, the Qur'an assures us, these tests will never be beyond our ability to bear: we should always have the God-given strength of making the right choice in any moral dilemma (Quran 2:86). Indeed, it is a privilege to be tested by Allah in this way, since it may give evidence that the Almighty Creator is taking a personal interest in us.

So, I emerged as a dedicated Muslim, no longer a Quaker in a traditional sense, but rejoicing in the many points of convergence between Islam and Quakerism. Islam is tolerant of monotheistic religions, and has a special affinity with Jews. Indeed, much of the Qur'an is addressed to Jews (with accounts of the lives and teachings of prophets common to both traditions). It appears to me that *Jews are a special kind of Muslim*. Both Muslims and Jews are descended from Prophet Ibrahim's two sons (either Isaac or Ishmael); and Allah promised the children of Isaac a special homeland in Canaan (now reckoned to cover Southern Lebanon, Northern Israel, and Western Syria). On this reading of the Qu'ran, the state of Israel is a righteous foundation, but may not incorporate Judea and Samaria (as Israelis term the Palestinian West Bank) [17].

And if Christians (e.g. Quakers) accept that Prophet Isa was not the unique "son of God" and did not die upon a cross, Islam and Quakers may be spiritual friends. Thus Ziauddin Sardar in his account of Muhammad's life and teaching observes, of the Islamic sources: "The legacy of Jesus is gentleness, compassion and humility. The 'peace' of which Jesus speaks, in the words of The Qur'an is this: Peace be upon me the day of my birth, on the day of my death, and on the day I shall be raised up alive." [18]

Three books of monotheism

Consider three 'sacred' books: the Old Testament, including The Torah (OT), the New Testament (NT), and The Qur'an. The OT is a collection of some historical truths (affirmed by the Qur'an), but also contains many folk myths; sometimes the messages of The Prophets come through clearly, but oftentimes the details have been fudged or forged in the mists of transmission, perhaps for political and nationalist convenience. The NT contains conflicting and sometimes vague accounts of the life, teaching and apparent death of Jesus. Biblical scholarship [4] shows that accounts in the OT and NT were written many years after the presumed events, and contain many forgeries or obfuscations, textual corruption and additions reflecting ideologies which served the needs of various power groups in the four centuries after Christ's birth.

In the first three centuries CE, three 'Christian' groups struggled to obtain power and control over New Testament content: these were the Ebionites (Jews who believed that Christ was not in fact crucified, but remained a Jew, with a message primarily for Jews); the Gnostics, who believed that the Jesus (named Christ the Messiah, in the Qur'an) held special wisdom for an elect group; and the Paulites, who developed the ideology that Christ was crucified, was the son of God etc, and was relevant for all of humankind.

The Paulites won this power struggle and tried to erase all memory and writings of other Christian groups, and eventually merged spiritual and temporal power with the Roman empire, with important but often negative consequences [19]. The Ebionites were significant in number, but to escape the Paulite pogroms fled to the east, and many of their descendants may have eventually become Muslims [20]

There is a strong case for arguing that the OT and NT are mixtures of fact and fiction. Of the Qur'an this cannot be said: either it is true, in its absolute entirety, the final message of God to humanity; or it is a fabrication. If it is true (and I can't adduce any evidence showing otherwise) then its every syllable must be taken with the utmost seriousness by anyone who believes in God. Fortunately for Jews and Christians, Islam asks that their scholars and theists merely respect Muslims and The Qur'an; there is no imperative to convert, since Islam will protect and mutually respect monotheist groups in any Islamic state, provided that these Jews and Christians do not proselytize, respect local laws, and pay local taxes. Many Jews of the diaspora (e.g., after expulsion from Spain) found refuge in Muslim countries in North Africa and Asia, until this Qur'anically derived policy was usurped by colonial occupation by Western powers [8].

The Qur'an

Compared with the other two books of the Bible, the Qur'an is rather short, with 6,236 verses arranged in 114 books or Surahs. Conventionally the Surahs are listed by length, longest first. Each Surah has a characteristic name. Surah 19, for instance, has the title *Mary*, and its 98 verses give an account of Mary (Maryam), the birth of Jesus (Isa), and of incidents in the life of Prophet Isa.

The Message of the Qur'an was revealed by God's agency in the form of Angel Gabriel, to Muhammad over a 23-year period, beginning when Muhammad was engaging in religious contemplation when he was 40 years old, and ended in the year of his death. The Prophet was bewildered and anguished by the early revelations, but with the support of his wife Khadija repeated each segment of the message, which was in turn learned by heart by The Prophet's companions. The first complete and formal transcription of the message into an authorised written form was made about 18 years after Muhammad's death in 632 CE, when various oral versions and written transcripts made in earlier years were gathered together.

The Message given to Muhammad comes from a stern yet compassionate and merciful God. The penalties for rejecting the Message, and continuing with traditional polytheistic beliefs were seemingly severe, but for the faithful there remains repeated assurance of forgiveness. Sincere repentance results in forgiveness of all sins. The faithful however are enjoined to be humble, and no individual Muslim can be sure of entry to paradise: that decision is God's alone (but with the counsel of Prophet Isa, who sits at Allah's right hand). Good deeds count for much; rank, wealth and privilege in this life count for nothing. Sincere scholars however have special rank, both in The Qur'an and the Hadith. But scholars too must be humble, and simply reading and learning the Qur'an will count as scholarship. Although we may pray for Allah's mercy for a departed person, only the good deeds of a person in their lifetime can assure entry to paradise.

There is promised in paradise full indulgence of the senses; there are delicious fruits of trees, cool water, non-intoxicating wine, and wonderful linguistic companions. But in order for the believer to enter paradise they must follow the straight path, and surrender their being to God (*Islam*). Jews and other religions are acknowledged in God's revelation (and may enter Paradise, if God wills): but to be tolerated, they must follow their own precepts faithfully. God approves of pluralism, the mutual tolerance of diverse groups with different beliefs who live peaceably together (Qur'an 9:5-6). God may tempt people, challenge them with choices: the case of Prophet Job is the supreme example (Qur'an 21:83-84).

A dilemma exists concerning translation of The Qur'an into non-Arabic languages. God delivered his message to Muhammed, who repeated it to his companions in Arabic, so that the Prophet could spread this Message: and Muslims the world over try to teach Arabic to their children, whatever their local language. But translations are frequently used, and herein lies a dilemma. Each act of translation is an exegesis, an act of both scholarship and theological interpretation. Scholars try to be faithful to the original, but sometimes, according to critics, they often fail. Another problem of translation is that it rarely captures the beauty and the poetic cadence of the Arabic: the exquisite poetry of The Qur'an is said to be inter alia, evidence of its divine origin. Recited in Arabic, The Qur'an is often chanted, declaimed or sung: in the Sufi interpretation, this music itself is a pathway to God. For the adult convert to Islam, Arabic is hard language to learn, and this writer, certainly, will never be able to speak classical Arabic. Nevertheless, some prayers, Qur'anic verses and Hadith can be learned by heart. The best experience for this writer is to listen to a recording of Qur'anic verse sung in Arabic, and then declaimed (or subtitled) in English. But translations struggle to capture the poetry of The Qur'an, and many fail.

My favoured English translation is that by N.J. Dawood, who was born a Jew but died a Muslim [21]: careful scholarship has shown that his is both a beautiful and theologically faithful rendering of the original, and can be read as poetry.

Fundamentalism and jihad

Every Muslim, including myself, is a Fundamentalist. We believe absolutely in submission to Almighty God our creator, and the final word of God revealed to the Blessed Prophet, containing the fundamental rules which guide our lives. Jihad is a spiritual struggle, a form of self-discipline in which we strive through divine assistance to reach a spiritual goal whose essence is derived from the study of holy scripture, the Hadith of the Prophet, and the example of the Prophet's life [22]. The Qur'an makes it clear that Prophet Jesus too, brought a message and lived a life of goodness which we should follow.

The Quaker jihad is to find the spirit of God in everyone we meet, that is to find the answering light of God within ourselves in the silence of a Quaker meeting, and to act on the divine impulse within us to achieve good works in recognizing "the light of God in everyone" [23]. The Muslim jihad is to follow the five pillars (acknowledging One God and believing in the authority of the message to the final prophet; faithful prayers five times each day; giving to charity; fasting for a month each year; enabling oneself or another person to undertake the Haj pilgrimage; and being a good and dutiful citizen, helping and sustaining fellow citizens whatever their religion or social status.) Those who insist that Muslims, in order to "integrate" should stop being "fundamentalists" (and should abandon or neglect these 'fundamental' tasks) attack all Muslims. That may be their intention, in this age of Islamophobia [24].

The prophets of Islam

All of the biblical Prophets belong to the nation of Islam, including the 25 mentioned in the Qur'an by name, and many others whose existence is implied, but who are not named. The first prophet was Adam, and God's last prophet was Muhammad. A Prophet is one who brings aspects God's message to the people of earth. I mention here four of my favourite prophets, Adam, Joseph, Jesus and Muhammad.

The Prophet Adam in Islam is quite different from the Adam of the Jewish Old Testament. My view is that the Islamic Adam's nature and experience has profound theological implications. Adam and Hawwa (Eve) were created simultaneously and equally by God, and were given the Garden of Eden as a form of indenture, through introducing the fruits of Eden to life on the whole of the earth. God instructed that all of the angels should bow before God's human creation, Adam and Hawwa. One aspiring 'angel' or jinn, in the lust of pride, refused: this creature named Iblis or Shaitan was expelled, and ever since has tried to tempt humankind from "the straight path".

This idea of the straight path has a central place in Islam and is like the road which Pilgrim treads in Bunyan's allegory of good and evil [25]. The first verse of the Qur'an which emphasizes the straight path is repeated many times in a Muslim's prayers and is worth recording here: *Praise be to God, Lord of the Universe, The Compassionate, the Merciful, Sovereign of the Day of Judgement! You alone we worship, and to you alone we turn for help. Guide us to the straight path, The path of those whom You have favoured, Not of those who have incurred your wrath, Nor of those who have gone astray.* (Quran 1:1-7) This is the *Fathia*, the *Exordium*, which every Muslim recites on waking at dawn, on preparing for sleep, and several times in between.

Adam and Hawwa, according to The Qur'an, were instructed by God in the management of all living things, and of their environment: having served their apprenticeship they then set about recreating this heavenly garden upon earth. Crucially, the idea of 'original sin' is lacking in the Qur'anic account: Adam and Hawwa were born in a state of natural goodness, and they and their descendants remain in that blessed state. They transgressed in eating fruit from the tree of knowledge, but asked Allah's pardon, which was immediately granted. Given the knowledge from the tree of life, the first human couple began the task of stewardship of a green earth: from the beginning of human time, Adam and Hawwa were green stewards, 'vice-regents' of the earth. Hawwa was not created from Adam's spare rib: she was created independently and separately from Adam, and the two served one another equally in undertaking the tasks given to them.

From the very first, Islam established that genders are "separate but equal". Woman are revered as having the special task of nurturing a foetus, bearing and nurturing the child, and instructing him or her in ways of goodness until the child's seventh year, when the father will take an increasing responsibility for the education of boys. In the moments after a child's birth there is an exquisite ceremony in Islam in which the father gently sings the call to prayer, and the exordium into the child's ear. This is the most moving religious ceremony that I have ever witnessed.

Early in foetal life God breathes a soul into each human: the spirit or knowledge of God dwells in everyone. In this regard, most Quakers too have no concept of original sin, believing rather in original grace through God's inward light: in this they are at one with Islam, optimistically viewing the capacity of humans to achieve goodness in their lives, rather than evil [26].

Islam nevertheless has a clear image of Satan (Shaitan), who continuously tempts humanity to commit sin. God forbade Adam and Eve from eating of the tree of knowledge; however, such transgression may have been part of the divine plan, and God immediately forgave the penitent pair. This idea of the merciful God, ever ready to pardon the sins of all who ask for help and guidance, is a continuing theme throughout The Qur'an, and in the life and personal sayings (Hadith) of the Prophet Muhammad.

The Prophet Muhammad was, by the detailed accounts of his life [30], a warm and lovely man. He lived the Message given to him by God, in his numerous acts of forgiving, kindness, and advice concerning charity. He was kind and loving, frequently insulted and scourged, but forbad (as did Christ) his followers from retaliating. He was a trader by profession, literate only in the language of commerce. And not until his fortieth year did he begin to receive the Message from God.

Why was Muhammed chosen to receive "the final message"? Clearly he was a wise and profoundly good person, but the occasion of the Message was not dependent on Muhammad being a unique person: such good men exist in every generation. My theory of why Muhammad was chosen comes from a reading of Gibbon's *Decline and Fall of the Roman Empire* on the corruption of previous theologies and the spurning of God's prophets: the Roman takeover and distortion of Christianity as an imperial religion of organised cruelty and colonial enterprise (unfortunately followed by many Christian heirs) led God to choose a Prophet at a *particular time* to receive the Final Message: a set of theologies and instructions for worship, and of good conduct that was absolute and unambiguous. To deny the truth of the Message is to deny the truth of God's existence. And the Qur'an unambiguously declares that all Prophets are equal in God's vision (Quran 2:136), although each Prophet had his own particular mission: thus the blessed Prophets Jesus and Muhammad may deserve particular attention and study, and their Message resonates with our own times (Quran 2:253).

The character of Muhammad is endearing, and his companions and wives recorded many instances of his sweet and gentle nature. I love the accounts of his kindness to animals, and share his anger at those who mistreat or neglect animals. The story is told that on waking to say his dawn prayer, Muhammad found his cat sleeping on the robe he wanted wear. Rather than disturb his cat, he cut out the piece of his cloak on which the animal slept. Cats have special status in Islam and any food which a domestic cat touches does not lose its Halal (blessed) status. "He was beloved by God and an example among humans. He prayed, he contemplated. He loved, he gave. He served, he transformed. The Prophet was the light that leads to the Light, and in learning from his life, believers return to the Source of Life and find His light, His warmth, and His love." [30]

The Qur'an forbids the worship of relics, tombs and images, a precept not always followed, but a practice discouraged by reformers. One example is the writing of Abd al-Wahhab, who three centuries ago [31] advocated the abandonment of venerated "relics" (the bones and tombs of Prophets etc) with a return to the earliest principles of Islam – we might compare him in this regard with Martin Luther, or with Calvin in the Christian tradition.

The final guide to human conduct is The Shari'a, a system of canon law derived from Islamic teaching and the Hadith. In Islamic republics such as Saudi Arabia and Pakistan Shari'a law is also national law. In countries with Islamic minorities, national law (which is usually secular) prevails, and conformity with Shari'a principles is only for Muslims, and though often expected amongst the faithful, remains voluntary [32].

The Hadith (from the Sunnah) are fascinating and inspiring to read, as is the scholarship which supports the selection of "verified" Hadith – here I follow the *Textbook of Hadith Studies* by Kamali [33]. "Verification" means that the saying of the Hadith was verified by the Prophet's trusted companion, or wife, and was written down soon after the words were spoken. There have emerged in folk traditions many thousands of supposed Hadith which support one view or another, but whose attribution to a particular Companion may have been forged. The number of extant Hadith probably exceeds 10,000, but according to Khan [34] who collects together and translates the collection by Al-Bukhari, the true number may not exceed 6,000.

Khan proposes that the "true purpose of all Hadith" is to clarify and interpret the Qur'an in arriving at the *Shari'a*. In other words, the Blessed Prophet in his Hadith was either rephrasing part of God's message, or interpreting it in a consistent manner. A supposed Hadith which does not do this is in Khan's methodology, invalid, whatever the supposed chain of verification. Indeed, sometimes supposed Hadith contradict one another, or contradict the Qur'an, and have obviously been fabricated to serve the needs of particular groups.

Other scholars have selected groups of reliable Hadith on the basis of their direct relevance to everyday life, and their popularity amongst the faithful. Two excellent examples are Schemata's selection of 55 Hadith, and Ibrahim's translation of An-Nawawi's collection of 40 Hadith (first published in about 1250 CE) and which are very familiar to Muslims (the two collections are both worthy of consultation, and there is little overlap in the Hadith translated). [14]

I give a few examples here:

> Prayer is light; charity is a proof; patience is an illumination; and the Qur'an is an argument for or against you. Everyone starts his day as a vendor of his soul, either freeing it or bringing it to ruin. (An-Nawai, Hadith 23).

> ...Oh my servants, you sin by night and by day, and I forgive all sins, so seek forgiveness of Me and I shall forgive you ... (part of a long Hadith, the 24th of An-Nawami's collection).

> Narrated by Aisha [Prophet's wife] that she heard the Messenger of Allah say: There is not one person who seeks to make some night prayer and is overcome with sleep except that Allah writes for him the reward of the prayer that he intended to complete and the sleep that overcame him is a charity for him (from Allah to that person). (Shehata, Hadith 22).

Many of the Hadith in these two popular collections concern doing good deeds, helping one's neighbour, not returning evil for evil, and seeking and receiving God's forgiveness [14]: Islamic "sermons on the mount".

The message of prophet Jesus

The Qur'an makes it clear that Prophet Isa transmitted an *injeel*, a Message: but The Qur'an gives only gives glimpses of that Message. We might turn to the four gospels, and to the gospels suppressed or ignored by the Paulite faction, for a fuller account of the Message of Jesus. Unfortunately, as scholars have shown, these gospels were written many decades after the life of Christ (The Qur'an nominates Prophet Isa as "Christ", and also describes him as a Messiah). But there are contradictions and problems of interpreting the gospels *according to* (not by) the main gospel writers. Matthew, Mark, Luke and John were not the actual authors of the gospels attributed to them. Much of these gospels may have been distorted or actually forged to suit the ideologies of particular Christian factions [35].

With some hope of rescuing the core of the Message of Prophet Jesus I turn to the work of Robert W. Funk and his 24 colleagues (mostly, professors of divinity at American universities), members of "the Jesus seminar" [36], who compared no less than 22 gospels, or fragments of gospels, which list sayings and actions attributed to Jesus. Less than 20 percent of the supposed events in the life of Jesus could be verified through cross-textual analysis, and indeed many of these supposed events may have been imaginative accounts added many years after Jesus lived on earth.

It was crucially important for the Paulite faction that Jesus should be seen as the divine son of God who sacrificed himself through voluntary suicide in order to "redeem" man's original sin: but there is also clear possibility that the supposed events (and implications of Christ's divinity) were reconstructed or fabricated in order to fit this Paulite ideology. But Jesus did perform miracles (as The Qur'an affirms), and he did live a humble life, with profound teaching such as the Sermon on the Mount. The message of Jesus can be summed simply: love and obey God; nurture yourself and your family; love and serve your neighbour; and love your enemies. [28]

The Prophet Yousef ('Joseph') is another of my favourites (the interested reader will study The Qur'an, selecting their own favourites.) My Anglican childhood was full of the stories of Joseph, his jealous brothers, his dreams, and how he counselled the rulers of Egypt: The Qur'an too is full of these accounts. Prophet Yousef submitted himself to God and prayed that he be allowed to worship God each day and be admitted to the company of the righteous (Qur'an Surah 12). This is the mark of a true Muslim.

Maryam, the mother of Prophet Isa is revered and frequently mentioned in Islam, and there are also many Qur'anic passages on Maryam (within whose virgin body Allah created Jesus); and on John (also named as a Prophet), cousin of Jesus; and on Jesus himself, maker of miracles, preacher of forgiveness, and the receiver of God's light [27]. Mary gave birth to Jesus beneath a date palm, and the tree bended and fed her fresh dates (putting the possible moment of Christ's birth in early September, when dates ripen). Jesus, according to the Qur'an was "the anointed one" or "messiah", and thus earned the name Christ.

For Parrinder [28] who examines *Jesus in the Qur'an*, a crucial point of convergence between Christian and Islamic metaphysics is that of Light: "God guides to the light whomsoever God wills." (Qur'an 24: 35-37). The Qur'an does not mention the crucifixion of Jesus, but does not deny it: rather if Jesus was crucified, then he did not die on the cross [29]. He was *raised up to heaven alive*, and will assist God in making final judgements about admission to paradise. In this sense the Muslim idea of Christ the Messiah describes a fundamental member of the prophets of Islam; Muhammad was the final prophet in a chronological sense, but in my understanding from Muslim scholars is that Muhammad stands on an equal footing with all of the blessed prophets.

Tarif Khalidi in *The Muslim Jesus* [37] has gathered together the sayings of Jesus which have survived in Islam in a "gospel" which parallels The Hadith (sayings of Prophet Muhammad): "In its totality, this gospel is the story of a love affair between Islam and Jesus and is thus a unique record of how one world religion chose to adopt the central figure of another ..." (Khalidi, pp 5-6). Many of these collected sayings are also found in some apocryphal gospels of Christianity [38]. Some of the Muslim "sayings of Jesus" are also close to Christ's 'sermon on the mount'; and the 'infancy gospel' of Thomas has clear parallels with Qur'anic accounts of the deeds of young Jesus.

Women and Islam

"No human society has ever succeeded in promoting complete equality between women and men. We still have a long way to go ..." wrote Tariq Ramadan in *The Quest for Meaning: Developing a Philosophy of Pluralism*, 2010 [39]. In Islam women are "separate but equal": great women have nurtured The Prophet (Khadija, Fatima, Aisha), and the power of Muslim women is spread across the centuries. My insights into the role and status of women in Islam owe much to my (biological) sister Marjana who has been a Muslim (and a scholar of Islam) for 20 years, and with whom I discuss aspects of Islam almost every day [40].

Prophet Muhammad pronounced in a Hadith: "Every faith has an innate character. The character of Islam is modesty." [41]. This idea of *modesty* means that *both* men and women must present themselves to the world in humble and non-flamboyant ways. Women's modesty requires that limbs and body are covered, but the covering of face and head is voluntary. Many women like to wear the *hijab* (traditional head covering) but they often pay a price for this faithfulness to Islamic guidance: my sister, for example, is not alone in England in having her *hijab* wrenched off, being spat on, and told to "go back to your own ******* country, you Paki bitch, etc, etc."

Our recent studies of Muslim women in business organisations across the world, and in the Palestinian telecommunications industry [42] have introduced me to significant numbers of well-educated, highly skilled, multilingual Arab women occupying at least middle level posts in technical and service organisations (and senior posts in educational, health and aid organisations in Gaza), who simultaneously manage business roles with household and childcare, albeit with help from their sisters. These women seem to have struck a good balance between traditional Arabian or Islamic values concerning family and childcare, and pursuing high level careers.

Unlike Christianity and Judaism, in the Qur'anic account of creation women have equality with men. Eve (Hawwa) mother of all women was not created as a secondary creature from a spare rib, but created equally and simultaneously with Adam to continue the stewardship of nature. Nor, in the Islamic account, was Eve the instigator of "original sin", and therefore destined to suffer more than man. The roles of man and woman are, from the first joyous act of the creation of humankind, equally important and complementary.

The Sisterhood of Islamic women is separate from men: but it is a joyous, self-confident and caring community, and potentially free of male intrusion and control. For men, myself included, the brotherhood, the *Ummah* (the worldwide community of Muslim men) is also a joyful community: as I stand and kneel in the prayer line shoulder to shoulder with my brothers, I experience a special metaphysic, a humility in which we are all, regardless of rank, profession, education or ethnicity, equal.

From a Quaker point of view, this reaching out (in Islam) to the light of God within my fellow worshippers who stand in the prayer line with me, creates a spiritual experience of unity within the totality of divine wisdom. Women too, I am assured, in their separate prayers experience this gendered unity within the wisdom of God. We pray first to Almighty God, and then we pray with and for one another.

Men and women in Islam are indeed separate but they are also equal, and my feeling is that the benefits of the same-sex support within the Sisterhood and Brotherhood of the Ummah is one of Islam's strengths, and will not change. Each male, and each female may in weak moments be tempted by Satan to "lust after their neighbour". For some Christians this lust itself is an adulterous sin. In Islam having such thought is _not_ a sin: rather, resisting such temptation is a positive act of charity, to be recorded so by one's guardian angel.

Islam and education

Islam holds education in high regard, since education in its broadest sense helps the individual unlock their spiritual and cognitive potential as citizens. The Qur'an frequently enjoins us to observe and study the heavens, the earth, and the natural world: the Muslim as a spiritual being is also a natural scientist. All of the Hadith collections include sayings of The Prophet praising education. Khan comments: "According to one tradition, the ink of a scholar's pen is more precious than the blood of a martyr engaged in the task of defence, while an alim (scholar) builds individuals and nations along positive lines. In this way he bestows upon the world a real-life treasure ... An especially vital factor is the freedom to conduct research ... This great emphasis placed on exact knowledge resulted in the awakening of a great desire for learning of Muslims of the first phase." [43]

We have undertaken studies of how the Citizenship Education curriculum (which is required element of the English National Curriculum in state schools) has been implemented in schools with varying proportions of Muslim pupils, and in a number of Muslim-run schools; and how pupils themselves received and internalised instruction in how to be "good citizens". This work has shown that Muslim and non-Muslim pupils alike receive such education with some positive enthusiasm [44]. Moreover, Muslim pupils are particularly likely to bring from their homes and mosques, values that integrate well with National Curriculum values of what is a "good citizen".

We concluded that Muslim pupils were bringing positive elements of their religious education into the classroom in both secular and religious schools, in ways which strongly influenced their "integration", and their conduct as good citizens. In essence, being socialised in a Muslim family in England gives young people a set of Islamically grounded values which they apply in many of life's challenges, in doing "good deeds" and following the middle path in relating not only to fellow Muslims, but also to citizens of all religions, and cultural origins.

Consider one of the many Hadiths of The Prophet enjoining good behaviour: "Each person's every joint must perform a charity every day the sun comes up: to act justly between two people is a charity; to help a man with his mount, lifting him onto it or hoisting up his belongings onto it is a charity; a good word is a charity; every step you take to prayers is a charity; and removing a harmful thing from the road is a charity." [14]. The recorded sayings of The Prophet abound with such good advice, about walking abroad and seeing everyone, Muslim or not, as deserving God's favour, realised through human action: or, as Quakers say, "Seeking the light of God in everyone."

The five-times daily prayer of Muslims is not empty ritual, but is meant to keep the believer in a state of imminent grace, reminding one to carry out God's mission of good work on earth. Muslims take these teachings with great seriousness. For example, at Cheadle Mosque close to my former home in Manchester, there are monthly work groups who, following Hadith direction wander abroad "removing harmful things from the road" i.e. clearing litter from the pavement. Anyone who calls themselves Muslim is a religious person who prays frequently *and* is constantly seeking to perform good actions in relation to family, friends, neighbourhood and community. What exists for *all* citizens is an implicit social contract which binds good citizens together, in mutual bonds of cheerful co-operation [45].

Islam as a minority group in the West: The plural society debate

Muslims have a long history as a minority group, beginning with the movement from Mecca to Medina where, as refugees Muslims were a minority and worked out ethics and procedures for conduct in relation to the majority population. Thus was born the *Fiqh of Minorities*, or law of minorities. Since then in countries where Muslims have been minorities they have tried to apply this Fiqh, emphasising that in return for tolerance they will work hard to be self-sufficient and law-abiding. Muslims hope that the outcome of such mutual tolerance is that they will be allowed to worship and engage in the multiple religious practices of Islam, have access to halal food, be allowed to dress modestly, and to have their children educated either in Muslim-run schools, or in schools which respect their religious needs. These include principles of modesty, so that pupils will not be required to undress or change clothes other than in private, and that girls may wear religious dress, and sit separately from males if they choose.

Much is written about the "integration" of Muslims in European societies by critics who fail to define what they mean by integration. Sociologically speaking, "accepted integration" means that the minority group are tolerated in their customs of religion, dress, diet, clothing and personal language – and are legally protected from discrimination in services and employment, and from religious and racial hatred; reciprocally, the minority group will live peaceably with neighbours, according them the tolerance which they themselves enjoy [46].

In this model of integration, the minority group will maximise their talents through education and training, working hard to support their families and making (as all citizens should) minimal demands on state aid. Classic studies of "race relations" in Britain have pointed to Jews as an "ideal" minority group in this regard [47]. In more recent decades, Muslims now seek this ideal form of integration, often in the same areas which Jewish immigrants once occupied, including Bethnal Green in London where my Jewish great grandparents first settled. Like Jews, Muslims seek upward mobility on the basis of stable adaptation, retaining traditional languages for use in home and mosque or synagogue, wearing traditional religious dress, and seeking protection from discrimination through legal means.

Like Jews, Muslims are hardworking and law abiding, and draw on a set of values which are expressed as being good citizens, helping everyone regardless of their religion, who occupy their local community. However, often this seeking for acceptance through being model citizens has not been reciprocated by the "host" community [48].

The second form of adaptation is "assimilation", in which the immigrant group seeks to adopt the language and values of their new culture; usually these groups are Christian, although they may continue to worship in denominations they have traditionally known (such as my Jamaican wife's Seventh Day Adventist church). The most assimilated ethnic groups in Britain are probably those from Ireland and Europe, who have no problems in being stigmatized because of "racial" appearance. But African-Caribbeans are also assimilating rapidly, and at least a third of this group are in "mixed-race marriages" [49]

Tariq Ramadan, a leading writer on the adaptation of Muslims in Europe stresses that Muslims have choices in this matter of "plural accommodation", seeking forms of integration in adapting to Western cultures: "It is up to Muslim individuals to be and become committed citizens, aware of their responsibilities and rights. Beyond the minority reflex or the temptation to see themselves as victims, they have the means to accept a new age of their history. For those who were born in the West or who are citizens, it is no longer a question of 'settlement' or 'integration' but rather of 'participation' and 'contribution'" [50].

What Ramadan offers, with much brilliance, is a "post integration" role for Western Muslims who have:

> " ... multiple, moving identities, and there is no reason – religious, legal or cultural – a woman or man cannot be both American, or Muslim daily. Millions of individuals prove this daily. Far from the media and political tensions, a constructive, in-depth movement is under way, and Islam has become a Western religion ... Of course, there is only one single Islam as far as fundamental religious principles are concerned, but it includes a variety of interpretations and a plurality of cultures. Its universality indeed stems from this capacity to integrate diversity into its fundamental oneness" [51].

Today some notable Muslim theologians elaborate with eloquence the doctrine of religious tolerance and pluralism. Foremost among these has been the Algerian Mohamed Talbi [52]. Talbi goes to the roots of Islam, to its earliest practices in Makkah and Medina, and out of his puritan piety comes great wisdom, great tolerance, and much spiritual joy in the advocacy of tolerance between religions.

These liberal "political philosophers" have their critics amongst more conservative factions of Islam. But I respect (and indeed applaud, and sit at the feet of) Talbi, Esack and Ramadan, being in awe of their ability to return faithfully to the roots of Islam, and simultaneously forge a new political philosophy of plural accommodation without conceding the Islamophobic call for "assimilation", and denial of basic Islamic principles.

Islam and non-violence

> If having been treated with bitterness by neighbours or acquaintances, or after suffering any other kind of provocation, one refrains from reaction and retaliation and maintains pleasant relations unilaterally, this will also be a form of jihad. (Khan, Principles of Islam, 2012).

In its higher principles, "Islam is a religion of peace. And according to Islam peace is a universal law of nature. That is because God loves the condition of peace, and disapproves of any state of unrest. God's predilection for peace is quite enough reason for the believer also to love peace. In no circumstances will the true believer ever tolerate the disruption of peace." [34]

In making this statement, Maulana Wahiduddin Khan draws on several Surahs: God permits warfare only to repel attackers who are threatening the lives of one's family. Thus only defensive warfare is permitted, and in the conduct of war prisoners must be treated well, and the lives of non-combatants must not be threatened.

The teaching of Qur'an and Hadith is that of tolerance for others, forbearance in the face of insult, slowness in becoming angry, swiftness in forgiving (Qur'an 8:60-62; 9:5). Liberal Muslims such as Ramadan [51] argue that Islam should accept warfare only as a last resort, when a nation or group is under attack and threatened with extinction.

Karen Armstrong in her extensive survey of "religion and the history of violence" [53] discusses these circumstances in a chapter on "the Muslim dilemma". Armstrong characterizes random acts of terror in the West by Muslims as acts of self-destructive despair in the face of the war machines of Western states which have rendered so much disaster and the taking of innocent lives in the past three decades in Iraq and Afghanistan. These incursions by strongly armed states have resulted in the deaths of at least a quarter of a million innocent civilians, many of them children (in this view, the unleashing of the ISIS monster was directly attributable to failed Western interventions in the Middle East).

Considered on this scale, acts of Islamic terrorism in Europe and America, though profoundly wrong, are mere pinpricks, even though they violate the social contract between the state and minority groups [45]. My advocacy for peace-making for Christians, Jews and Muslims in these current conflicts is this: *Seize the moral high ground!* Choosing the higher order values of your religion as the basis for political co-operation is the only basis for ultimate success in achieving peace-making and social justice.

I emphasise that in this and in other areas of world conflict, the only just and lasting solution is that of pacifism based on the humanist principles embedded in the implicit social contract which prevails between individuals, groups, cultures and nations. This social contract may be derived from the philosophical values of Secular Humanists, Muslims, Christians, Hindus, Daoists, Buddhist and Jewish groups, and others. Each of these world religions or value traditions includes leading advocates of the peace doctrine.

Loving peace, as Karen Armstrong argues, is both a transcendent and logical human value [54]. So long as Christians (and other religions) condone violent warfare, "terrorism" (the warfare of the weak), will continue. "Forgiveness" is an outflow of love in the Christian canon, and Quakers who do not perceive original evil as corrupting the human soul, find both the currency and practice of "love" a joyous, inwardly comforting, cross of comfort.

Muslims and Quakers are enjoined by their respective theologies to be truth-telling, helpful, peaceful, conflict-avoiding, and mediating. Numerous accounts are given of The Prophet who forgave his detractors, and spiteful deceivers who made false accusations [55]. In modern times, Islam has produced a major pacifist activist Badshah Ghaffar Khan (known affectionately as Bacha Khan), who lived from 1890 to 1988. Khan was Pakistan's parallel to Gandhi (whom Khan compared to a Sufi mystic), who pioneered pacifist resistance to British colonialism, and continued his peace campaigning after Pakistan's independence. As a result he spent long periods either in British colonial prisons, or in the jails of Pakistani governments, in the period 1927 to 1983.

Bacha Khan declared:

> "There is nothing surprising in a Muslim or a Pathan like me subscribing to the creed of nonviolence. It is not a new creed. It was followed fourteen hundred years ago by the Prophet all the time he was in Mecca ... non-violence was the weapon of The Prophet" [56].

Today his campaigns are carried forward by brave Pakistani activists including the feminist campaigner Malala Yousafzai [57]. Amitabh Pal gives a full account of pacifist theologies and movements across the Muslim world today [58]. This pacifist movement in Islam draws directly on the examples of The Prophet's life, his endurance of persecution with stoicism and love, during the early years of Islam in Makkah, reflected in his many hadiths during all phases of his receiving the Qur'anic message: enjoining love, forgiveness and peace-making.

God's light shining

The Qur'anic account of Adam the first prophet and his wife Hawwa, shows that humankind and their descendants were not destined to bear the mark of original sin. Rather, humans through God's implant of the soul, are born seeking knowledge of and achievement of goodness. Humans in the Islamic message (as Quakers also generally believe) are born "naturally good", seeking the light that is Almighty God's loving will, and forgiveness. There are parallels too in the mystical insights of Quakerism and Sufi Islam in the evocation of God-awareness through accessing the inner power of Soul or Spirit, in self and others [59].

In Quaker theology the divine light within us which reflects the light of God, has a major role: through contemplation (e.g. in a silent meeting for worship) and through human interaction, Quakers reach out to "the light of God in everyone" – seeking the natural goodness that God has embedded in humankind. The Qur'an does not reveal much about "the spirit" or "the soul": that understanding is cloaked, in the message to The Prophet. But it is clear from the Qur'an that God breathes a spirit or soul into each human being soon after birth - but humans cannot presume that this is part of God: rather, this light or spirit comes *from* God (Qur'an 70:1). It is the means by which we understand goodness in self and others, and how we may communicate with God.

For Prophet Jesus, " ... we supported him by the Spirit of Holiness." Quakers assume that spiritual intuition has a power which transcends any instruction of scripture or sermon. This "inward light" is a powerful guide for Quakers. There is a mystical theology at the heart of Quakerism in which "life itself is the miracle". For

Muslims this miracle encompasses the whole of nature (whose flourishing honours God), and the human spirit which strives to serve God through acts of will in performing good deeds, crafted for each one of us each day, in acting upon the choices given to us by Allah.

The symbol of the cross is a major challenge for the Muslim who seeks a sympathetic understanding of Quakerism. In Qur'anic theology Jesus did not die on a cross, although a modern Muslim historian suggests that there may have been a crucifixion, but not a death [30]. The account of Jesus (the Messiah according to both the Qur'an and the Christian gospel) being raised up alive in order to sit to serve God concerning the judgement of sinners, is remarkably similar when New Testament and Qur'anic accounts are compared.

The Quaker William Penn wrote in 1699, that there is "no cross but the inward cross" which contains our inner submission to the divine message, in following the straight path towards God [61]. This metaphor of an inward, spiritual cross is also developed in the writings of the Muslim mystic Rumi [62].

Challenges for Islam's peace-making and the journey on the straight path

Studies in social science

Our idealistic understanding of how Islamic values may be translated into the proper ordering of society, in ways which protect the flourishing of all citizens, protecting their vulnerabilities, maximising their talents, and stimulating their ability to make free choices to follow their straight path, has been both challenged and enlightened by our social science studies in three Muslim-majority countries, Gaza, Bangladesh and Pakistan.

Our team of researchers in *Gaza* (and in Palestine and Jordan) has focussed on how women and children in particular, have survived the warfare imposed by Israel; have flourished psychologically; and have achieved success in the world of work [63].

Our team in *Bangladesh* has continued work begun in Canada and The Philippines on the rescue and nurture of young teenagers trapped in the degradations of commercial sexual exploitation, extending this work in trying to understand the very high rates of self-killing in young Bangladeshi women [64].

Our team in Pakistan has studied the status and exploitation of women and children, and the many departures from Islam through acts of corruption, rape, kidnapping, murder, and stoning to death [65]

We offer short summaries of this and our other fieldwork: all of the assertions made may be supported by our published studies, referenced in the *End Notes* for this Chapter.

Studies in Gaza

Gaza is the besieged sector of Palestine which endures frequent attacks of warfare from neighbouring Israel (against which Gaza ineffectually replies, and Israel counter-attacks with devastating impact on life, limb and property of Gazans). This has resulted in continued decline in economic welfare with reduced quality of life in the several refugee camps. Our first studies have been of how women teachers survive these bombardments, but also the many injuries and fatalities to family members and children that result. This work has shown how women draw on Islamic values and spiritual dynamics in enduring these events with dignity, calm and courage. They ask for comfort and protection from Allah, not for revenge against Israel.

We have also studied men and women employees in two telecom companies in Gaza, and found business models which served the goals of community service rather than of profitability. Women employees were welcomed (there are many well-qualified, bilingual graduate women who fill key positions). Firms and organisations support the welfare of women employees by generous work-life balance benefits which usually allow them to become successful both as family managers, and as professional employees.

We have studied "glass ceiling" effects which limit the occupational mobility of women in Gaza: such barriers exist, but women were skilful at developing special roles which enabled occupational advancement which allowed men to occupy nominal positions as industry leaders. Just as women in Gaza have developed as family leaders and managers, they have also used these strengths to quietly manage organisations: the managing director is male; the real power is held by those whom he nominally directs. In the changing social structure of Gaza, women's increasing strengths are acknowledged in Shari'a law judgements regarding divorce and inheritance.

All of this occurs within an orthodox Islamic structure of rules and organisation, in which principles of modesty for both genders are maintained, and the *zakat* (sharing of gifts) principle of a welfare state has fruitful realisation.

Studies in Bangladesh

The suicide rate in young women in this country is equal to or higher than that in young males, contrary to the pattern in virtually every country in which accurate statistics are recorded. Women in the Muslim-majority culture of Bangladesh appear to be an oppressed group, frequently subjected to sexual assault, group rape, and murder. Islamic rules regarding dowry at marriage (the groom must give the bride a monetary gift, as specified in Shari'a law) are only atypically observed: rather, the Indian custom of the bride's family having to pay the husband's family a substantial sum, is followed. This results, as in India, in events of 'wife murder' when her family fail to meet the marriage debt.

Bangladesh is notorious for its "brothel villages" which we have studied in detail, attempting to provide rescue services for girls and women. In these 'villages' hundreds of young women are trapped, and have to serve many males each week. Often they are sold into this sexual servitude at a young age and receive no income – rather, the payment for their degradation is shared between managers or pimps, as well as with police who are bribed to allow this business to continue. Men young and old, married or unmarried will enjoy these services, along with cheap liquor and drugs available in these villages, escaping the moral rigours of a conventional Islamic society. Corruption of public officials who should protect girls and women, is frequent. Our conclusion is that Bangladesh is in several ways, not a successful Islamic society.

Studies in Pakistan

Pakistan is a nominally "Islamic Republic", and whilst the adoption of Shari'a law into public law systems could in theory protect girls and women from sexual assault, it appears that these laws are not applied in a systematic manner. Shari'a law is, rather, applied in haphazard manner according to individual interpretations of local Imams and officials. Consider the example of stoning to death of those "taken in adultery" [65].

The American Islamic scholar Brown [66] argues that since four independent witnesses are required to attest actual acts of penetrative intercourse, in practice such witnesses are impossible to obtain, and so adulterers are never stoned. Unfortunately this is not true of Pakistan: women (but not men) are stoned to death in Pakistan, perhaps a dozen a year according to my research students. This is how it may happen: a single woman is raped, resulting in her pregnancy. She may accuse her rapist, but since she cannot call four witnesses, she is likely to receive 100 lashes for making an unprovable accusation. Meanwhile, her pregnancy begins to show, and now there are hundreds of witnesses to her "adultery", many more than four.

She is allowed to carry the pregnancy to term, and then she is stoned. This consists of being buried up to the neck in a pit in front of the Mosque, and a local elder or Imam will drop a large rock onto her head. She may now already be dead, but the surrounding men throw smaller rocks. Some Imams will also execute a new-born female on the grounds that the child is tainted with the lately-stoned mother's sin. Female infanticide is frequent in Pakistan, despite strict Qur'anic injunction against this practice. The grounds are not merely economic: females (as in India) have a devalued status, and are often unwanted additions to a family. The non-Islamic bride-price custom (of Indian origin) may also be a cause of this.

Our research describes the work of humanitarian groups who plead for female children to be given to orphanages rather than being killed: these same welfare groups tour the large cities each morning, picking up the bodies of female infants discarded into waste dumps and sewers, giving the child a proper Islamic burial. Child prostitution is common, and we have been successful in using funds from a Canadian charity which has enabled some of these children to be rescued, their families supported, and the girls returned to full-time education.

Sometimes grants are given to local officials to set up schools and employ teachers: these schools and teachers never exist. Or a school is simply a piece of ground without a building, no equipment, and no qualified teacher. Girls in rural areas who walk long distances to school risk sexual assault, kidnapping and trafficking. It is unsurprising that girls often avoid attending school.

In rural areas some girls are given in marriage at ages 12 or 13. The new 'bride' is sometimes treated as property, and will be raped by her husband's brothers and father. Intercourse imposed on immature girls can result in vaginal fistula, resulting in chronic pain, and infertility. These conditions are medically reversible, but rarely treated. A girl who produces no children (or only female children) may also have her own life at risk. Any young person complaining to police about sexual maltreatment is likely to be serially raped by policemen, and held in prison for a long period as a potential witness.

Pakistan contains many millions of former Dalits and their descendants (Hindu untouchables) who, prior to partition, tried to escape their 'untouchability' by converting to Islam [65]. But many impoverished Muslims try and wrest a degree of social power (or "social capital") by creating their own Muslim underclass (the former Dalits), and it appears that romantic relationships between 'real' Muslims, and formerly untouchable Muslims are sometimes grounds for 'honour killing'. In this practice families will put to death one or both of the young people engaged in a romantic relationship.

Pakistan produces many great scholars and politicians, but it seems that some of the best can no longer live in their birth country, since assassinations and political imprisonment are frequent. All that one can say is that Pakistan has the *potential* to become a great and fully-fledged Islamic republic.

It has far to go before this can be achieved. Finally, I stress that as a white westerner (albeit a Muslim) this is not fieldwork I have carried out myself. The work has been done by community activists and research students whom I have been able to fund and collaborate with. Pakistan is a dangerous place in which to do research. Pakistan (and India) have made the political mistakes of turning their backs on their pacifist founders, Bacha Khan and Mahatma Gandhi and have become instead nuclear states, at great expense and great risk. Pacifist pathways might have created prosperity and security.

Conclusions

I now believe that the life-path of each one of us is divinely inspired, in a process through which we are presented with numerous choices, leading to different pathways as we grow older [67].

Nothing in our lives happens by chance: all of the choices we make using our divinely given freedom of choice, are presented to us by God. My first major challenge occurred when I was a 17-year-old rating in the Royal Navy, reading the bible seriously for the first time: I decided that preparing for war was incompatible with Christ's teaching. I acted with determined impulsiveness following a sudden paradigm shift, a kind of awakening (my personality style), becoming a 'conscientious objector', and as a result endured twelve months in a naval jail, and much joy in Christ.

In that journey I was almost entirely alone, apart from God's company. Another major challenge occurred when I became a Muslim, and this time I have had joyous companionship, as well as friendly support from my Muslim and Quaker brothers and sisters. I am in awe of, and sit at the feet of liberal Islamic writers – John Esposito, Farid Esack, Mohamed Balbi and Tariq Ramadan – whose politically engaged Islamic views of the world return to the roots of Islam – The Qur'an, and The Hadith. As John Esposito (the Catholic authority on Islam) puts it, I am a religious journeyman with "multiple religious identities" [32]. These multiple identities are not simply additive, but synergistic in nature.

My most recent challenge has been the engagement with Palestinian brothers and sisters, which has significantly modified the way I think about myself as an ethnic Jew, and about Israel in general, but has certainly reinforced my pacifist confidence in Islam. Other challenges will come.

> "God is the Light of the heavens and the earth; the likeness of His Light is a niche wherein is a lamp (the lamp in a glass, the glass as it were a glittering star) kindled from a Blessed Tree, an olive that is neither of the East nor of the West, whose oil well-nigh would shine, even if no fire touched it; Light upon Light." (The Qur'an, Surah 24 Light, verse 35).

The image and metaphor of this *light* is shared by both Muslims and Quakers. The metaphor of the 'inward cross' may be shared too: "The way, like the cross is spiritual: that is, an inward submission of the soul to the will of God, as it is manifested by the light of Christ in the consciousness of men." (William Penn 1699/2014) [61].

My goal, as a religiously-motivated social scientist, is to understand and assist oppressed populations, including abused children, exploited girls and women, victims of racism and Islamophobia – and to understand and perhaps counter the negative social forces which initiate such oppressions. As a value-based social scientist, I follow ethical and moral principles derived from Islam, Judaism and Christianity.

A value-based approach to humanism and social science has led us to receive with enthusiasm new directions in the epistemology of social science, pioneered by Roy Bhaskar [68]. This value-based ontology has been used fruitfully by Muslim scholars [69], by Catholic educationists and social scientists [70], and by a Quaker child welfare advocate [71].

Critical realism has also enabled us to begin to understand the complex layers of value-based social structure embedded in the

Arabic society of Gaza, as this nation endures chronic siege and warfare [63].

End Notes

[1] William Penn (1699/2014). *No Cross, No Crown*. Project Gutenberg, online.

[2] For an understanding of the history and current state of Quakers in Britain, see:

Cary, M. S. & Pink-Dandelion, B. (2008). Three kinds of British Friends: A latent class analysis. *Quaker Studies* 12 (1), 11-20;

Pink-Dandelion, B. (2017). *The Liturgies of Quakerism. London*: Routledge;

Pink-Dandelion, B. (2007). *An introduction to Quakerism*. Cambridge University Press;

Angell, S. W. & Pink-Dandelion, B. (Eds) (2018). *The Cambridge Companion to Quakerism*. Cambridge University Press;

Abbott, M. P. & Abbott, C. (2020). *Quakerism: The Basics*. London: Routledge.

On Quaker Universalism, see:

Philpott, T. (2013). *From Christian to Quaker: A Spiritual Journey from Evangelical Christian to Universalist Quaker*. Quaker Universalist Group Publishing.

Randazzo, C. (2018). Christian and Universalist? Charting liberal Quaker theological developments through the Swarthmore Lectures. *Quaker Religious Thought* 131,(1). 4-20.

Randazzo, C. (2020). Liberal Quaker reconciliation theology: A constructive approach. *Brill Research Perspectives in Quaker Studies* 2(4), 1-2.

[3] For an account of William Penn's life in Quakerism, in Britain and in North America, see:

Fantel, H. (1974). *William Penn: Apostle of Dissent*. New York: William Morrow.

[4] The evidence on forgery, confusion, ideological and political obfuscation of Old and New Testaments seems overwhelming:

Allison, D.C. (2005). *Resurrecting Jesus: The Earliest Christian Tradition and Its Interpretation*. New York: Wiley.

Ehrman, B. (2003). *Lost Christianities: The Battle for Scripture and Faiths We Never Knew*. Oxford University Press.

Ehrman, B. (2003). *Lost Scriptures: Books that Did Not Make It into the New Testament*. Oxford University Press.

Ehrman, B. (2009). *Jesus, Interrupted: Revealing the Hidden Contradictions in the Bible*. New York: Harper Collins.

Ehrman, B. (2011). *Forged: Writing in the Name of God*. New York: Harper Collins.

Jenkins, P. (2001). *Hidden Gospels: How the Search for Jesus Lost Its Way*. Oxford University Press.

Keith, C. & Le Donne, A. (2012). *Jesus, Criteria and the Demise of Authenticity*. Continuum Books.

Long, J. (2005). *Biblical Nonsense: A Review of The Bible for Doubting Christians*. iUniverse Books.

Martin, D.B. (1995). *The Corinthian Body*. Yale University Press.

Tabor, J.T. (2007). *The Jesus Dynasty*. New York: Harper Collins.

Pagels, E. (2003). *Beyond Belief: The Secret Gospel of Thomas*. New York: Vintage Books.

Wright-Kunst, J. (2006). *Sexual Slander and Ancient Christianity*. Columbia University Press.

[5] Armstrong, K. (2007). *The Bible: The Biography*. London: Atlantic Books.

[6] An extraordinary "hysteria of false belief" swept European writing for three centuries from around 1700, claiming that virtually all Muslim males were 'sodomites', a libel which justified, inter alia, imperial conquest, suppression and slaughter of these 'infidels', which was carried over into Islamophobia in modern Europe, see:

Mater, N. (1999). *Turks, Moors and Englishmen in the Age of Discovery*. Columbia University Press; and

Goody, J. (2004). *Islam in Europe*. Cambridge: Polity Press.

Today, persecution of Muslims by various Christian groups is widespread, but is often reciprocated, as the Oxford Centre for Muslim-Christian Studies has documented:

MacCallum, R. (2019). *Christians, Muslims and Persecution*. Oxford: Hikmah Guide 3, Oxford Centre for Muslim-Christian Studies.

[7] For evidence supporting this thesis see:

Maccoby, H. (1998). *The Mythmaker: Paul and The Invention of Christianity*. New York: Barnes and Noble. Maccoby argues that from its very beginnings, Christianity involved a profoundly antisemitic ideology.

For an elaboration of this thesis, particularly for the post-crusade period, see:

Nicholls, W. (1995). *Christian Antisemitism: A History of Hate*. New York: Rowman & Littlefield.

On Europe's Christian antisemitism and the historical development of values supporting the Holocaust, see:

Ames, C. C. (2020). Christian violence against Heretics, Jews and Muslims. In *The Cambridge World History of Violence*; Volume 2, 470-491; and

Heschel, S. (2008). *The Aryan Jesus: Christian Theologians and the Bible in Nazi Germany*. Princeton University Press.

[8] On Islamic tolerance and co-operation of Christians and Jews, see:

Afridi, M. (2017). *Shoah through Muslim Eyes*. New York: Academic Studies Press;

Armstrong, K. (2002). *Islam: A Short History*. London: Phoenix Press;

Esposito, J. (1998). *Islam: The Straight Path*. Oxford University Press;

Lapidus, I. (2002). *A History of Islamic Societies*. Cambridge: Cambridge University Press;

Lewis, B. (2013). *The Jews of Islam*. Routledge.

Karabell, Z. (2007). *Peace Be Upon You: Fourteen Centuries of Muslim, Christian and Jewish Conflict and Co-operation*. New York: Random House-Knopf;

Lapidus, I. (2002). *A History of Islamic Societies*. Cambridge University Press.

Donner, F.M. (2017). *The Expansion of the Early Islamic State*. London: Routledge.

[9] Cohn-Sherbok, D. (2022a). *Antisemitism: A World History of Prejudice*. Cheltenham, UK: The History Press;

Cohn-Sherbok, D. (2022b). Two millennia of persecution started with the Christ-killer myth which Jews have suffered for 20 centuries – with Christian contempt lying behind most of the injustices and pogroms against Jews. *Jewish Chronicle,* January 14th, 2022.

We commend Daniel Cohn-Sherbok's many books as examples of enlightened Jewish humanism, seeing rapport with Christianity and Islam, and peaceful solutions to the Israel-Palestine conflict.

By coincidence, a few days after I wrote this paragraph a research report (using genome analysis) indicated the discovery of the remains of more than a dozen Ashkenazi Jews, including several children, who had been thrown into a well in Norwich, England, victims of a pogrom in CE 1190. Similar pogroms occurred during the periods of the Crusades, in London, York and Lincoln (and other Cathedral cities), perpetrated by Crusaders as they set out to liberate the Holy Land from Muslims, see:

Nicola Davis (2022). Jewish remains found in Norwich well are medieval pogrom victims. *Guardian Online*, August 30th, 2022.

For an historical and contemporary overview of English antisemitic ideologies and violence practised against Jews in England, see:

Cardaun S. (2015). *Countering Contemporary Antisemitism in Britain*. Leiden: Brill.

[10] Adam-Bagley, C. (1973). *The Dutch Plural Society: A Comparative Study of Race Relations*. Oxford University Press;

Adam-Bagley, C., & Abubaker, M. (2017). Muslim woman seeking work: An English case study with a Dutch comparison, of discrimination and achievement. *Social Sciences*, 6(1), 17-30;

Adam-Bagley, C. & Al-Refai, N. (2017). Multicultural integration in British and Dutch societies: education and citizenship. *Journal for Multicultural Education*, 11(2), 82-100;

Abubaker, M. & Adam-Bagley, C. (2017). Methodology of correspondence testing for employment discrimination involving ethnic minority applications: Dutch and English case studies of Muslim applicants for employment. *Social Sciences*, 6(4), 112-121;

Adam-Bagley C. & Abubaker, M. (2019). Muslim women (and men) and youth seeking justice: English and Dutch Case studies of prejudice, racism, discrimination and achievement. In *Muslim Women Seeking Power, Muslim Youth Seeking Justice: Studies from Europe, Middle East and Asia* (pp 162-181). Cambridge Scholars Publishing.

[11] Qudah-Refai, S. (2014). *Dogmatic Approaches of Qur'an Translators: Linguistic and Theological Issues*. Leeds: University of Leeds doctoral thesis.

[12] On social occasions, and in popular entertainment Muslim men dance with men: so should it be. https://youtu.be/Pzx6XTSGCXM

There is an active group arguing the case for Gay Muslims – see:

Kugle, S. S. A. H. (2010). *Homosexuality in Islam: Critical Reflection on Gay, Lesbian, and Transgender Muslims*. London: Oneworld Publications.

Shah, S. (2016). Constructing an alternative pedagogy of Islam: the experiences of lesbian, gay, bisexual and transgender Muslims. *Journal of Beliefs & Values*, 37(3), 308-319.

Shah, S. (2017). *The Making of a Gay Muslim: Religion, Sexuality and Identity in Malaysia and Britain*. London: Palgrave-MacMillan.

[13] Miller-White, B. (2004). The journeyman – the making of a Muslim Quaker. *Quaker Theology*, 10, 1-4.

See too another American viewpoint, Naveed Moeed's account of the unity of Islamic and Quaker worship, and mutually reinforcing Quaker and Islamic writings:

Moeed , M. (2019). Muslim? Quaker? Speak! *Friends Journal*, August 1 (FriendsJournal.org).

[14] See the Hadith collections of:

An-Nawani's *Forty Hadith* (translated by Ibrahim, E. & Johnson-Davies, D. 1976). Lebanon: The Holy Koran Publishing House;

Sardar, Z. (2012). *Muhammad*. Hodder Education; and

Shehata, A. (2007). *The Trade Which Shall Never Fail: A Collection of 55 Hadith on Actions with Immense Rewards*. Hedaya Publications.

For an account of scholarship in verification of Hadith, see Kamali, M. H. (2009). *A Textbook of Hadith Studies*. Markfield, UK: Islamic Studies Centre.

See also for an extensive list of Hadith and their English translations:

As-Sanani, M.B.I. (1996). *Bulugh Al-Maram Attainment of the Objective according to Evidence of the Ordinances*. Riyadh: Dar-us-Salam Publications, with Arabic and English text, and commentary on 1,358 Hadith, in the realm of law and social progress; and

Khan, M.M. (Translator and Editor) (1996). *The Meanings of The Ahadith Summarized by Al-Bukhari*. Riyadh: Dar-us-Salam Publications, with Arabic and English text, and commentary on 2,330 Hadith, in the realm of 'spiritual progress.'

For an important account of Hadith influence on mediaeval and modern history see: J.A.C. Brown. J.A.C. (2009). *Hadith: Muhammad's Legacy in the Medieval and Modern World*. OneWorld Books.

[15] Robert Frost's poem "The Road not Taken" is included in numerous anthologies, and is freely available on the internet. For philosophical implications, see:

Hollis, M. (2014). Edward Thomas, Robert Frost and the road to war. The *Guardian online*, August 8, 2011.

Islam's account of human free will seems similar to Hume's idea of "compatibility and will" in which our choices are presented by a previous matrix of social relations and choices made earlier. See:

Hume, D. (1998). *Enquiry Concerning Human Understanding* (Ed. T. Beauchamp). Oxford University Press;

Russell, P. (2008). *Hume on free will. Stanford Encylopedia of Philosophy*. Stanford, CA: Stanford University Press.

Macksood, A. (2015). Is Islam committed to dualism in the context of the problem of free will? *Journal of Cognition and Neuroethics* 3(1) 1-12.

[16] Page, D. (2011) *Consciousness and the quantum.* Journal of Cosmology, online journal at: www.journalofcosmology.com.

See too the work of the Anglican priest, quantum scientist and theologian John Polkinghorne for an exposition of God's miraculous power in moulding a complex universe:

Polkinghorne, J. (2005). *Quarks, Chaos and Christianity: Questions to Science and Religion.* New York: Crossroad Books.

For a Quaker-universalist perspective on quantum theory, see Isham, C. (2013) Quantum theory and the concept of reality. *Universalist: Journal of the Quaker Universalist Group* 98, 36-49.

[17] I argue for this case - of Jews being given a promised land through Allah's will, more fully in:

Adam-Bagley, C. (2019). Gender equality and peace-making: Challenges for the human rights achievement of Muslim women, men and youth. In *Muslim Women Seeking Power, Muslim Youth Seeking Justice: Studies from Europe, Middle East and Asia* (pp 296-317). Cambridge Scholars Publishing.

[18] Sardar, Z. (2012). *Muhammad.* London: Hodder Education.

[19] Gibbon, E. (2003). *The Decline and Fall of the Roman Empire.* New York: Random House (Chapter 15).

[20] On the fascinating Ebionites, the Jewish/Christian forerunners of Islam, and their survival amongst pre-Islamic and early Islamic cultures see:

Ehrman, B. (2003). *Lost Christianities.* Oxford University Press;

Skarsaune, O. (2007). *Jewish Believers in Jesus.* Peabody, MA: Hendrickson Publishers;

Petri, P. (2011). *Recovering Jewish-Christian Sects and Gospels.* Leiden: Brill;

Mustafa, A. (2011). *The Islamic Jesus: How the King of the Jews Became a Prophet of the Muslims.* St. Martin's Press, 2017;

Chekovikj, T. & Chekovikj, E. (2020). Jesus and monotheism, the similarity and relations between early Judeo-Christian credence and Islam. *Journal of Modern Islamic Studies* 2, 45-53; and

Hartog, P. (2012). Ebionites. *The Encyclopedia of Christian Civilization*. Oxford: Blackwell.

[21] Dawood, N.J. (Translator) (2003). *The Koran*. London: Penguin Books.

[22] Sardar, Z. (2012). *Muhammad*. London: Hodder Educational;

Armstrong, K. (2007). *Muhammad: Prophet for Our Time*. London: Harper;

Ramadan, R. (2007). *The Messenger: The Meanings of the Life of Muhammad*. Oxford University Press.

[23] Fox, G. (1656/2015). *Quaker Faith and Practice*, 19:32. London: Society of Friends.

[24] Massoumi, N., Mills, T., & Miller, D. (2017). *What is Islamophobia? Racism, Social Movements and the State*. London: Pluto Press.

[25] Bunyan, J. (1678/2014). *The Pilgrim's Progress from This World to That Which is to Come*. Project Gutenberg, online.

[26] Spencer, C.D. (2007). Early Quakers and divine liberation from the universal power of sin. In J.L. Scully & B.P. Dandelion (Eds.) *Good and Evil: Quaker Perspectives*. London: Routledge-Ashgate.

Calvinists accused early Quakers of being "atheists" for denying the doctrine of original sin: Gillman , H. (2014). Transformation, redemption, salvation. *The Friend*, October 31, 13.

[27] In Islamic theology "receiving the spirit" means that the individual receives a message from God which invokes the soul already implanted in the individual. The idea of "spirit" and "word" from God are used in The Qur'an with similar meanings.

[28] See Parrinder, G. (2013). *Jesus in the Qur'an*, London: One-World Books, pp 8, 49-50, 54, 68, 139. Each Muslim, in prayer, reaches out to God through the gift of the implanted spirit, as do Quakers in their ritual silence.

See too Winter, T. (2009). Jesus and Mohammad: new convergences. *Muslim World*, 99, 21-38.

See too: Akyol, Mustafa (2017). *The Islamic Jesus: How the King of the Jews Became a Prophet of the Muslims*. New York: St Martin's Griffin Books.

[29]. The Quaker theologian Stuart Masters writes of "the inward cross" which inspires Quakers [60]. I like this idea: it is symbol of service which makes no theological assumptions about the deity or death of Christ, but acknowledges this Prophet's teaching as a force within our lives.

A Muslim historian suggests that Prophet Isa (Jesus) may actually have been crucified, but did not die on the cross:

Azlan, R. (2013). *Zealot: The Life and Times of Jesus of Nazareth*. New York: Random House.

See also the discussion by Siddiqui, M. (2013) Christians, Muslims and Jesus. Yale University Press, pp 225-248.

[30] Ramadan, T. (2007). *The Messenger: The Meanings of the Life of Muhammad*. Oxford University Press; and

Sardar, Z. (2012). *Muhammad*. London: Hodder Educational.

[31] Esposito, J. (1998). *Islam: The Straight Path*. Oxford University Press, Chapter 4. "Wahhabism" has popular profile among Islamophobes who assume that this puritan group of theologians is the source of much evil across the world. *Inter alia*, Wahhabism shares with Quakerism a distaste for the Muslim equivalent of "steeple worship". Followers of Abd al-Wahab's theology, dislike being called Wahhabists since they see themselves as "true Muslims", returning to The Qur'an and The Prophet's Hadith in a fundamental way. And this, of course leads them to follow teaching on ethical and peace-loving relationships:

Bowen, I. (2014). *Medina in Birmingham, Najaf in Brent: Inside British Islam*. London: Hurst, Chapter 3.

[32] Deen, M.H. (2012). *Shari'ah in Britain: The Biblical Forbidden Fruit*. Vienna: United Publishers. Deen advocates, as do others, forms of "legal pluralism" for British Muslims.

Archbishop Rowan Williams makes somewhat similar proposals:

Williams, R. (2007). *Islam, Christianity and Pluralism*. London: Association of Muslim Social Scientists (UK).

See also the "legal Hadith" collection, referenced in Footnote [14], above.

See too:

Eaton, H.G. (2004). *The Concept of Justice in Islam*. London: The Book Foundation: "Believers are warned again and again that if they hope for mercy from their Lord – as all must – then they have to show mercy to their fellows and to 'every creature that has a living heart' including the beasts and the birds. 'God gives a reward for gentleness which He will never give for harshness', said the Prophet. It is clear that, for the Muslim, there is a powerful restraint upon justice if justice is understood merely as a weighing of relevant facts and that is why the human judge, fallible and himself in need of mercy, trembles when he gives judgement. In Islam mercy always has the last word." (Eaton, 2004, p.8).

[33] Kamali, M.H. (2009). *A Textbook of Hadith Studies*. Markfield, UK: Islamic Studies Centre.

[34] Khan, M.M. (1996). *The Meanings of the Ahadith*. Riyadh: Dar-us-Salam Publications.

[35] Ehrman, B. (2011). *Forged: Writing in the Name of God*. New York: Harper Collins.

[36] Funk, R., Hoover R. & The Jesus Seminar (1993). *The Five Gospels: What Did Jesus Really Say?* San Francisco: Harper.

[37] Khalidi, T. (Editor and Translator) (2001). *The Muslim Jesus: Sayings and Stories in Islamic Literature*. Harvard University Press.

[38] Ehrman, B. (2003). *Lost Scriptures: Books that did not make it into the New Testament*. Oxford University Press.

[39] Ramadan, T. (2010). *What I Believe*. Oxford University Press (Chapters 9 to 11 on women and Islam). See too:

Ghadanfar, M. A. (2001). *Great Women of Islam*. Riyadh: Darussalam.

Haddad, Y. Y., & Esposito, J. L. (Eds.) (2001). *Daughters of Abraham: Feminist Thought in Judaism, Christianity, and Islam*. Gainesville: University Press of Florida.

[40] See:

Kultab, E. (2006). The paradox of women's work. In L. Taraki (Ed.) *Living Palestine: Family Survival, Resistance and Mobility Under Occupation* (pp 231-270). Syracuse University Press;

Wadud, A.(1999). *Qur'an and Women: Rereading the Sacred Text from a Women's Perspective*. Oxford University Press;

Taraki, L. (Ed.) (2006). *Living Palestine: Family Survival, Resistance, and Mobility Under Occupation*. Syracuse University Press.

There is a welcome and growing literature on the Ummah sisterhood, and Islamic feminism. See, for an introduction to relevant issues:

Hudson, A.M. & Rozana, S. (2006). Special Issue on Islam, gender and human rights: Introduction. *Women's Studies International Forum*, 29, 331-338;

Brown, K. (2006). Realising women's rights: the role of Islamic identity among British Muslim women. *Women's Studies International Forum*, 29, 417-430;

Joseph, S. & Najmabadi, A. (2003). *Encyclopedia of Women and Islamic Cultures*. Leiden: Brill;

Siddiqui, M. (2018). *The Routledge Reader in Christian-Muslim Relations*. London: Routledge (on feminist dialogue on shared issues).

See also al-Dakkar, K. (2012). Reconciling traditional Islamic methods with liberal feminism: reflections from Tunisia; and on Mohamed Talbi, see:

Talbi, M. (1998). Religious liberty. In C. Kurzman (Ed.) *Liberal Islam: A Sourcebook*. London: Oxford University Press; and:

Lovat T. (Ed.) (2012). *Women in Islam: Reflections on Historical and Contemporary Research*. Doordrecht: Springer – for an exposition of the work of Talbi, a brilliant modernist in the debates on Qur'anic and Hadith interpretation.

[41] See Sardar's (2012) translation (End Note 22) of selected Hadith of The Blessed Prophet: "Every faith has an innate character. The character of Islam is modesty." See Qur'an 24: 30-31, and 33-35, for sources.

[42] See our review and conceptualisation of Muslim women's achievement in professional and business roles:

Adam-Bagley, C., Abubaker, M. & Shahnaz, A. (2018). Women and management: a conceptual review, with a focus on Muslim women in management roles in Western and in Muslim-Majority countries. *Open Journal of Business and Management*, 6, 485-517.

[43] See Khan, M.W. (2012). *Principles of Islam*, p. 22. Birmingham, UK: Islamic Vision.

[44] Al-Refai, N. & Adam-Bagley, C. (2008). *Citizenship Education: The British Muslim Perspective.* Leiden: Brill.

Al-Refai, N. & C. Adam-Bagley, C. (2012). Muslim youth and citizenship education: idealism, Islam and prospects for successful citizenship education. In Ahmed, F. & M. Siddique-Seddon, M. (Eds.) *Muslim Youth: Challenges, Opportunities and Expectations.* London: Continuum Books.

Adam-Bagley. C. & Al-Refai, N. (2013). Citizenship education: a study of ten Islamic and state secondary schools. In C. Tan & Y. Suleiman (Eds.) *Reforms in Islamic Education.* London: Bloomsbury.

Adam-Bagley, C. & N. Al-Refai, N. (2019). Muslim youth in Britain: Becoming good citizens in the age of Islamophobia. In *Muslim Women Seeking Power, Muslim Youth Seeking Justice: Studies from Europe, Middle East and Asia.* Cambridge Scholars Publishing.

[45] On the implicit social contract between the state, and Muslim minorities, see: Ceric, M. (2008). *Toward a Muslim Social Contract in Europe.* London: Association of Muslim Social Scientists. Mustafa Ceric casts the mutuality of rights and duties in spiritual terms, drawing on Qur'anic sources.

On philosophical and political assumptions in such a social contract, see the writings of a leading British Muslim:

Ramadan, T. (2010). *The Quest for Meaning: Developing a Philosophy of Pluralism.* London: Pelican Books.

[46] Rose, J. & Associates (1969). *Colour and Citizenship.* Oxford University Press.

On Muslim settlement patterns in London see:

Peach, C. (2006). Islam, ethnicity and South Asian religions in the London 2001 Census. *Transactions of the Institute of British Geographers*, 31, 353-

370. Peach found that British Muslims were "... much less segregated than Sikhs, Hindus and Jews", even though pockets of ethnic density (such as the Bengalis) existed.

[47] Endelman, T. (2002). *The Jews of Britain: 1656-2000*. University of California Press. For an interesting comparison of Jewish struggles against racial exploitation in the 1930s, and Muslim struggles of a similar nature in the 1970s in Bethnal Green, London, see:

Glynn, S. (2005) East end immigrants and the battle for housing: a comparative study of political mobilization in the Jewish and Bengali communities. *Journal of Historical Geography*, 31, 528-545.

[48] Greenslade, R. (2005). *New Jews: Scapegoating Muslims*. London: Institute of Public Policy Research.

[49] For studies on "mixed race" children and their parents see:

Sawyerr, A. & Adam-Bagley, C. (2017). *Equality and Ethnic Identities: Studies of Self-Concept, Child Abuse and Education in a Changing English Culture*. Leiden: Brill.

Christian Joppke argues that despite an official policy of multiculturalism, which should in theory ameliorate feelings of alienation in religious and racial minorities, the current fugue of Islamophobia in Britain results in a significant degree of disenchantment with British culture by the Muslim population, especially as right-wing elements, including the press, denigrate multiculturalism as an accommodation with a "terrorist" religion:

Joppke, C. (2009). Limits of integration policy: Britain and her Muslims. *Journal of Ethnic and Migration Studies*, 35, 453-472.

Even prior to 11/9 a strong current of anti-Islam ideology pervaded Christian countries of Europe and North America:

Strabiac, Z. & Listhaug, O. (2008). Anti-Muslim prejudice in Europe: a multilevel analysis of survey data from 30 countries. *Social Science Research*, 37, 268-286.

In Britain a long-standing prejudice against foreigners in general, and Arabs in particular evolved into a more coherent Islamophobia, even before 9/11, after which it increased markedly:

Poynting, S. & Mason, V. (2007). The resistible rise of Islamophobia: anti-Muslim racism in the UK and Australia before 11 September 2001. *Journal of Sociology*, 43, 61-86.

The purveyors of extreme prejudice are typically the "white" third of the population who are nominally adherents of Christian "values", and have lower social status in society:

Fetzer, J. & Soper, C. (2003). The roots of public attitudes towards state accommodation of European Muslims' religious practices before and after September 11. *Journal for the Scientific Study of Religion*, 42, 247-258.

Our earlier studies of racial prejudice in Britain and Europe had identified a similar typology, a third of the population (nominally Christian whites) were very hostile to all kinds of minorities; a third had unclear or unfocussed attitudes which could be swayed by right wing press and demagogues; and a third who were generally younger and better educated, were more accepting of both minorities as individuals, and of multicultural policies.

Interestingly, in The Netherlands the most accepting were those with an "intrinsic" commitment to Christian values:

Adam-Bagley, C. (1979). *Personality, Self-Esteem and Prejudice*. London: Routledge- Ashgate, on the cultural and social psychological dynamics of racist, and non-racist individuals. The links of intrinsic commitment to religious values and social and interpersonal behaviours are explored further in English and Dutch contexts in:

Adam-Bagley, C. (2019). Gender equality and peace-making: Challenges for the human rights achievement of Muslim women, men and youth. In *Muslim Women Seeking Power, Muslim Youth Seeking Justice: Studies from Europe, Middle East and Asia* (pp 296-317). Cambridge Scholars Publishing.

[50] Ramadan, T. (2012). *The Quest for Meaning: Developing a Philosophy of Pluralism*. London: Pelican Books, p. 6.

[51] Ramadan, T. (2010). *What I Believe*. Oxford University Press, p. 6.

[52] Talbi, M. (1998). Religious liberty. In C. Kurzman (Ed.) *Liberal Islam: A Sourcebook*. London: Oxford University Press.

For an interpretation of Talbi's contribution to Islamic scholarship see:

Nettler, R. (2004). Muhammed Talbi on understanding The Qur'an. In S. Taji-Farouki, S. (Ed.) *Modern Muslim Intellectuals*. Oxford University Press.

Another well-known Muslim advocate of plural accommodation in the modern world is the South African Farid Esack (Esack, F. (1997) *Qur'an, Liberation and Pluralism*. London: OneWorld Books).

[53] Armstrong, K. (2014). *Fields of Blood: Religion and the History of Violence*. London: Bodley Head.

[54] On the "high ground" of Jewish (and other religious) values, see:

Armstrong, K. (2011). *Twelve Steps to a Compassionate Life*. London: Bodley Head.

For a comprehensive account of Jewish values see:

Novak, D. (1992). *Jewish Social Ethics*. Oxford University Press.

For reason and rhetoric on this issue I recommend all of the books by Marc Ellis – for example:

Ellis, M.H. (2002). *Israel and Palestine out of the Ashes: The Search for Jewish Ethics in the Twenty First Century*. London: Pluto Press.

On humanist principles of peace-making see:

Butler, J. (2020). *The Force of Non-Violence*. Fayard.

[55] Al-Mubarakpuri, S-R (2008). *The Sealed Nectar: Ar-Raheequl-Makhtum*. London and Riyadh: Darussalam.

[56] Easwaran, E. (1999). *Nonviolent Soldier of Islam: Badshah Khan, a Man to Match His Mountains*. Berkeley, CA: Nilgiri Press.

[57] Yousafzai, M. (2019). *We are Displaced: My Journey and Stories from Refugee Girls Around the World*. London: Weidenfeld & Nicolson.

[58] Pal, A. (2011). *Islam Means Peace: Understanding the Muslim Principle of Nonviolence*. Santa Barbara, CA: Praeger. See too Izzeldin Abuelaish's pacifist memoir, reflecting on the death of his daughters through Israeli tank fire in Gaza:

Abuelaish, I. (2011). *I Shall Not Hate*. London: Bloomsbury.

[59] Morgan, A.E. (2010). Islam from a Quaker perspective. www.LAQuaker.blogspot.com

For introduction and overview of Sufism's spiritual nature, see:

Baldick, J. (2012). *Mystical Islam: An Introduction to Sufism*. New York: I.B. Tauris; and

Arberry, A.J. (2002) *Sufism: An Account of the Mystics of Islam*. London: Dover Publications.

[60] Masters, S. (2014). The transformative power of God: the cross in Quaker faith and practice. *The Friends Quarterly*, 41 (2) 4-16.

[61] Penn. W. (1699/2014). *No Cross, No Crown*. Project Gutenberg, online; and QFP (2022). *Quaker Faith and Practice 5th Edition*. London: The Society of Friends.

[62] Mokrani, A. (2022). The cross in Rumi's *Matnawi*. *Religions*, 13(7), 611 Online.

[63] Abubaker, M. & Adam-Bagley, C. (2016). Work–life balance and the needs of female employees in the telecommunications industry in a developing country: A critical realist approach to issues in industrial and organizational social psychology. *Sage Open: Comprehensive Psychology*, 5, Online.

Adam-Bagley, C. (2017). Women graduates as human relations counsellors and researchers in Gaza, Palestine: 'Beyond Brokenness' – a planned research framework. *Open Journal of Political Science*, 5(1), 16-22.

Abubaker, W. (2019). Muslim women and the children of Gaza: Teacher support for children under stress- evidence from elementary school case studies. In *Muslim Women Seeking Power, Muslim Youth Seeking Justice: Studies from Europe, Middle East and Asia* (pp 74-119). Cambridge Scholars Publishing.

Luobbad, M. & Adam-Bagley, C. (2021). Work-life balance policies and traditional culture in a competitive market: Three Jordanian case studies. *Journal of Human Resource & Leadership*, 5(1) 25-45.

Abubaker, M., Luobbad, M., Qasem, I. & Adam-Bagley, C. (2022). Work-Life-Balance policies for men and women in an Islamic culture: A Palestinian case study of the telecommunications sector. *Businesses*, 2 (3) 319-338.

[64] Adam-Bagley, C. (1989). Adolescent prostitution in Canada and the Philippines: Statistical comparisons, an ethnographic account and policy options. *International Social Work*, 42(4), 445-454.

Adam-Bagley, C, Madrid, S., Simkhada, P., King, K., & Young, L. (2017). Adolescent girls offered alternatives to commercial sexual exploitation. *Dignity: A Journal on Sexual Exploitation and Violence*, 2(2), Online.

Adam-Bagley, C., Shahnaz, A. & Simkhada, P. (2017). High rates of suicide and violence in the lives of girls and young women in Bangladesh: Issues for feminist intervention. *Social Sciences*, 6(4), 140-115.

Adam-Bagley, C., Kadri, S., Shahnaz, A., Simkhada, P., & King, K. (2017). Commercialised sexual exploitation of children, adolescents and women: Health and social structure in Bangladesh. *Advances in Applied Sociology*, 7(4), 137-150.

Shahnaz, A., Adam-Bagley, C., Simkhada, P., & Kadri, S. (2017). Suicidal behaviour in Bangladesh: A scoping literature review and a proposed public health prevention model. *Open Journal of Social Sciences*, 5(07), 254.

Adam-Bagley, C., Kadri, S, & Shahnaz, A. (2019). Chapters 8 to 11 on exploitation of girls and women in Bangladesh and Pakistan. In *Muslim Women Seeking Power, Muslim Youth Seeking Justice: Studies from Europe, Middle East and Asia* (pp 212-296). Cambridge Scholars Publishing.

[65] Adam-Bagley, C. (2008). An end to apartheid? The oppression and educational inclusion of India's Dalits. In *Challenges for Inclusion: Educational and Social Studies from Britain and the Indian Sub-Continent* (pp165-182). Liden: Brill.

Adam-Bagley, C. & Abubaker, W. (2019). Child marriage as traumatic rape: A cause of PTSD in women in Bangladesh and Pakistan? In *Muslim Women Seeking Power, Muslim Youth Seeking Justice: Studies from Europe, Middle East and Asia* (pp 255-262). Cambridge Scholars Publishing.

Adam-Bagley, C. (2019). Pakistan: The hard struggle for the Islamic equality of women and girls. In *Muslim Women Seeking Power, Muslim Youth Seeking Justice: Studies from Europe, Middle East and Asia* (pp 263-295). Cambridge Scholars Publishing.

[66] Brown, J.A.C. (2016). *Stoning and Hand Cutting: Understanding the Hudud and the Shariah in Islam*. Irving, TX: Yaqeem Institute for Islamic Research.

[67] A challenge I have failed, is to understand and cope with the question of why some alienated Muslim youth in Europe volunteer to serve the Isis movement (which violates the basic principles of Islam, and distorts and betrays The Prophet's message).

I give an account of my unsuccessful attempt to counsel a young man (Salman Abedi) in my Manchester Mosque, who was a paranoid schizophrenic, and who was subsequently sucked into the maw of Isis as a 'suicide bomber':

Adam-Bagley, C. (2019). Gender equality and peace-making: Challenges for the human rights achievement of Muslim women, men and youth. In *Muslim Women Seeking Power, Muslim Youth Seeking Justice: Studies from Europe, Middle East and Asia* (pp 296-317). Cambridge Scholars Publishing.

[68] English social philosopher Roy Bhaskar who died in 2014, was a Hindu mystic and Marxist-Humanist. See:

Bhaskar, Roy (2015). *From East to West: The Odyssey of a Soul*. London: Routledge, 2015; and:

Bhaskar, Roy (2016). *Enlightened Common Sense: The Philosophy of Critical Realism*. London: Routledge.

[69] Professor Matthew Wilkinson is a leading criminologist, and Muslim social advocate in Britain. See:

Wilkinson, M. L. N. (2015a). *A Fresh Look at Islam in a Multi-Faith World: A Philosophy for Success Through Education*. London: Routledge, and:

Wilkinson, M. L. N. (2015b). The metaphysics of a contemporary Islamic Shari'a: A meta-realist perspective. *Journal of Critical Realism* 14 (4): 350–365.

[70] Professor Margaret Archer, an English sociologist, has been adviser to the Pope on women's issues, and head of The Pontifical Academy of Social Sciences. See:

Archer, M. S. (2017). *Morphogenesis and Human Flourishing*. New York: Springer; and

Archer, M. S. & Morgan, J. (2020). Contributions to realist social theory: An interview with Margaret S. Archer. *Journal of Critical Realism* 19: 179-200.

[71] Professor Emerita Patricia Alderson is an English Quaker, and researcher on behalf of physically challenged children. See:

Alderson, P. (2021). *Critical Realism for Health and Illness Research: A Practical Introduction*. London: Policy Press.

Chapter 4
Explaining Evil in a World Where Humans are Motivated by a Spirit of Inward Goodness
Chris Adam-Bagley

> Human beings will never be delivered from evil. Our only hope is not to eradicate it definitively but to try and understand it, to contain and name it, recognising that it is also present in us.
> Tzvetan Todorov, *Memory as a Remedy for Evil* (2010) p. 82.

The problem

We have offered the argument that human beings at birth, are "born with goodness in their being, with the impulse to seek the light of goodness which God has placed within them". If this is true, then why are not the communities of adults more perfect? That would be the Panglossian sequel (Voltaire, 1758/2005), but it is clearly not true, as our accounts of the travails of childhood in, for example, Bangladesh and Pakistan in the previous Chapter argues. But we take heart from a powerful writer on evil, Tzvetan Todorov (2010), who makes the case for restorative (not punitive) justice in dealing with malefactors: those 'evil' men and women who have succumbed to an evil spirit that tries to control all of us.

This argument leads us to ponder on the existence of an external force which takes different guises to pull us from The Straight Path: this is the creature whom Muslims call *shaitan*, the evil one. Nevertheless, in our reading this devil who lays in wait for Muslims (and for everyone else, of course) is a jumped-up jinn, one of the invisible creatures who were mired in jealousy at the progress of Adam and Hawwa, and whose approach and temptation can be resisted by conversations with Allah, which follow reciting the Muslim's daily prayer. This Islamic satanic figure seems less powerful, more easy to resist, than the satan of Christianity.

The best solution would be for adherents of monotheist religions (as well as secular humanists) to recognise evil in themselves and others, and to strive non-violently to seek together (across personal, cultural and national boundaries) to proceed on the basis of good will, putting the temptations of evil-doers behind them. This is, of course a major challenge: and so we review relevant literature, and some possible solutions.

Start with stable families, loving parents, and children who flourish

Parental abuse and neglect can for the child result in "soul murder", according to the psychodynamic case material presented by Lawrence Shengold (2000), following Schatzman's (1973) earlier work. Shengold focusses on adults whose rational optimism had been destroyed by profound and prolonged child abuse:

> " ... human beings who are prone to violent emotions, impulses, and actions (sadistic and masochistic) and a relative failure (some combination of too much and too little) of the defenses against them ... " Shengold (2000), p. 300).

These themes are also elaborated by the Canadian psychiatrist Paul Steinhauer (1989 & 2016), who shows that the crimes of psychopathic individuals often reflect failures in the child welfare system, in which a child is moved from a chaotic and abusing family by social services, but then loses the ability to bond and empathise (with self and others) through numerous movements from one foster family to another, through child care institutions, back into foster care or natal family, and then out again.

This perpetual breaking of affectional bonds sometimes results, as Bowlby and others have also shown, in the creation of antisocial and sometimes psychopathic personalities (Bowlby, 1982; Howe, 1995). Although the absence of a figure to whom the child can bond emotionally in the first two years of life may cause long-lasting emotional damage (sometimes reflected in brain alterations), nevertheless adoption into stable, loving families combined with expert intervention and support from therapists (which may be required for many years) may result in very positive psychological outcomes. This is shown clearly in the studies of Romanian children adopted in England, and studied systematically over several years by Michael Rutter and colleagues (Rutter et al., 1998 to 2010; Mehta et al., 2009; Sonuga-Barke et al., 2017; Mackes et al., 2020). Earlier studies had shown the positive outcomes for children from very deprived or abusing backgrounds, when they were adopted in their first two years of life by stable and caring parents (Adam-Bagley et al. 1993). The exception in our studies was the case of Native Canadian children adopted by European-Canadian parents, in which failure to give cultural support for their children in an environment which was hostile to Native identity, often led to unsuccessful outcomes (Adam-Bagley et al., 1991a).

We advocate once again, the idea of *Child-Centred Humanism* (CCH) (Adam-Bagley, 1997; Sawyerr & Adam-Bagley, 2017; and Chapters 1 & 2, above) as the humanist foundation for just societies. This principle asserts that all institutions of any society must first serve the welfare needs of *children and young people*. A just society fosters the self-esteem of each child as a sound foundation for esteeming not only themselves, but others also. Adults who lack self-esteem are likely to devalue others as a means of gaining some self-respect: this is one way in which racist identities are created (Adam-Bagley et al. 1979).

Good and stable parenting creates good self-esteem in children and adolescents. This is a simple formula, bolstered by a wealth of research (Coopersmith, 1967; Mruk, 2006, 2013 & 2017; Adam-Bagley et al., 1979). In this model, parents need to provide two elements which can be represented by "orthogonal" axes. A vertical axis represents *structure and stability*. This is represented at one end by families in which father and mother figures are stable figures, present throughout the child's development into adulthood (this can be one parent; or a new parent). The parent(s) are consistent in the rules they provide in their socialization, including the rewards they offer for good conduct (physical punishment for 'bad' behaviour is almost always harmful, and as an act of cruelty begets hatred and violence in future generations – Strauss & Donnelly, 2017).

At the opposite end of the *stability* spectrum are families marked by inconsistent parent figures who come and go, imposing difficult to anticipate or understand types of reward and discipline, and even physical, emotional and sexual abuse of the child by parent and other figures, which is likely to have very negative consequences for self-esteem and mental health development (Finkelhor & Tucker, 2015; Sawyerr & Adam-Bagley, 2023).

The horizontal axis in this developmental model of healthy self-esteem development is represented at one end of the axis by *warmth, love and acceptance* of the child's total being. The parent loves each and every child in their family, albeit tailoring their modes of affection according the child's individual character - as shown in a longitudinal study of children into young adulthood, testing the ideas of Chess et al. (1976; 2013) that "your child is a person", with unique requirements for love, care and socialization (Adam-Bagley & Mallick, 2000a). At the opposite end of this axis are children suffering both inconsistent and harsh discipline, which makes the child fearful of ever being successful in everyday tasks.

The first axis measures "consistent warmth *versus* inconsistent and often harsh discipline". The second, cross-cutting axis measures "household stability, including parent figure(s) who are constant in the child's life, providing basic but consistent material support *versus* instability of parental figures and of home life."

In the upper left-hand quadrant are children who experience not only structure and consistency in the attitudes and behaviour of their parent, within a stable household; these are children who also receive consistent love, warmth, support and guidance from their parents. These children will do well in life, loving themselves and others, overcoming in pacific ways through inner strength, the pathway which life opens up for them. These children enjoy structure and stability in their family lives. This combination, of loving warmth with family stability and structure produces self-confident, friendly children who will tackle the tasks of life with openness, joy and awe.

Hopefully, there are many more children in this quadrant in any population, than in any other quadrant. But consider the bottom left-hand quadrant in this model: this contains children who have experienced much inconsistency in the presence of parent-figures, both physically and emotionally. They may be moved from family to family, or to institutional or foster care. Often they experience both inconsistent and severe punishments, and a lack of love and comfort. Worse yet, quite often these parent figures (or other adults who have easy access to vulnerable children) may abuse the child, physically, emotionally and even sexually.

How many children in a population have experienced these latter conditions of development depends largely on how well their culture supports (and prevents) disruption of family life through poverty, disease and addiction. Cross-national studies (such as those cited by Sawyerr & Adam-Bagley, 2017a) indicate that some cultures (e.g., Finland, The Netherlands, and Scandinavian countries) have done well in this social policy enterprise. Others (e.g., USA, UK) have done much less well. The evidence is clear: families who endure chronic poverty are more likely to be neglectful or abusive towards their children.

(a) Child is born into a family that gives inconsistent forms of caring, sometimes warm, sometimes punitive; sometimes even abusive & neglectful. *Outcome*: lower self-esteem. (b) Child's family structure is unstable and disorganized, with parents & siblings leaving, new adults entering the family; child is moved between families in kin network, or into & out of child and foster care. *Outcome*: lower self-esteem	(c) Child is born into a stable, loving family with consistent caregivers who nurture the child with unconditional love. *Outcome*: higher self-esteem. (d) The family has structural quality, with enduring parental and sibling figures, and stability of residence & schooling. *Outcome*: higher self-esteem
When conditions (a) and (b) are combined: *Self-Esteem* levels are very low, and the child becoming an adult, struggles to give warmth, empathy and respect to fellow citizens. Some, very damaged have "devastated self-esteem", with aggression turned towards self or others.	When conditions (c) and (d) are combined: *Self-Esteem* levels of child are high, and the child becoming an adult, engages with warmth, empathy and respect with peers, and fellow citizens.
Research supporting this model derived from: Coopersmith (1967); Young & Adam-Bagley (1982); Adam-Bagley et al., 1997; Adam-Bagley & Mallick, 2000a & 2001; Mruk, 2003; Ziller, 2013; Steinhauer, 2016; and Sawyerr & Adam-Bagley (2017).	

Table 4.1 *Types of Parenting and Family Environment: Outcomes for Healthy Self-Esteem*

Many families stressed by chronic economic hardship survive as being excellent parents; but many do not, and aggressive and antisocial behaviour in children and adolescents is a known outcome. Poverty makes the devil's work in corrupting human nature, much easier. That is why, as social democrats in T.H. Green's legacy we should develop and deliver intervention programmes at preschool level, and later which can counter the malicious legacy of poverty upon child care and development (Adam-Bagley & Pritchard, 1998 & 2000; Sawyerr & Adam-Bagley, 2017b).

An important factor in evaluating cultures with many children with families in relative poverty (with attendant disruption of stable and loving family life) is the *Gini coefficient of inequality*: societies in which much wealth is held by a small upper class elite, have a large pool of degraded adults, struggling against permanent poverty, and many challenges to child-rearing (Adam-Bagley, 2022).

Thus for Britain we have advocated what Margaret Archer (2017) calls *morphogenesis* through which alienation of the economically neglected population can be "unmasked". Another kind of movement involves Keltner et al's (2010) movement for happiness and self-compassion (which shows that economic growth and equity is associated with "net happiness" levels). This is similar to developmental model of Neff et al. (2007 to 2011) in which adults can learn self-compassion, " … which entails being kind to oneself in instances of pain and failure: perceiving one's experiences as part of the larger human experience; and holding painful thoughts and feelings in balanced awareness." Developing such self-compassion is part of what Maslow calls "self-actualization" (Maslow, 1956). Self-compassion is a form of self-disciplined exercise in recognizing the potential for evil in oneself, as part of the straight pathway to success, and to personal transcendence.

Secular scholars on 'human goodness'

For secular humanists "The question of evil remains unanswered." (Fasching, 1983; McAlmont, 2020). Indeed, philosophers (e.g. Bernstein, 2005; Roth, 2015) are deeply critical of the whole body of writing on "ethics" from ancient times until the present, in its failure to explain how and why humans, *en masse*, sometimes engage in group murder of stigmatised peoples, century after century.

It may however be that social and clinical sciences can elucidate why some individuals engage in cruel and ruthless behavior, and it is a matter of law and politics, guided by psychological studies, to contain such brutality (Midgley, 2003a; Focquaert & Glenn, 2015). This is an uphill task, but hopefully not a Sisyphean one. Yet much of the world seems mired in a pseudo-religion, the norms and ethics of capitalist enterprise which McCarraher (2019) likens to "a religion", in which freedom of enterprise allows the exploitation of many, and the amassing of wealth by a few. In a review of capitalist exploitation and wealth (Adam-Bagley, 2022) this writer cites studies showing the huge amount of international wealth held by a small number of companies and individuals: and the massive poverty of at least a third of the world's population.

Doesn't being a trillionaire and using accumulated wealth to manipulate and exploit millions of individuals, cultures, and nations towards non-ethical ends, involve acts of "wickedness"? A few individuals (such as Bill Gates) have used their wealth to support the health and well-being of children in Africa and other continents. But many of the very rich have not acted for the public good.

Mary Midgley (2001) persuades us that extreme wickedness (of individuals, groups, and cultures) involves the arbitrary and unnecessary taking of human life; and being rich through capitalist exploitation, in ways which leaves many billions with a wretched and foreshortened existence. The poor are left to prey on one another, to steal, and to engage in corruption so as to survive. We have chronicled this occurring in India, Bangladesh and Pakistan (Adam-Bagley & Abubaker, 2019). This may lead to a debasement of the lives of children and adolescents, in which adults have "knowledge of evil". Thus Brown & Barrett (2002) use this concept in their focus on sexual exploitation of children and adolescents for commercial purposes, a societal evil we have only begun to recognise in the late twentieth century (Adam-Bagley, 1997; Sawyerr & Adam-Bagley, 2023).

Social structures and psychohistory: Ways to explain both good and evil in human affairs?

Psychohistory, pioneered by the psychological anthropologist Lloyd deMause (1982 & 2002) offers explanations for the rise of dictatorial and pathologically wicked leaders and dictators through a simultaneous examination of child-rearing practices (and child abuse) both at a universal, cultural level; and in the development of leaders of particular kinds. deMause had particular success in predicting pathways in 19th century American history using this model. He died before the advent of Donald Trump and the fantasies of Q-Anon, but his psychohistory model derived from Freudian psychology, would likely have had much to say on these developments (Connolly, 2022).

A startling but not totally implausible application of psychohistory (using Freud's ideas) to explain some historical events (such as the rise of Nazi power) is this: a powerful but immoral charismatic leader (such as Hitler) persuades a mass of people that id drives are actually super-ego drives, so that a nationalist, id-driven evil represents itself in super-ego form, and this becomes part of a normalised "national socialist" regime.

One facet of the group psyche, when evil has been dethroned, is a national mood of "forgetting evil", a process of mental suppression when normal civilization returns. This may have been the case in France (and other European nations), where collaboration with Nazis and complicity in deportation of Jews was quickly forgotten (Mehlman, 1983). But the average citizen in these totalitarian states often retained a core of humanity and goodness. There have been many "Schindlers", and many acts of goodness by those who could not undo the fascist or totalitarian state (Crowe, 2007).

The pacifist writer Judith Butler (2020) also considers the dark forces of the id which Freud describes as a factor in human violence and wickedness, but discounts the idea of permanent universal wickedness in the human psyche. The spiritual dimension in the human psyche described by Jung (Jung, 1958; Schott & Maslow, 1992) certainly has more heft for social scientists seeking to explain why some groups and sectors of society are pursuing good and rightful goals, of seeking compromise, universal social justice, and peace-making. Erik Erikson (1977) also presents us with a version of psychohistory which is altogether more optimistic than the approach of deMause, and offers a different type of Freudian-based theory which leads to, for example, his focus on the childhood development and spirituality of Mahatma Gandhi (Erikson, 1993a).

Writing about evil and its origins is a difficult and unsatisfactory experience. One grasps at the logic of contemporary social science: but these studies can only explain the origin of antisocial behaviours, wrong-doings which are not usually evil in any fundamental way. Psychoanalytic theories offer *post facto* explanations, but their logic can rarely be tested, or lead to practical programmes of prevention. Mary Midgley (2003a & b) offers humane rationales of how society may treat "wickedness" in individuals, and how we can exclude and humanely treat these evildoers in our midst. But what if the evil person is President of a powerful nation, who holds in thrall a 'mindless' mass of followers? We have no practical answer, but instead move to existential accounts of those who have experienced evil at the hands of others, and have emerged as fine people with lessons for us all.

Goodness emerging from evil: Humanist accounts of the Holocaust by Etty Hillesum, Elie Wiesel, Eugene Heimler and Viktor Frankl

Etty Hillesum

The remarkable Etty Hillesum was Dutch and arrested along with her brothers and parents by the Dutch quisling government, she was interned awaiting transportation to Auschwitz, where she and her whole family were murdered in Autumn, 1943. Etty's journals were not published in English until 1982, since publishers in the decades of "forgetting" genocide seemed reluctant to remind their public of the sufferings of Jews who had been persecuted in The Netherlands for centuries, and were best now forgotten. Etty's writings have been sympathetically analysed and presented by a Christian scholar Patrick Woodhouse (2009) who shows that Etty's Jungian analysis awakened in her a spiritual power, enabling her to transcend suffering, offering love to the forces of evil in the fascist movement which swept Europe for more than a decade. Etty was a spiritual humanist, not attached to any particular religion, but powerfully motivated by a power of goodness. She wrote in the days before deportation, knowing that death was almost certain:

> … I am filled with a sort of bountifulness, even towards myself …
> And a feeling of being at one with all existence. No longer: I want

this or that, but: Life is great and good and fascinating and eternal ... It is in these moments – and I am so grateful for them – that all personal ambition drops away from me, that my thirst for knowledge and understanding comes to rest, and a small piece of eternity descends on me with a sweeping wingbeat. (Hillesum, 1985, p. 365).

In October, 1942 a few hours before she and her family were herded in to a cattle truck enroute to Auschwitz she handed her diary to a friend. The last entry was:

"We should be willing to act as a balm for all wounds." (Hillesum 1985, p. 463).

Through small acts of kindness and comfort, she loved her enemies, and her spirit transcended. "She offered warmth and care, humour and kindness. Even in the face of death she would not be daunted." (Woodhouse, 2009, p. 150). The dynamic power of Etty's "thinking heart" is acknowledge by humanist psychology (Piechowski, 1992).

Eugene Heimler

Some people survived death camps, such as Anne Frank's father, Otto Frank whom I was privileged to meet in Amsterdam in 1969. A death-camp survivor from whom I learned much was Eugene Heimler, Professor of Human Social Functioning and my colleague in the Faculty of Social Welfare at the University of Calgary, for five years. Eugene was not a pacifist (he supported the fight against Soviet occupation of his native Hungary; and Israel's fight for survival against what was seen by many as a new form of attempted Holocaust). But he supported the 'dignity of struggle' as a way of surviving oppression, finding the best motives in those who oppressed him and his family, as he explains with both dignity and enthusiasm in his book *Night in the Mist* (reprinted in 1997) on how he survived Nazi brutality.

Eugene died in 1990 and is best known for his successful social work method, explained in his book *Human Social Functioning* (1967 & 2014). This model draws directly on Eugene's survival experience in Auschwitz, and reflected the intellect, bravery and social skills of Heimler's extraverted approach to life. Experiencing Nazi rule, and then life in Auschwitz he identified five bases for human flourishing and survival (which, theoretically were derived from his mentors Adler and Jung): personal satisfaction, from engaging emotionally with others; connection to family, or quasi-family; friendship stability; work stability and reward; and intrinsic rewards from any other vocation. Eugene developed a scale from these five levels of potential satisfaction, which was used to guide social work and psychiatric practice, the purpose being for social practitioners to enhance functioning in at least three of these domains. This model was warmly received, and put into successful practice by his students (Burnell & Norfleet, 1983). Heimler's model of practice has been absorbed into broader methods of supporting patients and clients, but his synergistic energy lives on in the humanistic psychology movement (Heimler 2014; & www.heimler-international.com).

Elie Wiesel

Elie shared Eugene's death camp experiences (though in Buchenwald, rather than in Auschwitz), and both survived. Their shared efforts to engage with the Holocaust memory in constructive ways were addressed to Europe and North America, whose people had largely "forgotten" the evils of antisemitism (now that 'the problem' had been shifted to Israel - Wiesel & Heimler, 1971). Elie Wiesel is best known for his trilogy of autobiographical novels, published together as: *Night, Dawn, Day* (1985), for which he was awarded The Nobel Prize for Literature, in 1986. The oration for this prize honoured Wiesel " ... for being a messenger to mankind: his message is one of peace, atonement and dignity" Though Romanian-born, he settled in America and was for many years Presidential Advisor on Holocaust remembrance.

Elie Wiesel argued that for the world to remember and learn from the Holocaust was not the only goal. He thought it equally important to fight indifference and the attitude that "it's no concern of mine". Elie perceived the struggle against indifference as a struggle for peace. In his words, "The opposite of love is not hate, but indifference". (www.nobelprize.org/1985)

Viktor Frankl

Austrian-born Viktor Frankl trained as a psychiatrist in Vienna, becoming a student of Alfred Adler. Not an overtly religious man, he was an active socialist in pre-war Austria. After the Nazi putsch he and his whole family were deported to Buchenwald, and Auschwitz. Only Viktor survived. In America he developed the theme of "the unconscious God" in all of us (Frankl, 1975), and pioneered a therapeutic system called logotherapy: "Only when the emotions work in terms of values can the individual feel pure joy." (Frankl, 1986, p. 40)

His research and autobiography (Frankl, 1988 & 2000) have also influenced a form of "community psychotherapy", in which groups tell and retell their stories, their cultural psychohistory as part of group identity enhancement (Lantz & Harper, 1992). Frankl's humanistic model has parallels with Heimler's approach, and involves self-recreation by accepting challenging tasks which are undertaken in a spirit of love for oneself and others: 'God within' is the driver of "logotherapy", moving towards personal, group and cultural re-creations.

Learning to be empathic: Simon Baron-Cohen and transcending the evil of the Holocaust

The English scholar Simon Baron-Cohen is a psychiatrist whose work on the neurology of autism spectrum disorders is well-known. But his remarkable book *Zero Degrees of Empathy: A New Theory of Human Cruelty and Kindness* (2011) is not about autism (although he does describe the neurological bases of empathy and kindness). This book according to Matthew Ridley (2011) " ... combines his creative talent with evidence and reason to make the case that evil is essentially a failure of empathy. It is an understanding that can enlighten an old debate and hold out the promise of new remedies."

Baron-Cohen grew up in a Jewish household in which the Holocaust was often mentioned, with ironies of humour that are exquisitely Jewish. In his book Baron-Cohen analyses the failures of empathy which characterised the work of Nazi scientists in Dachau. He draws too on autobiographies of death camp survivors showing that empathy was not totally lost: it is a natural human spirit which kept breaking to the surface, in both victims and guards.

From his neurological studies Baron-Cohen maps "the empathy circuit". His experimental work identifies brain mechanisms which lead to some individuals having "zero degrees of empathy", and why this pathological state is, fortunately, quite rare. Nevertheless, psychopathic personalities survive in modern society, probably as a function of the interaction of early neurological damage, and profoundly abusive parenting. Our work with sex-offenders in England, for example identified a type of person who inflicted cruelty without conscience, and obtained pleasure in doing so (Pritchard & Adam-Bagley, 2000 & 2001). These men who also often injure and kill their victims, might have found gainful employment as concentration camp guards in another culture: they are often products of a disordered and unloving socialization.

One challenge is to identify these conscience-less psychopathic and narcissistic personalities, in order to campaign against them holding custodial or political power. Another task Baron-Cohen presents us with is seeking to strengthen parenting which fosters empathy; and diminishing social conditions which undermine good parenting:

> My paraphrase of Bowlby's theory is this: what the caregiver gives his or her child in those first few critical years is like an **internal pot of gold**. The idea – which builds on Freud's insight -is that what a parent can give his or her child by way of filling the child up with positive emotions is a gift more precious than anything material. That internal pot of gold is something the child can carry inside throughout their life, even if they become a penniless refugees or are beset by other challenges. This internal pot of gold is what gives the individual the strength to deal with challenges, the ability to bounce back from setbacks, and the ability to show affection and enjoy intimacy with others. It overlaps with what the London child psychiatrist Michael Rutter refers to as 'resilience'. (Baron-Cohen, 2011, pp 50-51)

Baron-Cohen develops a complex model on how empathy develops in later life, stemming firstly from the degree to which parenting early in the child's life has developed the capacity to make enduring affectional bonds (as Bowlby termed them), and how in turn this "ego-strength" (i.e. good self-concept and self-esteem) is fostered or hindered by eleven domains of influence and interaction derived from culture, neurophysiology, hormone levels, types of stress, extended family, social groups, educational and career environments, and choice domains (e.g. choosing available options, and dealing with the consequences of choice.)

The journey of each individual is unique, and those experiencing disordered childhoods often have difficulty reaching the highest state of "super-empathy" (which seems akin to Maslow's self-transcendence). Nevertheless, given "normal" or "good" socialization, every individual is capable of achieving some state of empathy which is sufficient to support the citizens' social contract on which successful societies are grounded. He cites the supporting ideas Jeremy Rifkin's political science account of *The Empathic Civilization* (2009); and Frans de Waal's *The Age of Empathy* (2010) on how empathy-based human co-operation arises naturally from the process of evolution.

Baron-Cohen (2011) ends his challenging book with case histories from Israel, inspired by his grandfather Michael Greenblatt, a founder of the new Jewish state. There have been multiple "failures of empathy" in the past 75 years by both Jews and Muslims in Israel-Palestine (a land which one day may become a co-operative, single state). The Qur'an tells us that Jews are a special kind of Muslim (Qur'an 2:62); and the land of Israel (Canaan) was promised to both Jews and their Muslim cousins (Qur'an 5:20-21; 17:104; 26:59). Co-operation based on empathy would have avoided the Six-Day war of 1967, and Israel would certainly have developed as a different country if this needless war had been avoided.

> "It is clear that military solutions have not worked, and I argue that **the only way forward will be through empathy**. Fortunately, there is evidence that those in the Middle East have not lost their empathy in any permanent or enduring way." (Baron-Cohen, 2011, p. 131)

Baron-Cohen gives a powerful account of two visitors to his synagogue (who also made their joint presentation to other Jewish and Muslim places of worship) to illustrate his thesis on the meaning of empathy:

> Two men went up on the stage. The first one spoke: 'I am Ahmed, and I am a Palestinian. My son died in the Intifida, killed by an Israeli bullet. I come to wish you all Shabbat Shalom'. Then the other man spoke: 'I am Moishe, and I am an Israeli. My son also died in the Intifada, killed by a homemade petrol bomb thrown by a Palestinian teenager. I come to wish you all Salaam Alaikem ... Moishe told Ahmed 'We are the same: we have both lost our son. Your pain is my

pain.' Ahmed had replied, 'This suffering must end before there are more fathers like you and me who come to know the awful pain of losing a son. (Baron-Cohen, 2011, pp 131-132).

Ending hatred: Goodness stemming from tragedy in Izzeldin Abuelaish's account of Palestinian and Israeli conflict

Izzeldin Abuelaish's (2011) book titled *I Shall Not Hate* is a *story*, a true story. In the tradition of communicating stories including a life history marked by profound tragedy, he unburdens his emotional life in order to achieve a peace-making solution, for himself and for others including the warring peoples of Israel and Palestine. He begins by telling of a life of material poverty in a refugee camp in Gaza, his educational struggle to achieve a place in medical school in Egypt, and his postgraduate work at Harvard University in America. He opted to leave the comfortable life of a highly rewarded obstetrician in America, and returned to Gaza to serve his people, and endure the ever-present risks of military bombardment by Israel.

In January 2009 the Israelis once again attacked Gaza, and the tanks rolled in "looking for Hamas". A tank stopped outside of Izzeldin's house, but in which there was no-one from Hamas (the civilian authority administering Gaza). The tank fired into his house at point-blank range, into an upper bedroom where his teenaged daughters were sleeping.

Izzeldin then describes how he pieced together the dismembered bodies of the girls, and tended his wounded son:

" ... I was trying to sort out who else was injured. Shehab had shrapnel in his head and back. I was trying to check his wounds while I held Shartha in my arms, when I looked up to see Mohammed, and was stricken by the thought that he had just lost his mother and now three of his sisters were gone ... Then

Mohammed said 'Ghaida took a breath.' Before that I thought that she too was dead ... My neighbors lifted Shartha, Ghaida, Nasser, and Shehab onto stretchers and wrapped the bodies of Mayar, Aya and Noor in blankets ..." (Abuelaish, 2011, p. 178)

For many months afterwards the remaining children suffered from post-traumatic stress; one boy recovered from physical wounds but had frequent seizures. PTSD frequently occurs in Gazan children who have experienced Israeli rockets, bombs and tank fire (Wesam Abubaker, 2019). It is worth noting that in these recurrent conflicts the 'kill ratio' is 500 to 1 in favour of Israel: that is, for every Israeli killed in these acts of warfare, 500 Gazans (most of them women, the elderly and children) are killed (Mahmoud Abubaker et al., 2022).

Izzeldin recovered from the tragedy of his murdered children through the bravery of political activism, speaking and writing about the need for peace-making in his resolve that "I Shall Not Hate":

"This catastrophe of the deaths of my daughters and niece has strengthened my thinking, deepened my belief about how to bridge the divide. I understand down to my bones that violence is futile. It is a waste of time, lives and resources and has been proven to beget only more violence. It does not work. It just creates a vicious cycle. There's only one way to bridge that divide, to realize the goals of two peoples: we have to find the light to guide us to our goal. I am not talking about religious faith here, but light as a symbol of truth. The light that allows you to see, to clear away the fog – to find wisdom. To find the light of truth, you have to talk to, listen to, and respect each other. Instead of wasting energy on hatred, use it to open your eyes and see what's really going on ..." (Abuelaish, 2011, p, 196)

These are not new ideas born out of Izzeldin's grief. Rather, they are an eloquent expression of the Islamic ideas he held all of his life. Now he compares himself with Prophet Ayoub or Job, described in Qur'an, Talmud and Bible, who faithfully suffered terrible tribulation:

"I believe everything happens for a reason, and that even my family's terrible loss serves a purpose. The deaths of my daughters and niece opened the Israeli's eyes to the suffering on the other side … I believe that there is a better future for us because of what this tragedy has taught the world. There is hope; the past is only there to learn from." (Abuelaish, 2011, p. 198)

Fifteen years after this event there is still, alas, no peace for Gaza (Gelvin, 2021). But we agree profoundly that pacificist politics by Israel and Palestine, including acceptance of the Oslo Accords might bring lasting peace. To continue spousing warfare is to continue spousing evil.

Mehnaz Afridi's *Shoah Through Muslim Eyes*: A story of empathy and tolerance

Mehnaz Afridi is an American-based scholar who was born in India, but as an infant was taken by her parents into what is now Pakistan at the time of partition in 1948. This personal *hijra*, the fleeing of persecution experienced by Muslims in what became India, has formed the basis of her story, which she retells in her sparkling monograph *Shoah Through Muslim Eyes* (2017), a remarkable book of empathy and conciliation for Jews and Muslims. She begins her book with by quoting a Sufi poet Mayuddin Ibn Arabi, writing in about 1150 of the Common Era. We reproduce this poem here since it sums up the humanist spirit of tolerance and discovery (*Tazkiya*, intellectual growth or self-purification) which lies at the heart of Islam, and which is relevant for all humanists:

> My heart has become capable of every form: it is a pasture for gazelles and a convent for Christians; And a temple for idols, and for pilgrims to the Kaaba, and for the tablets of The Torah, and the books by the Qur'an; I follow the religion of love, whatever way love's camels take, it is my religion.   (From the collection edited by Mahmood Jamal, 2015).

Mehnaz is director of the Holocaust, Genocide and InterFaith Center at Manhattan College New York, and for the past decade has been recording accounts of death camp survivors, now resident in New York. She retells these stories in her book, and also offers a historical account of the Shoah (the movement which led to the Nazi death camps), and the organized mass-killing using the sophistication of industrial states with the passive or active help of 22 different countries (Afridi & Smith, 2021). As a Muslim she is deeply offended by these mass murders, and offers empathic support to her Jewish friends.

> I decided to write this book as I began to interview Holocaust survivors because I wanted to tell their stories, but also to join their stories with my experience of antisemitism today ... As Muslims we are taught to accept justice, truth and equality. It is time that people of all faiths, and even the faithless, started listening to the voices that speak for the 'other' – those with a message to all of our shared humanities ... An example is the universal message that came to Muslims as believers of Abraham and his family, which is similar to that of Jews and Christians. (Afridi, 2017, p. 4)

Mehnaz Afridi observes that Muslims (unlike Christians) have been welcoming of Jews of the diaspora, a welcome which the Qur'an directs (Lewis, 2013). But colonial occupation in the past two centuries usurped the finely balanced tolerance of Muslim cultures, imposed antisemitic ideologies, and usurped the peace of Palestine through a brutal foundation of the State of Israel. True, Israel ("Canaan") is the land which the Qur'an promises for the Jews who are the first cousins of Christians and Muslims descended from Abraham (Adam-Bagley, 2019c) – but the nature of this European colonization imported a conflict between Jews and Muslims which, unfortunately, endures. Afridi argues that the antisemitism generated through modern Middle Eastern conflicts is not her main concern. Her role is rather to educate both Christians and Muslims on the history and nature of the Shoah in making " ... connections between the importance of accepting each other's narratives in creating dialogue and reconciliation." (p. 20). This is a noble example of "telling of stories".

Ken Plummer's critical humanism, and 'the telling of stories'

Critical humanism is enervated by the sharing of our *stories* with others. This process is liberating for ourselves, and may be inspiring for others too (Plummer, 2019). Ken Plummer was my beloved teacher (at the University of Essex) who died in 2022: he grounded his humanism (termed "a manifesto for the 21st century") in the discipline of the shared telling of stories, a form of reflexive anthropology in which we learn both empathy and tolerance (Plummer, 2020).

Arthur Frank also persuades us that: "Stories animate human life: that is their work. Stories work with people, and for people; and always stories work on people affecting what people see as real, is possible, and what is worth doing or best avoided … A good life requires living well with stories. When life goes badly, a story is often behind that too … Narrative makes the world habitable for human beings." (Frank, 2010, p. 3)

There are true stories; there is noble fiction; but there are also false stories. False stories involve rumour and hatred, such as the slandering of an ethnic group. An example is the fugue of antisemitic stories which swept through the city of Orleans in 1968 (Morin, 1971); and the media-fuelled false stories which led to the Rwanda massacres of 1994 (Thompson, 2007). At the time of writing (2023) America is still awash with false and cruel stories from the MAGA movement.

Our stories (like the stories of refugee girls retold my Malala Yousafzai, 2019) must be true, and have an implicit but unmistakeable moral purpose. We must have humanistic stories, not dehumanized ones. We must also use reason and critical intelligence in reading and interpreting the stories offered by the great religions. In analysing these stories, these metaphysical accounts of human endeavour, Ken Plummer observes:

> "... the world's multiple, schismatic and pervasive religions become deeply woven narratives of what it means to be human. For most of humanity's more recent history, they have provided central canopies of meaning. They have served to define who we are and what our purpose is. They have provided narrative frames for our routines and rituals, our codes and cultures, our hierarchies and symbols, our beginning, middle and ends. They are not just narratives of the past. These axial narratives of humanity live on today, shaping the lives of the vast majority of people on Planet Earth." (Plummer, 2020, p. 114)

Plummer (2020) takes the concept of "the axial age" from the philosopher Karl Jaspers (Peet, 2019) to describe human evolution into an age of telling stories about humankind's origins, and our place in the universe, a process which began to be recorded about 8,000 years ago in the writings of the earliest known religions. The humanist scholar (like Plummer) looks for the universal elements in these stories, seeking tales of goodness and self-sacrifice in the expansion of human identity and culture (Plummer, 2019). Seligman (2012) in pioneering a new science of optimism, has also followed this path in analysing the higher values and behavioural practices of the great religions and philosophical traditions, in deriving modal pathways for the aspiring rationalist seeking the most hopeful ethical domains of behaviour.

The Muslim needs to read The Bible and The Torah: we all need to read and listen to one another's axial stories. An example of such a critical exercise is Tom Wilson's deconstruction of the text of St. Matthew's Gospel, which is taken by some as a 'blood libel', to justify the continued persecution of "Christ killers". Wilson (2022) shows clearly that Matthew neither intended nor implied any such interpretation.

And what of our beloved Qur'an, which we read with such joy and inspiration, as a book which inspires human goodness, pacific deeds, and the dignity of women. Alas, there are still today warring and dissident factions within Islam who regularly murder one another, and the innocents of other religions (as the continued hostility between Sunni and Shia; and the rise of ISIS, exemplify).

We have looked to the Islamic nations of Pakistan and Bangladesh as potential havens of spiritually-driven moral and political cultures which might enable the flourishing of men, women and children. Alas, our research in these countries has proven that often the opposite is true, and women and children are physically and sexually exploited and killed, in ways entirely contrary to the teachings of Islam (Adam-Bagley et al., 2017 to 2019; Shahnaz et al, 2017).

The positive psychology movement: Overcoming evil by 'learning to be good'

The positive psychology movement of the present century offers us behaviourist techniques for 'learning to be good', through which the neuroses imposed by problems of childhood development can be overcome. Thus Lomas (2015) using Bronfenbrenner & Ceci's (1994) ecological model of personal and cultural development, offers an interesting and challenging model of how the positive psychology movement may be effecting positive changes at the level of cultural values, which in turn effects positive social changes in a variety of social institutions. Lomas focuses on education and human interchange which can promote "positive thinking" in a variety of cultural institutions, especially those which involve economically poor and disadvantaged people.

His "positive school psychology" involves, for instance the 'mindfulness' approaches of educating and enabling individuals to 'think for themselves', and in engaging with like-minded others, promoting first better self-esteem level; second better levels of co-operation; and finally dialogue and joint action to provide mutual help in addressing social change issues. Lomas reviews a number of important English studies which are attempting to achieve this (the parallels and connections with Margaret Archer's morphogenesis are clear).

What have these approaches to do with evil? They are hopeful attempts to work with and develop the essential goodness in human beings, who despite their oppression and disadvantage in class-exploited or warfare-threatened societies, can make positive changes in themselves and in their social structures. But it remains possible also that these techniques could be manipulated by evil actors, such as politicians who seek to enhance the welfare of the majority through scapegoating minority groups. This "positive thinking" must embrace ideas of non-discrimination, and 'fair play' in all our dealings.

We must, in Matthew Ridley's dictum, be "rational optimists" (Ridley, 2010). Ridley, a polymath scholar steeped in genetics, history, demography, economics and sociology anticipated many of the social and climatic changes which have influenced human development in the past decade. He charts the historical movement towards greater prosperity and flourishing of the human spirit and its endeavour, *despite* problems of overpopulation and climate change:

> "Human nature will not change. The same old dramas of aggression and addiction, of infatuation and indoctrination, of charm and harm, will play out ... the human race will continue to expand and enrich its culture, despite setbacks and despite individual people having much the same evolved, unchanging nature. The twenty-first century will be a magnificent time to be alive." (Ridley, 2010, p. 359).

Ridley's optimism is based on his analyses of human nature and human endeavour across the centuries, and the steady improvement in human societies, because "ideas have sex" (i.e. good ideas beget more good ideas). "Wickedness" breaks out like pus across the world's body, but the survival instinct of humans according to Ridley, overcomes these temporary manifestations of evil in human society. The fundamental, universal drive towards achieving goodness is why we should remain optimistic, and why we should strive towards maximising that goodness in ourselves and others.

We may now embark in this century on a phase of ending poverty and extremes of wealth, and the deprivation and exploitation of children and childhood, echoing Keltner's thesis (2009) that since humans are "born to be good", positive social policies can through supporting programmes of child welfare and humanist education, enhance the social bonding necessary for the development of the working social contract which is the essence of civilised society, but works imperfectly when the evil of ethnocentrism inserts itself (Ziller, 2015).

An optimistic mapping of general human progress also comes from the Swedish group led by Hans Rosling (Rosling et al., 2018), using worldwide public health data which shows continuous improvement in child and adult health, and children's survival into healthy lives. Now "less than" six percent of the world population endure dire poverty which shortens life, according to these data. The policy implication is that we should overcome political biases, in helping all countries of the world reach acceptable levels of public health – which in Rosling's optimistic view is achievable. This valuable idea of addressing behavioural goals for promoting "human flourishing" in developing countries as a way of reaching UN Sustainable Development Goals, is advocated by Brasso & Krpdn (2023)

Evil remains: But humanity can transcend evil

Evil has been, and will remain part of human civilization, and motives towards evil actions are embedded in each one of us. We must be "mindful" of these drives, and imagine goodness, good deeds, in ourselves and others: contemplating, with awe, the wonders of nature and of humanity's complex nature, and the potential in each one of us not only for ethical actions, but also of spiritual joy that is the privilege for each one of us, Secular Humanist and Religious people alike. The potential of this *awe* is available to all people, whether they be Muslim, Jew, Christian or of other religions, including the 'secular religious' such as Quaker non-theists.

Dacher Keltner and his colleagues in elaborating their ideas that humans and their civilizations are ultimately serving goals of seeking the best outcomes for all of humankind (Keltner et al, 2009 to 2022), asked 2764 people in 20 countries to record their experience and understanding of "awe". From this material emerged "the eight wonders of life" that stimulate humans to experience awe: moral beauty; collective effervescence; nature; music; visual design; spirituality and religion; life and death; and epiphany. All kinds of people – artists, prisoners, sports-people, musicians, spiritual leaders – reported an experience of awe. Keltner & Bai (2022) also report work with PTSD survivors, in which "mindful awe" helped military veterans to transcend and lose their symptoms.

This "Mindful Pursuit of Awe" through self-disciplined thought and dialogue is a welcome movement which flourishes through many different approaches in philosophy and the social sciences (Ridley, 2010): we read with satisfaction and hope the writings of Dacher Keltner (2009), Kenneth Gergen (2010 & 2016) and William Irvine (2008) each of whom develop different (but compatible) philosophies and techniques on how to develop our innate goodness, through a variety of self-directed reflections and interactions. Thus for Keltner & Piff (2020) "Self-transcendent awe is a moral grounding of wisdom."

The person experiencing awe of others, in the ruddy wealth of human kindness and the richness of nature, becomes a "diminished self", less proud but more co-operative in the new political state that Keltner envisages (which bears an interesting resemblance to Islam's ideal state grounded on *zakah* principles – Zakaria & Malek, 2014). This state of awe is both an emotional state and a cognitive skill which may be acquired through education and self-directed knowledge-seeking; and also, of course, through prayer, in which Muslims have a 5-a-day head start.

Conclusions

Writing about evil is both easy and hard. It's everywhere, and its multiple forms in individuals, groups and occasionally in nations is easy to describe: but hard to understand. Two themes emerge in the literature on how to combat evil. First, we must start with those most precious beings, our children and treat them not only with love and tenderness, giving them warm clothing and a safe environment, with an education which enables them to cope with life's challenge. We must also nurture them with love, systematic structures, guidance and praise. We need also to emphasise their moral education, enabling them to become good citizens, able to take part in a social contract which avers: *I am, because you are; I serve you, my fellow citizen, with respect and esteem and I know that you will value me likewise.* We can offer treatment, moral education and perhaps gentle confinement for some who have not absorbed this message.

When I lived in Reading in the UK, our local Quaker Meeting visited the nearby Broadmoor Special Hospital every Sunday, visiting men who had no family visitors – this hospital houses those who committed serious crimes (usually murder) but had been judged "unfit to plead" in Court, because of their serious mental illness. I developed an affection both for the men I befriended; and also for Broadmoor, its people and its lovely rose bushes grown by patients, and the gentle and relaxed regime which prevailed.

In the same period I spent time in a monastery, and learned that monks loved two things (in addition to the seven daily offices): good food and warmth, physical and emotional. My proposal has been that all prisons should become like religious institutions, full of good food and warmth for those contained for long periods, and not places of punishment. But I know, from participating with the group *Quakers in Criminal Justice*, that prisons are cold and sad places, in which evil is allowed to fester and grow. I am impressed therefore by the work of Muslim colleagues, led by Matthew Wilkinson (Wilkinson et al, 2015 to 2022) on enriching the lives of Muslim prisoners in Britain. Through this work the *spiritual power from within* is redemptive, just as Vincent de Paul, the former slave, energised the redemption of prisoners through the enactment of small acts of kindness (Pujo, 2003).

Within the most evil person, the light of the spirit is never entirely extinguished. I intuit that Adolf Hitler (whose soul I pray for) might have earned redemption through a final act of love, such as marrying Eva Braun. There is always hope, as the death camp survivors have shown. And the humanist movement pioneered by the scholars described in this Chapter, give grounds for hope, working on the assumption of the basic goodness of humans, showing in a variety of ways how to make the best of ourselves, and the best of society.

This book has not focussed as much as it should on the brilliant philosopher and political scientist Mahatma Gandhi (Allen, 2007; Parekh et al., 2008) whose pacifist ideal is still highly relevant for the world's future development. His Pakistani contemporary Bacha Khan (Easwaran, 1999) declared an Islamic philosophy of peacemaking which meshes with Gandhi's Hindu-inspired philosophy of peace. May these two philosophies entwine and grow!

Chapter 5

The Retelling of Our Stories - Abraham Maslow, Religion and Human Transcendence
Chris Adam-Bagley

Beginning with Edward Said ...

In the preface to his study on ethnocentric perceptions of non-European cultures, titled *Orientalism*, Edward Said (2016) wrote that

> "...humanism is the only – I would go so far as saying the final – resistance we have against the inhuman practices and injustices that disfigure human history...my arguments ... based on a humanist position that places the well-being of the historical, embodied human struggling for a better world at the heart of its analysis: it puts our species to the forefront of critical thinking. Humanism is the world philosophy that considers what it means to be a human being across the globe. It sees that the world we live in is a human world: it is created through human beings, organized and disorganized by human beings, and ultimately transformed by human beings. It is people doing things together that make states, economies, institutions happen. It is people together who change the world and make it a better or lesser place .... Humanistic research starts with the people around the world living their daily lives of difference. At the core of our concerns lies the talk, feelings, actions, bodies, vulnerabilities, creativities, moralities, sufferings, joys, and passions of people as they share communities and social worlds, create human bonds, and confront the everyday constraints of history and a material world of inequalities and exclusions." (Said, 2016, p. 1)

Edward Said was born a Palestinian Christian, but his intellectual bond with the secular humanists on whom Ken Plummer (2020) focuses, is clear. Muslims too acknowledge the thrust and integrity of Said's scholarship (Aruri & Shuraydi, 2006).

Said was for many years a leading critic of the Western world's islamophobia and its biased and prejudiced portrayals of Muslim cultures. Like his fellow-Christian Yasser Arafat, Said also advocated peaceful solutions for relations between Israel and Palestine. In his autobiography Said tells his life's story, of being a wandering intellectual whose dispossessed identity gave him powerful insights into both epistemology and peace-making; and in the uncovering of Western cant and prejudice regarding Islam, and Palestine (Said, 1992 to 2016). There is prescience in his writing of Ken Plummer's (2019 & 2020) masterful account of recounting stories to redeem ourselves and others. As Christians, Muslims, Jews and Secularists seem to agree: if you can save one life, it's as if you have saved the whole world. Think big, start small, and go on from there. The "stories" from Israel and Palestine recounted by Barren-Cohen (2011) and Izzeldin Abuelaish (2011) add moral force to this dictum.

The life-stories of ourselves and others have two elements: the adoption of common values through emotional bonding; and the shared critical rationality embedded in stories. Our stories must be true, loving and humane (i.e. humanist in character) – showing how in this sharing we can help one another. If you help your neighbour in both dialogue and action, you are on the straight path to mending the world. As Keltner (2010) advises, "focus on the moral beauty of others". This may be part of Margaret Archer's (2017) *morphogenesis*, remaking ourselves and others through dialogue, through the telling of stories.

The most powerful stories are those which stem from suffering, but develop great optimism and profound spirituality in the telling. This is the case in particular with the stories of death-camp victims and survivors, such as Anne Frank, Etty Hillesum, Elie Wiesel, Eugen Heimler, Primo Levi, Viktor Frankl and other brave souls who faced the most dreadful assault upon human civilization, but emerged with dignity, love, transcendence, and the advocacy of restorative justice. This is also the social movement advocated and sponsored by Todorov (2010). Searching for "the keys to kindness" is a way of healing oneself, and a broader network of social relationships and their implicit cultural values (which is how the social contract works) (Hammond, 2022). [8]

Varieties of religious experience: Their purpose and meaning

William James and modern research on religious experience

> "We can experience union with something larger than ourselves and in that union find our greatest peace." (William James, The Varieties of Religious Experience 1982, p, 204).

The father of modern humanistic psychology, William James in his *Principles of Psychology* (1983), is also well known for his work on *Varieties of Religious Experience* (1982) in which he mapped and described different kinds of religious and transcendental experiences which humans can achieve: suffice to say, his intellectual heir Abraham Maslow's peak experiences and self-transcendence, can take a variety of forms, both philosophical and experiential.

---

[8] Being through marriage, part of an extended Jamaican family I am fascinated by the syncretism of African and Christian religions and culture which survives in Jamaica today. The story of Anansi, the spider-man who always outwitted his potential captors, was one of the many folkways through which African slaves survived and founded a new culture, and a new religion (Rastafarianism), and the culture of *juk*, the thrust of survival. Alice Sawyerr and I discuss this cultural survival in our book on ethnicity (Sawyerr & Adam-Bagley, 2017).

According to Butler-Bowdon (2005):

> "For William James ... spiritual ideas should be judged on three criteria: 1) immediate luminousness; 2) philosophical reasonableness; and 3) moral helpfulness. Put simply, do they enlighten us, do they make sense, are they a good guide to living?" (Butler-Brown, 2005, p. 10)

James' ideas have stimulated much research in the field of "religious sociology", and in reviewing and synthesising this work David Yaden and Andrew Nuberg (2022) borrow James' title and update his themes in their book *The Varieties of Spiritual Experiences: 21st Century Research*. They find that about 30 percent of people in a variety of cultures report having had some kind of "spiritual experience". While some neurological correlates of such experience have been established, it has proved impossible to predict when such an experience might occur. Around 80 percent of those having a spiritual experience regarded it as positive or enlightening, although only some ten percent of these individuals had experiences of a divine presence.

Benefits of being religious?

Some neuroscientists and philosophers (e.g., Eccles and Popper on *The Self and Its Brain*; and Beauregard and O'Leary on *The Spiritual Brain*) have argued that the "urge to be spiritual" is embedded as Descartes would aver in the human neuro-system. Is "being spiritual" part of both human goodness, and human survival, as Eccles and Robinson (1984) have argued?

All the themes touched on in our book have resonance with David Robson (2022) on how being religious (or at least, having an active religious affiliation) can benefit personal life – although it's not clear how many people are religious merely because of social and health benefits. Robson gathers together two decades of social science research which shows that individuals actively associated with a church, chapel, mosque, synagogue, temple or other religious venue (in physical, emotional or social ways) live, on average about 5 years longer than the "non-religious". They have lower rates of heart disease and cancer, are less likely to be psychiatrically depressed or anxious, less likely to be suicidal, or hypertensive. Why should this be so?

The most likely reason seems to be that religious people are less likely to use or misuse alcohol or drugs; less likely to practise unsafe sex; less likely to smoke; they are less socially isolated: and in difficulty are supported by their religious communities. Furthermore, the acts of being helpful to others, and praying for others (as well as for oneself) seems to bring health benefits.

In reaching these conclusions Robson cites studies from North America and Europe, which in the main do not control for the effects of class and ethnicity. Being conventionally religious could merely be a beneficial side effect of class privilege. Nevertheless, experience with my Jamaican wife Loretta, of attending the Seventh Day Adventist Church is persuasive. This American-origin (and female-founded) church has evangelised many disadvantaged communities in the Caribbean, The Philippines, Hong Kong and elsewhere. The documented benefits in health in Adventist church members through its world-wide network of health-promoting clinics, hospitals and colleges, does offer the model of a religious movement whose insistence on alcohol avoidance, self-care and vegetarian diet has had the benefit of excellent health, and longevity (Kwok et al., 2014; Galvez et al., 2021). But as my Adventist friends say: When the Good Lord calls you, it's your time! We – Christians, Muslims, Jews, Secularists and Others – serve on earth "so long as the good Lord spares us": and there is much joy in this.

Abraham Maslow: The scholar of transcendence

Maslow's short but productive life, 1908 to 1970

After a rather miserable childhood in New York City, where his Jewish parents had settled following emigration from Russia, Maslow studied law at university. He quickly abandoned this "dry" topic for what he hoped would be the more warm-blooded discipline of psychology. In this too he was disappointed, being directed in his doctoral work into studies of sexual dominance in imprisoned primates (Maslow, 1936). Maslow moved in a radical direction, teaming with noted anthropologists Ruth Benedict and Margaret Mead in using new, qualitative methodologies in describing how people survive often wretched childhoods, to become fulfilled individuals making 'the best of themselves', becoming good citizens in terms of the implicit social contract, and finally (for some) achieving self-transcendence (Maslow, Honigmann & Mead, 1971; Maslow, 1971). His work is now widely cited, and used in many settings including clinical psychology, social work, industrial psychology, and management.

Maslow's work resonates with new generations in the fields of health care, counselling and management (e.g., Bridgman et al., 2019), and his ideas have been taken forward in fresh thinking, evidenced by Kaufman's *Transcend: The New Science of Self-Actualization* (2020), which we discuss later.

> "Abraham Maslow was always looking at the 'big picture.' Whereas most social scientists of his day seemed to wear blinders that riveted their attention to narrow concerns, Maslow's own vision was far-reaching. His lifetime of discoveries in motivation and personality transcended academic psychology, and extended into the major business fields of management and marketing." (Hoffman, 2011, p. 4)

Maslow's view of the world, and of the role of psychology in creating a new world which transcends the evils and the cruelties of the past world is lyrically expressed in his 1956 essay (Hoffman, 2011 & 2016):

> "I believe that the world will either be saved by the psychologists or it won't be saved at all ... All important problems of war and peace, exploitation and brotherhood, hatred, love and sickness and health, misunderstanding and understanding, the happiness and unhappiness of humankind will yield only to a better understanding of human nature... Hard science is a means, not an end. The **end** is human fulfilment, human betterment, growth and happiness... By psychologists I mean all sorts of people, not just the profession of psychology ... I include some sociologists, linguists, anthropologists, educators, philosophers, artists, publicists, linguistics and business people." (Maslow, 1956a, p. 19).

In this model, psychology "should have an intrinsic value commitment: the meaning and betterment of human endeavour in all spheres of society ... Psychology and philosophy *must* go hand in hand in focussing on and speculating about human actions and endeavours, and moral and behavioral choices." (Maslow, 1956a, p. 20) Psychology should, in this model, not offer generalisations from a large, anonymised group of "subjects": it should present a series of linked case studies which enable "John Smith" to be the "best John Smith in the world."

In the master's footsteps

The Blackfoot nation, living in what is now Southern Alberta, Canada (part of the Plains Cree civilization) is also known in Northern Montana as the Blackfeet people. North and south of the border, they are part of the same nation, whose traditional land was cruelly cut by the 49th Parallel which the colonial powers used to divide Canada from the USA. Blackfoot people are humiliated when their sacred "medicine bundles" are searched by US or Canadian border guards, as peoples of this First Nation journey to tribal gatherings, north or south of the artificial border.

Soon after I arrived in Calgary, Alberta to join the Faculty of Social Welfare at the University there, I was introduced to a meeting of elders of the Blackfoot Nation, in 1981. As a naïve newcomer having lunch with an Elder, and searching for a topic of conversation I observed that Moose were stupid animals, since they stood on the highway without moving, staring the car down. "No," the Elder replied. "They are wise. The Great Creator has given them to us as sustenance which is easy for us to harvest". This first lesson in theology of the First Nations began a wonderful journey, with many friendships.

I later worked with the Blackfoot (and more northern Native communities) as a social work consultant doing 'expert witness' assessments of Native children seized from their homes by social services and placed with white foster parents. This also involved an assessment of Native children adopted by white foster carers, and I was able to show that this cultural mismatch often proved harmful to children's psychosocial development (Adam-Bagley, 1991a).

I didn't know it then, but I was treading in the footsteps of the human-centred psychologist Abraham Maslow who in 1937 (the year in which I was born) came to Calgary to begin work on the psychological anthropology of The Blackfoot Nation, on behalf of the anthropologist, Ruth Benedict. Abraham Maslow was a refugee from the barren and cruel experimental work that his doctoral studies had involved, and he sought intellectual sanctuary with the well-known social anthropologist Ruth Benedict (who lived from 1887 to 1948), and who sent Abraham on a field-trip to Alberta to undertake qualitative work on understanding the psychological embodiment of culture in an indigenous First Nation, the Blackfoot of Southern Alberta. His understandings of the culture and social psychology of an indigenous people stimulated the development of his now famous writings on self-actualization, and synergy in self and culture (Benedict, 1940; Maslow, 1937; Maslow & Honigmann, 1944; Maslow, 1951; Maslow, Honigmann & Mead, 1970; Takaki et al, 2016; Feigenbaum & Smith, 2020).

For Native peoples, synergy (giving support and praise to others, and receiving this support and praise in return, in relation to both functional and overarching goals); and unity with the natural world within a metaphysical system of animism, is a fundamental behavioural ethic. For the Blackfoot still retaining their original language, with strong vestiges of traditional culture and leading a full and culturally-contained life, led to mental contentment which in elders Maslow recognized as "self-actualization", concepts which he developed in his later writing. Kaufmann (2020) also acknowledges the Blackfoot experience of Maslow in developing the important concept of synergy, in which "virtue pays", in the traditional medicine wheel of aboriginal culture. [9]

In postscript to the ideas of synergy and actualization embedded in Native people's social structure and values, it is clear that Canada's colonial policies of attempting to suppress Native language and

---

[9] David Peat (2002) a quantum physicist visited and absorbed Blackfoot culture for several years: " ... hitherto having spent all of my life steeped in and influenced by linear Western science, I was entranced by the Native world view and, through dialogue circles between scientists and Native Elders, I began to explore this in greater depth ... I offer a "Blackfoot Physics" through a synthesis of anthropology, history, metaphysics, cosmology and quantum theory ... I compare the medicines, the myths, the languages, indeed the entire perceptions of reality of two peoples, Western and Indigenous. What became apparent was the amazing resemblance between Indigenous teachings and some of the insights that have emerged from modern science ... a congruence that is as enlightening about the physical universe as it is about the circular evolution of man's understanding."

culture through removal of children into notorious residential schools, where many died (Truth & Reconciliation Commission, 2015; Austin, 2023) has meant that Native cultures have struggled to survive. Alcoholism became common, giving social workers an excuse to remove children from parents, even though a member of the extended family was almost certainly available to provide childcare.

Our thesis that high recorded suicide rates in Native peoples reflected levels of poverty was borne out in research in Alberta (Adam-Bagley et al., 1991a & b; 2009) which showed that when oil was discovered on tribal lands in the 1960s, the welfare and mental health of Band members improved, and suicide rates diminished. When prosperity returned, so did a resurgence in traditional Native culture and values.[10]

Maslow's well-known pyramid of human needs and their achievement

Most text-books for professionals in the fields of human service and management psychology reproduce the famous pyramid of developmental challenges and achievements. We don't reproduce it here since Maslow never designed such a pyramid – it was recreated after his death by interpreters of his published writing (Kolkto-Rivera, 2006; Bland & DeRobartis, 2020a).

---

[10] Writing on management applications of his models, Maslow wrote some 35 years after his fieldwork with the Blackfoot: "For a Blackfoot Indian to discover a gold mine would make everyone in the tribe happy because everyone would share benefit from it. Whereas in modern society, finding a gold mine is the surest way of alienating many people who are close to us." (Maslow et al, 1998, p. 30). When Blackfoot people discovered not gold, but oil on their land, wealth from revenues was in fact shared, and the communities grew and prospered, and alcoholism and suicide diminished with prosperity!

Although widely used in education of human service professionals, the 'pyramid' of human needs does not include the setting in which children spend "15,000 hours" of their lives (Rutter, 1979; Sawyerr & Adam-Bagley, 2017), namely their secondary schools. Good education is crucial for healthy emotional and cognitive development and must build upon the earlier stages of development in Maslow's model (1987). That is why we've added Educational and Leisure Needs in the model which we offer in tabular form, in Table 5.1 below. We add two final stages to Maslow's initial model: self-transcendence (Maslow, 1971); and the more recently developed "collective-transcendence" from the work of Viktor Frankl (1988).

We begin at the first level, rather than inverting the model of needs as the pyramid does. This seems more logical. We also add to the model by inserting "educational fulfilment" as an important developmental stage. Education for every citizen should not merely enable the acquisition of knowledge: it should enable the learner to explore and enjoy their environment with an inquisitive mind, seeking knowledge and refreshment in nature, in sport, in exercise, and in exploration. Kaufman (2020) in his presentation and reframing of Maslow's ideas, comments:

> "Imagine if schools weren't only places to learn standardized academic material but were also places full of wonder, awe, and self-actualization – as well as hope for humanity." (Kaufman, 2020, p. 229)

At the peak of the popular pyramid is "self-actualization", making the most of one's talents in enjoying a successful life, stressors and checks at previous levels having been overcome. But in his final writing (Maslow, 1971) identified a final stage beyond self-actualization, which he termed "self-transcendence", in which the individual seeks to focus on a cause or goal which is beyond the mere maximization of talents. It involves a communion beyond the boundaries of the self, through "peak experiences" which lead to great satisfaction for selfhood in achieving the maximum of potential goals. This may, but certainly not always, involve religious or spiritual experiences and goals.

Our model retains, of course, all of the elements in the original model, including the very important goal of self-actualization:

> "Self-actualization does not mean a transcendence of all human problems. Conflict, anxiety, frustration, sadness, hurt, and guilt all can be found in healthy human beings; on the other hand, with increasing maturity, one's focus shifts from neurotic pseudo-problems to the real, unavoidable existential problems." (Maslow, 1987, p. 230).

Maslow emphasized that the ability to adapt to circumstances beyond one's control in constructive ways, remaining calm when faced by crisis, treating setbacks as opportunities for growth did depend *to a certain extent* on experiencing some success in having Safety and Esteem needs met: "The child with a good basis of safety, love, and respect-need-gratification is able to profit from . . . frustrations and become stronger thereby." (Maslow, 1987, p. 220). Maslow (1996) also accentuated that tragedy is often conducive to growth insofar as it "confronts [individuals] with the ultimate values, questions, and problems that [they] ordinarily forget about in everyday existence" (p. 56).

Maslow (1987) identified several interrelated qualities of self-actualizing people. They have:

> " ... clearer, more efficient perception of reality; more openness to experience; increased integration, wholeness, and unity of the person; increased spontaneity, expressiveness, full functioning, aliveness; a real self, firm identity, autonomy, uniqueness; increased objectivity, detachment, transcendence of self; recovery of creativeness; ability to fuse concreteness and abstractness; democratic character structure; ability to love ..." (Maslow, 1996 pp. 172-173)

1. Basic Physical Needs	Being born alive, and healthy; good infant nutrition; adequate warmth and shelter; close bond with a loving caretaker; toileting cared for; sound sleep.
2. Safety Needs	Security of body; safe employment, with stability & security, and adequate reward from work. Consistency of caregiving in family; developing freely chosen sexual intimacy & pregnancy; affordable, high quality health care; affordable & comfortable dwelling place.
3. Love and Belonging Needs	Love of partners in sexual fulfilment; good friendships and peer support; warm and fulfilling family life; engagement with supportive religious mentors and peers.
4. Educational and Leisure Needs	Affordable access to high quality basic and higher education; availability of aesthetic and leisure pursuits, in music, art and dance; access to sports as participant & spectator; access to natural world.
5. Esteem Needs	Good self-esteem from interaction with parents, & peers; self-concept supported by local culture and national values; achievement of confidence and respect in the wider, non-discriminating society; development of talents, fostered and esteemed by cultural values; being respected as a unique and free citizen.
6. Self-Actualization	Successful achievement of a life guided by chosen moral values; achieving creative excellence and spontaneity; acceptance of fulfilment of self-identity in social relationships; understanding of the meaning of one's personal life; pleasure in the achievements of family, children and others.
7. Self-Transcendence	Seeking to serve a cause 'beyond the self', with an experience of communication beyond the boundaries of the self, through 'peak experiences'
8. Collective-Transcendence	Self-transcendence takes place within a community of peers who share the same beliefs and goals, sometimes as part of a shared religious identity; or a shared value commitment to offer service, or achieve social change.

Table 5.1 *Adaptation, Expansion & Restatement of Maslow's 'Pyramid' of Universal Needs & Achievements*

In our adaptation of the Maslowian stages in Table 5.1, Stages 2 to 5 often influence (in memory at least) in parallel; they are *mutually reinforcing* factors in healthy psychosocial development, as we ponder on and retell to our life's story, to ourselves and to others. Maslow (1996) commented that " … the ability to be aggressive and angry is found in all self-actualizing people, who are able to let it flow forth freely when the external situation 'calls for' it" (p. 216). They are accepting of the full range of human impulses without rejecting them in the interest of reducing tension.

Viktor Frankl (1988) working independently of Maslow developed a rather similar idea of "self-transcendence" (responding to the God or the spirit within oneself). This idea has been taken forward by Wong (2017) who, melding the ideas of Frankl and Maslow, develops the idea of "cultural transcendence", which involves various motivations including spiritual response, but may also reflect ideological commitment to higher order value (Llanos and Verduzco, 2022). This idea of cultural transcendence is added as the final phase in the Maslowian model of the ideal pathway in human development and achievement.

Maslow and 'peak experiences'

In studying stories, histories and accounts of *peak experiences*, in a variety of individuals Maslow (1965 & 1971) identified a form of thinking, self-reflection, personal achievement and values which he termed "Being-cognition" (or "B-cognition"), which is holistic and accepting of self, which is contrasted with the evaluative dimension termed "Deficiency-cognition". The B-values, which often describe the "self-transcendent" person in Maslow's case studies are characterized by people who frequently manifest:

a) *Commitment to Truth*: reaching for the values of honesty, reality, simplicity; richness of thought and aesthetic interests, which recognise beauty; development of personal values which imply a moral purpose in one's life; and the search for a completed and fulfilled life.

b) *A Search for Goodness*: seeking 'oughtness' and moral obligations; seeking justice for oneself and others; being forthright and benevolent.

c) *A Search for Beauty*: finding richness in simplicity; finding wholeness, completion and perfection in the moral beauty of humans.

d) *Finding Wholeness*: integration of complexities in a unified form; interconnectedness; simplicity in organization and structure of organizations.

e) *Sense of 'Being Alive'*: spontaneity combined with self-knowledge and self-regulation.

f) *Being Unique*: idiosyncrasy; individuality in personhood and enterprise.

g) *Seeking Perfection*: completeness through achievement of just goals; getting things in the right order, to achieve a sense of completeness.

h) *Achieving Completion*: achieving a sense of ending tasks and endeavours; finding justice for others; accepting fulfilment through 'fate'.

i) *Achieving Justice*: seeking fairness; orderliness; lawfulness; "oughtness"

j) *Finding Simplicity*: finding honesty in the abstract being of people and their institutions.

k) *Finding Richness*: finding both complexity and intricacy in people and their institutions.

l) *Achieving Effortlessness*: developing a life which lacks strain, striving or difficulty; finding grace, perfection and beauty of functioning in self and others.

m) *Being Playful*: enjoying fun, joy, amusement, sport and exercise, gaiety and humour in enjoying life, and exuberant interaction with others.

n) *Being Self-sufficient*: achieving autonomy and independence through self-determination, enabling environment-transcendence in oneself; achieving 'personal separateness' and uniqueness, living by one's own values.

This fascinating account of 'ideal types' of personhood is at once simple and complex. Some of them overlap, sometimes they slightly contradict one another, but mostly they reinforce one another as the bedrock of humanistic personality psychology. Achieving these goals is part of both self-actualization and transcendence (personal and cultural).

Maslow, personality theory and 'the Big Five' (OCEAN) dimensions

Personality theory has by and large developed separately in mainstream psychology, with Maslowian humanistic psychology models, and 'hard science' behaviourist approaches being addressed in 'parallel' academic streams (Koltko-Rivera, 2006). But an important study has linked Maslow's model with the 'Big 5' personality profiles, the latter now being which widely used in research and counselling (Montag et al., 2020). The 5-factor personality dimensions (OCEAN) measure of: *Openness to Experience; Conscientiousness; Extraversion; Agreeableness;* and *Neuroticism*, and their polar opposites (since these profiles are fitted to a normal curve when measured, most people, about 50%, fall into the middle range of these five personality profiles).

Montag and his colleagues (2020) found that Neuroticism was *inversely* linked to successful achievement of life satisfaction (including self-actualization) on Lester's (2013) measure which operationalized the Maslowian 'stages' into a standardized questionnaire. All of the other Big 5 dimensions had statistically significant links to success at each stage of the Maslowian levels of development. But the data also showed that the successful achievement of Maslowian stages occurred *simultaneously* (at the point of data collection), and not sequentially. This is important, since it contradicts the assumption of some practitioners that successful achievement of one stage is crucial before the next stage can be achieved. Individuals in this model may frequently review their life's progress, and come to terms with the past (according to personality strengths), in making an onward journey of success ('self-actualization') in life.

This implies that the developmental schema of Erikson, Dabrowski and Loevinger (McRae et al., 1980; Erikson & Erikson, 1998; Hy & Loevinger, 1996; Loevinger, 1983; Mendaglio, 2008; Piechowski`, 2003 & 2008) should also guide our knowledge of how individuals overcome earlier life hazards, and incorporate them into a meaningful, ongoing identity. Webb (2008) explains that Dabrowski and Maslow were collaborative colleagues in developing models of identity achievement (Piechowski & Dabrowski, 2003). Simultaneously with achievement of basic needs, there is a struggle for all individuals in the form of "disintegration", a form of review leading to "reintegration" before the achievement of making the best of oneself finally emerges (Table 5.2). The actual numbers in any population who actually achieve this higher level of integration is a challenge for future social science research.

Kaufman (2020) integrates both Loevinger's and Erikson's ego-development models in his rewriting of Maslow's 'stages' model, and has developed a research instrument (Kaufman, 2018 & 2019b) identifying morally creative and soul-full individuals. This is a challenge for a much larger study to estimate levels of 'goodness' in human populations. Another excellent example of how individuals face challenges, including Eriksonian "identity crises" in achieving long-term happiness and transcendent old age, comes from the Harvard longitudinal studies (Malone et al., 2016; Waldinger & Shultz, 2015 & 2016).

LEVEL I: PRIMARY INTEGRATION • Individuals are governed by the "first factor" of developmental needs and are primarily influenced by heredity, basic impulses, and/or social, environmental forces. • This level is marked by selfishness and egocentrism; individuals often seek self-fulfilment through "ends justify the means" behaviour.
LEVEL II: UNILEVEL 'DIS'-INTEGRATION • This level is characterized by a lack of inner direction, submission to the values of the group, socially accepted values and beliefs, with the emergence of ambiguities about "popular" and "moral" courses of action. • This "Second factor" serves as the organizing principle of social factors, and individual conformity to social system groups.
LEVEL III: MULTILEVEL 'DIS'-INTEGRATION • Within this level, individuals begin to get a sense of the ideal, of moral concerns, and of the existence of conflicting values within themselves. • The individual's inner tension between "What is" and "What ought to be" is responsible for the process of an unfolding 'positive maladjustment' or 'creative psychoneurosis'.
LEVEL IV: DIRECTED MULTILEVEL 'DIS'-INTEGRATION • The individual begins to move towards self-actualization and holds a strong sense of responsibility concerning others' well-being, through personal inner growth. • This becomes the primary motivator of growth, spurring individuals to work towards agreement between their actions and their ideals.
LEVEL V: SECONDARY INTEGRATION (SELF-ACTUALIZATION) • The "personality ideal" is achieved, and individuals experience harmony and are at peace with themselves. Lower forms of motivation have been surpassed and are replaced by higher forms of awareness, insight, empathy, autonomy, and 'self-compassion'.

Table 5.2 *Summary of Dabrowskian Developmental Levels (based on & Dabrowsi & Piechowski, 1977; Piechowski, 2003 & 2008; & Smith, 2013)*

Maslow's (1971) developmental model does suggest that longitudinal studies of the type pioneered by Waldinger and his colleagues over a 40-year period, should be an ongoing research agenda:

> "The idea that ... if one need is satisfied, then another emerges . . . might give the false impression that a need must be satisfied 100% before the next need emerges. In actual fact, most individuals are partially satisfied in all their basic needs and partially unsatisfied in all their basic needs at the same time. A more realistic description of the hierarchy would be in terms of decreasing percentages of satisfaction as we go up the hierarchy of prepotency. . . . The emergence of a new need is not a sudden phenomenon, but rather a gradual emergence by slow degrees." (Maslow, 1971, pp. 27-28)

Anne Smith (2013) uses the Maslow-Dabrowski schema to great effect in enabling refugees in London to re-achieve 'lost identities' through drama and story-telling, recreating their lives in a new environment, in the direction of self-actualization. Dabrowski's model seems to merge with Erikson's (1993) eight stages of development, with a tension or struggle between ideals and achievements at each stage: in the final stage is the struggle between "wisdom" and "stagnation". Dabrowski's idea of individuals recreating themselves with fresh, onward identities as they review their development and face new tasks, is described as "a personality theory for the 21st century" by Piechowski (2008).

Big Five personality profiles: Occupational success, Maslow and Islamic ideals

The Big Five model reliably predicts some of the success in employment and work experienced by individuals across time, and *Openness to Experience* (which portrays individuals as being ingenious, inquisitive, and novelty seeking - McCrae & John, 1992) is the strongest of the OCEAN dimensions predicting an individual's success. This personality trait includes " ... being inventive, cultivated, questioning, unusual, forward-thinking, intellectual and imaginatively complex. Individuals with a high degree of openness appreciate new concepts and viewpoints, and create new ideas, both practical and spiritual ... Such successful individuals tend to be exceptionally accountable, trustworthy, tough-minded when necessary, and prompt in meeting deadlines." These individuals are also highly *Conscientious* people and are result-focused, enthusiastic and task-focused (Templer, 2012).

The Big 5 (OCEAN) personality profiles have validity and application across a wide range of world cultures (Saroglou, 2010). But in the Islamic world there have been challenges to the idea of abstracting personality traits from the whole person: rather, the individual is treated as a unique individual following a straight path on their particular journey to enlightenment. Thus Maslow's idea of self-actualization is seen as being appropriate for describing success in employment (Zakaria & Malek, 2014).

A comparison of Maslowian and OCEAN profiles in predicting personal success has been usefully addressed by Abdullah et al. (2019) in a study of personnel in four Islamic banks in Malaysia. By far the strongest personality profile predicting occupational success was *Openness to Experience*, which the authors link to the Maslowian profile of Self-Actualization. In another interesting Malaysian study Saeednia & Nor (2013) found that individuals were able to achieve self-actualization even though their 'lower' needs in the Maslowian 'hierarchy' had not been fully met. In other words, adults through an act of will, and with the help of others, are able to overcome early disadvantage. This is an optimistic conclusion, since it suggests that individuals may be constantly 'reinventing' themselves, through G.H. Mead's (1964) "I-Me" self-dialogue, healing their identities (as both Maslow and Dabrowski suggest), as part of the natural will of humans to survive, and make the best of themselves. In joining with others in this task, this identity-remaking is part of *morphogenesis* in Archer's critical realism.

How do the OCEAN profiles link to self-disciplined religious journeys? Saroglou (2010) answers this question by further analysis of previous data sets (from 71 samples in 19 different countries, including 21,715 individuals) in which questions about religiosity and religious observance were also asked. Results were consistent across gender and age groups, for every type of religion studied (Christianity, Islam, Hinduism, Buddhism, Daoism et al.): high scores on A (Agreeableness) and C (Conscientiousness) predicted *becoming* religious. Religious affiliation or socialization did not seem to cause these character traits. Rather, individuals took advantage of existing religious institutions to become more fully committed people, sharing with others the doing of good deeds. Others high on Agreeableness and Conscientiousness in these cohorts were committed ethical humanists without any particular religious affiliation. However, profile O (Openness to Experience) had a small but significant negative association with being part of a fundamentalist religion.

These interesting results bring into focus the question of intrinsic and extrinsic commitment to religious values, a concept identified by Gordon Allport (Allport & Ross, 1967; Gorsuch, 2019). *Extrinsic* attachment to religion involves affiliating with a religion for reasons of social prestige, self-aggrandisement, or escaping strictures of social control. Most 'national' religions permit affiliation of this type. In England the state church, the Church of England is used by many as a matter of convenience for baptisms, weddings and funerals by individuals who rarely if ever, attend the parish church for devotional reasons. In contrast, the minority of the population who have an *intrinsic* commitment to religious worship and values may lead more spiritually disciplined and ethically committed lives. Allport & Ross (1967) argued that individuals who scored highly on measures of prejudice would be more likely to treat religion as a matter of convenience, part of the armamentarium of social capital. We confirmed this view in studies of Dutch attitudes to minorities (Adam-Bagley, 1973).

It is problematic to cast most Muslims as having only an extrinsic attachment to their religion, praying and fasting and conforming to norms of dress and diet, because of social controls and social pressure within their family and their local social structures. Our working hypothesis, supported by research from Malaysia (Tekke et al., 2015 & 2017) is that Islam involves *both* extrinsic and intrinsic religious commitments simultaneously. Praying five times daily, usually with others, is an extrinsic duty, but one's personal prayer to Allah during these prayers is an intrinsic commitment. And the experience of group worship each day aids the exercise of personal, moral self-discipline and purpose in 'doing good deeds'.

Developmental pathways: Overcoming early disadvantage in achieving self-actualization and beyond

The quotations in this Chapter from Maslow show that he was keenly aware of how emerging successfully from each level of development (in the 'pillar' in Table 5.1 above) often involves struggle and setback: we need the help, counsel, advice and support of others in making these steps as we develop, grow and age (Dabrowski & Piechowski, 1977). The first five levels are crucially important, and need policy and practice guided by child-centred humanism, outlined earlier. The work of Bowlby (1982) and Rutter (1998) and others is important in showing the kinds of parenting, family environment and social structure which enables healthy psychological and neurological development, with the crucial bonding to a caring figure in the development of good levels of self-esteem and adjustment. These developmental psychology pathways fit neatly with the Maslowian stages, discussed below. British research continues to show that disrupted, cruel or abusive experiences in childhood often have an adult sequel in violent or other maladaptive behaviour (Bellis et al., 2013).

There are other complementary and interlocking schemas of healthy and challenging development which stem from the work of Erik Erikson, Jane Loevinger, and Kazimerz Dabrowski, discussed earlier. These address issues of experiencing trauma and challenge, and recovering from these challenges. Freud had observed that the infant and young child must suppress the memory of the pseudo-erotic contact (breast feeding, washing etc) which early care involves, so that by the time that 'latency' begins at age four or five, the child develops an ego, and then a super-ego which suppresses all memory of these practices of early care.

Indeed, the close physical interaction of older children with their siblings and parents is not overtly erotic, and there develops a natural aversion to within-family erotic contact (this is true for all mammals, whose pheromone-based aversion to mating with close kin is functional for species survival). Sometimes as the case material we have presented (Adam-Bagley, 1969) shows, the boundaries of incest are crossed by a predatory or psychotic older person, often with devastating results for the mental health of the young victim (Adam-Bagley & King, 2003; Sawyerr & Adam-Bagley, 2023). In the context of humanist psychology the family therapy model developed by Hank Giarretto (1981 & 1982) seeks to restore the nuclear family to a 'normal balance', in which the incest is 'forgiven and forgotten' if all family members agree to this. We found that this therapeutic approach did generally work in a study of Canadian families (Adam-Bagley & LeChance, 2000).

Erik Erikson (1993) like Maslow, observed that healthy development involves not only the meeting of the child's basic needs, but also involves their ability to withstand some level of deprivation that enables individuals to "withstand food deprivation" because they "have been made secure and strong in the earliest years," which enables their psychological strength and emotional security afterwards (Maslow, 1987, p. 27). On physiological needs, Erikson (1993) suggested that a key developmental task for infants is to establish confidence in caregivers. Thus, secure interactions between parent and child mediate the relationship between low socioeconomic status and healthy development (Bronfenbrenner & Ceci, 1994). As Kaufmann (2020) observes, "We can work on multiple needs simultaneously." (p. xxix)

Scott Barry Kaufman's transcend: *The New Science of Self-Actualization* (2020)

In the master's footsteps ...

Kaufman dedicates this remarkable book " ...to Abraham Maslow, a dear friend I've never met." The book received multiple positive reviews from scholars, counsellors and activists such as "What a masterpiece! Maslow 2.0" (Angela Duckworth); and "This splendid book is a twofer. It's a retelling of the life of Abraham Maslow woven through an insightful updating of Maslow's theory" (Martin Seligman). We can't summarise the contents of this 390-page book here, but certainly recommend scholars, social scientists and theologians to read it. We begin a brief overview by referring to Kaufman's earlier journal articles which are woven into the text of his book.

Kaufman (2018a) begins his introduction to the search for human goodness ("the Light Triad") with this quotation from the diary of Anne Frank, the Dutch Jewish girl who was hidden in Amsterdam, trying to escape transportation to a death camp: "I still believe, in spite of everything, that people are truly good at heart." (Anne

Frank,1995 p. 332). Kaufman bonds intellectually with the victims and survivors of the Holocaust (Frankl, Wiesel, Heimler and others) who transcend these experiences with enlightened world views, and psychological and social therapies based on the transcendent intuition that the spirit and practice of goodness, appealing to the best in every individual, must be the only way forward that civilization can proceed.

Kaufman follows directly Maslow's footsteps in offering us a lyrical mixture of social science analysis and ethical advocacy, in studying "self-actualizing people in the 21st century, together with an integration with contemporary theory and research on personality and well-being." (Kaufman, 2018).

This enterprise begins with Kaufman et al's (2018a & b, & 2019) development of measures of a concept called the *Light Triad*, the search for a measure of human motivation that identified

> " ... a loving and beneficent orientation toward others ("everyday saints") that consists of three facets: Kantianism (treating people as ends unto themselves), Humanism (valuing the dignity and worth of each individual), and Faith in Humanity (believing in the fundamental goodness of human beings)." (Kaufman, 2018, p. 4)

Individuals with high scores on this measure

> " ... reported more satisfaction with their relationships, competence, and autonomy, and they also reported higher levels of secure attachment style ... in their relationships ... the light triad was related to being primarily motivated by intimacy and self-transcendent values. Many character strengths correlated with the Light Triad, including curiosity, perspective, zest, love, kindness, teamwork, forgiveness, and gratitude ... Individuals scoring higher on the LTS also reported higher self-esteem, authenticity, and a stronger sense of self ... unlike the Dark Triad, the Light Triad was uncorrelated with bravery or assertiveness." (Kaufmann, 2020, p. 121-122)

Kaufman's (2020) book is shot through with the energetic epistemology of optimism, drawing on and reframing Maslow on synergy, self-actualization, and peak experiences – such experiences may just happen to us; but also, through Kaufman's advocacy we can discipline ourselves to achieve them, share them with others, and work for a spiritually-enhanced betterment of our entire civilization:

> "It's time for us to take responsibility for the society we live in, and to help create the conditions that will help all people not only self-actualize, but also transcend. We can simultaneously work on making the good society and making **ourselves** better. Improving the good society starts from **within**, as we shift our own perspective on human nature. In so doing we can even transcend our own physical experience, impacting future generations long after we've gone." (Kaufman, 2020, p. 333)

While Kaufman expands on William James' ideas of peak experiences, he is not an advocate of any particular religious approach. His model will appeal to both secular and religious humanists. But for Kaufman as for Maslow, "heaven", the immanence of spiritual goodness, keeps breaking through into our lives, in ways which overcome basic evil in our natures:

> "Heaven, so to speak, lies waiting for us through life, ready to step into for a time and to enjoy before we have to come to our ordinary life of striving. And once we have been in it, we can remember it forever, and feed ourselves on this memory to be sustained in time of stress." (Maslow, 1962 in Toward a Psychology of Being, p. 120) [11]

---

[11] This idea of immanence reminds me of the experience of being an Anglo-Catholic for several years: when the bell is rung at the point of elevation of The Host, I know that God is immanent, and I am bathed in the glory of this light. I still believe this, Quaker-Muslim that I am, and still slip into a Catholic Mass for this never-lost feeling of excitement that I am being absorbed into the Body of God. Sectarian boundaries cannot separate me

Kaufman's latest offering is a self-help book titled *Choose Growth: A Workbook for Transcending Trauma, Fear, and Self-Doubt* (2022). Long may you flourish, Dr. Kaufman.

Interpreting Maslow's ideas for human service and management professionals

It is noteworthy that American capitalism, for all its brusque and aggressive search for profit, has in some significant ways humanised itself through accepting many of Maslow's ideas, and Maslow responded by writing several articles specifically intended as guides for how businesses should conduct themselves, and service both customers and employees in ethical ways. James Atfield has gathered together these writings (Maslow et al, 1998), and they have served to guide both public service, health management, and business organisations.

Succinctly, Maslow and his colleagues wrote:

> "This business of self-actualization via a commitment to an important job and worthwhile work ... could be the path to human happiness ... the happy people I know are the ones who are working well at something they consider important ... enlightened economics must assume good will among all of the members of an organisation, rather than rivalry or jealousy ... We need a culture in which what is beneficial for the individual is beneficial for everyone ... Assume that there is a 'natural' trend towards self-actualization, the freedom to effectively realise one's own ideas, being and nature ... Assume that everyone can enjoy good teamwork, friendship, good group spirit, good belongingness, organizational loyalty, and group love ... People can always do better: trust them ... Enable workers to do their best, to maximise

---

from this experience. God is everywhere, available to all people, and watches kindly on the deeds of the non-religious!

their talents, to self-actualize ... Assume that growth occurs through delight, and through avoiding boredom ... Work should involve a zest for life ... Managers, identify every worker and their needs and aspirations, talents and goals ... Charisma of leadership is crucial." (Maslow et al., 1998, pp 6 to 87).

We can't summarize the whole of this remarkable book here, but Maslow's philosophy of management in which he elucidates principles of fairness, justice and creativity for employees, clients and customers from the perspective of his humanist social psychology, seems to us to be a treatise that fits well with the premises of democratic socialism. But Maslow (unlike his contemporary George Mead) was careful to avoid any kinds of political advocacy or affiliation (although he had written that "Marx ... was the first thinker who saw that the widespread realization of the universal can only occur together with social changes which lead to a new and truly human economic and social organisation of mankind." – Maslow (1996c), p. 81.)

There are numerous expositions and evaluations of applying Maslow in the world of business, and we won't review them here. But we must mention Chip Conley's (2017) book: *Peak: How Great Companies Get Their Mojo from Maslow*, which gives numerous examples of how Maslowian principles are applied in practice. Two themes *energy* and *optimism* characterise these enterprises, themes which have lessons for politicians, entrepreneurs, leaders of all kinds, and all of us in the human service professions.

Applying Maslowian principles in human service and health care

Maslow's ideas which have influenced how "public servants" (politicians, civil servants, teachers, health care workers, and administrators) maximise benefit for the people they serve, have been carried forward by Simon Stretton (1994). Stretton first advocates the application of Maslowian principles (including fulfilling all of the needs in the well-known hierarchy) for employees' security and welfare, as a basis for applying the principles of ensuring that the psychosocial needs of clients, pupils and patients shall, in Maslowian terms be met, with movement towards self-actualization. These themes are taken forward and applied in the research and programme development described by Benson & Dundis (2003), and Castro-Molina (2018).

Inspired by Maslow, the authors of the present monograph (Adam-Bagley, Sawyerr and Abubaker) have undertaken longitudinal research on the career achievements and stresses of a group of English nurses, examining how they have managed to cope with the challenges of covid pandemic nursing (Adam-Bagley et al., 2018 to 2021). The studies (based on interviewing each nurse several times over three years) was undertaken within a critical realist model, in which we framed the reality of nursing within the emotional life of nurses, and the stories they told about their identity and coping strategy as nurses, identifying "absences" in order to create a coherent story of the challenges of nursing.

We can best summarise progress in this research through citing the summary of the most recent publication on this research:

> "...these findings are from a 2020 follow-up study of 159 senior hospital nurses involved in the front-line care of COVID patients in urban centres in Northern England, prior to the "second wave" of COVID patients in November 2020. A typology of nurses from measures interviewed in 2018 identified four types: a. 'Soldiers'; b. 'Professionals'; c. 'Highly Stressed'; d. 'High Achievers'. In 2020 further measures of adjustment stress (including PTSD), and self-actualization were added to earlier measures of personality, adjustment, work-life stress, and career intention ... analyses identified three main types in the 2020 follow-up cohort: 'Actualizing

Professionals'; (N=59); 'Strong Professionals' (N=55); 'Highly Stressed Nurses' (N=30). Highly stressed nurses identified in 2018 had mostly left nursing, so the 30 highly-stressed nurses in 2020 were mainly a newly-identified group, who included all nurses identified as having PTSD symptoms. The research model driving this research is that of Critical Realism which identifies the process of morphogenesis which creates a constructive dialogue for social change on behalf of nurses, who faced almost overwhelming stress in caring for COVID patients. We have identified two types of dedicated nurses with a hardy personality style which has helped them face severe stress in emerging as psychologically strong, self-actualizing individuals, dedicated to the higher values of nursing." (Adam-Bagley et al., 2021, p.125)

Nursing (the first profession of both CAB and AS) is a value-based vocation, in which humanistic values enable professionals to give dedicated service under difficult and often highly stressful conditions. We are pleased to have identified a group of successful nurses who have achieved self-actualization, and based on their personal or religious values, are also often achieving self-transcendence within the shared energy and ethic of nursing.

Conclusions

We leave evil behind (to chew its own tail), and turn to the spiritual power of humanism, religious and secular, impressed and inspired by scholars writing about a "post-holocaust" world in which both spiritual excellence and social harmony seem attainable. If we treat our children well, there is hope for all of humankind. Through stories, humanist case studies of adversity, struggle, triumph and transcendence, we share values and critical rationality, a form of morphogenesis, the remaking of ourselves. Evil still lurks, in the telling of false and malicious stories that beget hatred and violence. It is therefore essential that *our* stories must focus on "the moral beauty of others" (Keltner, 2010). The stories of holocaust victims and survivors are the most moving. The experience of extreme poverty, slavery and genocide does not defeat us, nor eliminate our goodness of spirit.

"Religious experience" enervates humankind, giving us awe and transcendence. Being religious brings many unexpected benefits in physical and emotional health. Evidence shows that the sharing of religious bonds and rituals helps rather than hinders the survival of humankind, in constructive ways. An *intrinsic* commitment to religion is important, as well as the sharing of our "religious stories" with one another. The stories from Judaism and Islam often overlap, and we can accept the cloak of another religious identity as pathways to peace-making, as in the case of Israel-Palestine.

We honour the great scholar Abraham Maslow, ostensibly a secular Jew, but whose psychology nevertheless has much spiritual healing power for those of all religions, and for secular humanists. This humanism, of treasuring the worth in each other regardless of ethnic or religious origin, is the only way forward for the social contract of a civilized world.

Maslow's model of development has much overlap with and support from the developmental models offered by Dabrowski, Loevinger and Erikson. All of these models show us pathways along which all of humanity can transcend evil in "the making the best of ourselves". This synergy is part of the universal social contract, in which the two of us relating creates a third force, a metaphysical goodness in which goodwill begets goodwill, with a growing synergy. Martin Seligman's positive psychology movement is an excellent example of how humanist psychology increasingly informs mainstream psychological research and practice.

We experience with delight Scott Barry Kaufman's taking forward Maslow's models of fulfilment through self-other relationship. Maslow tossed his ideas forward in 1968 like a 'Hail Mary' throw.

Kaufman caught the ideas, and has enlarged them in forging towards the touch-down.

Abraham Maslow began his humanist journey with the Blackfoot people, and the synergy and transcendence of this people inspired him in a career as a psychologist. Blackfoot eschatology has also provided creative energy for the quantum physicist David Fell (2002); and for others including myself, working for the support and restoration of Blackfoot families.

Evil lurks everywhere, but so does goodness which shines through and transcends in all human institutions and religions, including secular humanism. What matters on the final day is that God believes in you, not that you believe in God. But loving and worshipping the divine is an excellent way to go forward:

In My Soul

There is a temple, a shrine, a mosque, a church where I kneel.

Prayer should bring us to an altar where no walls or names exist.

Is there not a region of love where the sovereignty is illumined by nothing,

But where ecstasy gets poured into itself and becomes lost,

Where the wing is fully alive but has no mind or body?

In My Soul

There is a temple, a shrine, a mosque, a church that dissolve,

That dissolve,

That dissolve in God.

(Poem by Sufi Rabia Basri, obit 801 CE, in the collection of Jamal, 2015; translation by Daniel Ladinsky.)

General References and Bibliography

Abdullah, H., N. M. Arifin and A. M. Mohammed Salleh. Can the new fusion of Maslow and Maqasid Al Sharia explain the linkage of Big Five personality traits on job satisfaction? *International Journal of Innovation and Creative Change* 7 (2019): 17-32.

Abubaker, Mahmoud and Chris Adam-Bagley. Work-life balance policies in Jordanian telecommunication companies. *Eurasian Journal of Business and Management* 4 (2016a): 13-18.

Abubaker, Mahmoud and Chris Adam-Bagley (2016b). Work-Life Balance and the needs of female employees in the telecommunications industry in a developing country: A critical realist approach to issues in industrial and organisational social psychology. *Comprehensive Psychology* 5 (2016b): 1-12.

Abubaker, Mahmoud and Chris Adam-Bagley. Methodology of correspondence testing for employment discrimination involving ethnic minority applications: Dutch and English case studies of Muslim applicants for employment. *Social Sciences* 6 (2017)): 112-121.

Abubaker, Mahmoud and Chris Adam-Bagley. Islamic ethics, sociology and social justice – A Critical Realist perspective and a feminist viewpoint. In *Muslim Women Seeking Power, Muslim Youth Seeking Justice: Studies from Europe, Middle East and Asia* (pp 1-35). Cambridge Scholars Publishing, 2019.

Abubaker, Mahmoud, Mousa Luobbad, Ismael Qasem and Chris Adam-Bagley. Work–Life Balance policies for women and men in an Islamic culture: A culture-centred and religious research perspective. *Businesses* 2 (2022): 319-338.

Abubaker, Wesam. Muslim women and children of Gaza: Teacher support for children under stress – evidence from elementary school case studies. In *Muslim Youth Seeking Power, Muslim Youth Seeking Justice* (74-119). Cambridge Scholars Press, 2019.

Abuelaish, Izzeldin. *I Shall Not Hate: A Gaza Doctor's Journey on the Road to Peace and Human Dignity*. Bloomsbury, 2011.

Acevedo, Alma. A personalistic appraisal of Maslow's needs theory of motivation: From "humanistic" psychology to integral humanism. *Journal of Business Ethics* 148 (2018): 741-763.

Adam-Bagley, Chris. Incest behavior and incest taboo. Social Problems 16 (1969): 505-519. Reprinted in B. Armour (Ed.) *Treatment of Family Sexual Abuse*. University of Minnesota Press. 1975.

Adam-Bagley, Chris. *The Dutch Plural Society: A Comparative Study of Race Relations*. Oxford University Press, 1973a.

Adam-Bagley, Chris. The welfare of the child: an examination of judicial opinion about medical and social work evidence in adoption cases. *British Journal of Social Work* 3 (1973b): 79-90. (Reprinted in S. Curtis (Ed.) *Child Adoption*. London: Association of British Adoption and Fostering Agencies, 1977.)

Adam-Bagley, Chris. Adolescent prostitution in Canada and the Philippines: Statistical comparisons, and an ethnographic account and policy options. *International Social Work* 42 (1989): 445-454.

Adam-Bagley, Chris. Adoption of Native children in Canada: A policy analysis and a research report. In Howard Alstein & Rita Simon (Eds) *Inter-Country Adoption: A Multinational Perspective* (55-72). New York: Praeger, 1991a.

Adam-Bagley, Chris. Poverty and suicide among Native Canadians: A replication. *Psychological Reports* 69 (1991b): 149-150.

Adam-Bagley, Chris. The urban environment and child pedestrian and bicycle injuries: interaction of ecological and personality characteristics. *Journal of Community and Applied Social Psychology* 2 (1992): 1-9.

Adam-Bagley, Chris. The urban setting of juvenile pedestrian injuries: a study of behavioral ecology and social disadvantage. *Accident Analysis and Prevention* 24 (1993): 673-678.

Adam-Bagley, Chris. *Children, Sex and Social Policy: Humanistic Solutions for Problems of Child Sexual Abuse*. Routledge Ashgate, 1997.

Adam-Bagley, Chris. An end to apartheid? The oppression and educational inclusion of India's Dalits. In *Challenges for Inclusion: Educational and Social Studies from Britain and the Indian Sub-Continent* (pp 165-182). Brill, 2008.

Adam-Bagley, Chris. Women graduates as human relations counsellors and researchers in Gaza, Palestine: 'Beyond Brokenness' – a planned research framework. *Open Journal of Political Science* 5 (2017: 16-22.

Adam-Bagley, Chris. Pakistan: The hard struggle for the Islamic equality of women and girls. In *Muslim Women Seeking Power, Muslim Youth Seeking Justice: Studies from Europe, Middle East and Asia* (pp 263-295). Cambridge Scholars Publishing, 2019a.

Adam-Bagley, Chris. Gender equality and peace-making. *Muslim Women Seeking Power, Muslim Youth Seeking Justice: Studies from Europe, Middle East and Asia* (pp 296-317). Cambridge Scholars Publishing, 2019b.

Adam-Bagley, Chris. Neurodiversity as status group, and as a class-within-a-class: Critical Realism and dyslexia. *Open Journal of Social Sciences* 10 (2022): 117-129.

Adam-Bagley, Chris, Gajendra K. Verma, Kanka Mallick, and Loretta Young. *Personality, Self-Esteem, and Prejudice*. Routledge Ashgate, 1979.

Adam-Bagley, Chris and Loretta Young. Long-term evaluation of group counselling for women with a history of child sexual abuse: focus on depression, self-esteem, suicidal behaviors and social support. *Social Work with Groups* 21 (1988): 63-73.

Adam-Bagley, Chris, Loretta Young and Anne Scully. *Intercountry Adoption: A Multinational Perspective*. Routledge Ashgate, 1991.

Adam-Bagley, Chris, Loretta Young, and Anne Scully. International and transracial adoptions. *Journal of Sociology and Social Welfare* 21 (1994): 180-190.

Adam-Bagley, Chris., Floyd Bolitho and Lorne Bertrand. Norms and construct validity of the Rosenberg Self-Esteem Scale in Canadian high school populations: Implications for counselling. *Canadian Journal of Counselling and Psychotherapy/Revue Canadienne de counseling et de psychothérapie* 31 (1997): 82-92.

Adam-Bagley, Chris and Colin Pritchard. The reduction of problem behaviours and school exclusion in at-risk youth: An experimental study of school social work with cost–benefit analyses. *Child & Family Social Work* 3 (1998): 219-226.

Adam-Bagley, Chris and Marguerite LaChance. Evaluation of a family-based programme for the treatment of child sexual abuse. *Child & Family Social Work* 5 (2000): 205-213.

Adam-Bagley, Chris, and Kanka Mallick. Spiralling up and spiralling down: Implications of a long-term study of temperament and conduct disorder for social work with children. *Child & Family Social Work* 5 (2000): 291-301.

Adam-Bagley, Chris and Colin Pritchard. The billion-dollar costs of troubled youth: Prospects for cost-effective prevention and treatment. *International Journal of Adolescence and Youth* 7 (2000): 211-225.

Adam-Bagley Chris and Kanka Mallick K. Normative data and mental health construct validity for the Rosenberg Self-Esteem Scale in British adolescents. *International Journal of Adolescence and Youth* 9 (2001): 117-126.

Adam-Bagley, Chris and Kathleen King. *Child Sexual Abuse: The Search for Healing*. Routledge-Taylor and Francis, 2003.

Adam-Bagley, Chris, Michael Wood, and Helda Khumar. Suicide and careless death in young males: Ecological study of an aboriginal population in Canada. *Canadian Journal of Community Mental Health* 9 (2009): 127-142.

Adam-Bagley, Chris., Susan Madrid, Padam Simkhada, Kathleen King and Loretta Young. Adolescent girls offered alternatives to commercial sexual exploitation: A case study from the Philippines. Dignity: A *Journal of Analysis of Exploitation and Violence* 2 (2017): 8-18.

Adam-Bagley, Chris, Sadia Kadri, Afroze Shahnaz, Padam Simkhada and Kathleen King. High rates of suicide and violence in the lives of girls and young women in Bangladesh: Issues for feminist intervention. *Social Sciences* 6 (2017): 140-115.

Adam-Bagley, Chris, Sadia Kadri, Afroze Shahnaz, Padam Simkhada and Kathleen King. Commercialised sexual exploitation of children, adolescents and women: Health and social structure in Bangladesh. *Advances in Applied Sociology* 7 (2017): 137-149.

Adam-Bagley, Chris and Nader Al-Refai. Multicultural integration in British and Dutch societies: education and citizenship. *Journal for Multicultural Education* 11 (2017): 82-100.

Adam-Bagley, Chris and Mahmoud Abubaker, M. (2017). Muslim woman seeking work: An English case study with a Dutch comparison, of discrimination and achievement. *Social Sciences* 6 (2017): 17-30.

Adam-Bagley, Chris., Sadia Kadri, Afroze Shahnaz and Wesam Abubaker. Chapters 8 to 11 on exploitation of girls and women in Bangladesh and Pakistan. In *Muslim Women Seeking Power, Muslim Youth Seeking Justice: Studies from Europe, Middle East and Asia* (212-296). Cambridge Scholars Publishing, 2019.

Adam-Bagley Chris and Mahmoud Abubaker, M. Muslim women (and men) and youth seeking justice: English and Dutch Case studies of prejudice, racism, discrimination and achievement. In *Muslim Women Seeking Power, Muslim Youth Seeking Justice: Studies from Europe, Middle East and Asia* (162-181). Cambridge Scholars Publishing, 2019.

Adam-Bagley, Chris and Nader Al-Refai, N. Muslim youth in Britain: Becoming good citizens in the age of Islamophobia. In Adam-Bagley, C. & Abubaker, M (Eds.). *Muslim Women Seeking Power, Muslim Youth Seeking Justice: Studies from Europe, Middle East and Asia* (120-161). Cambridge Scholars Publishing, 2019.

Adam-Bagley Chris and Mahmoud Abubaker, M. Muslim women (and men) and youth seeking justice: English and Dutch Case studies of prejudice, racism, discrimination and achievement. In *Muslim Women Seeking Power, Muslim Youth Seeking Justice: Studies from Europe, Middle East and Asia* (162-181). Cambridge Scholars Publishing, 2019.

Adam-Bagley, Chris and Mahmoud Abubaker. Discrimination in action: Three case studies of Muslim women seeking work in England and the Netherlands. In *Muslim Women Seeking Power, Muslim Youth Seeking Justice: Studies from Europe, Middle East and Asia* (182-211). Cambridge Scholars Publishing, 2019.

Adam-Bagley, Chris, Mahmoud Abubaker and Alice Sawyerr. Personality, work-life balance, hardiness, and vocation: a typology of nurses and nursing values in a special sample of English hospital nurses. *Administrative Sciences* 8 (2019): 79-85.

Adam-Bagley, Chris, Sadia Kadri and Afroze Shahnaz. Exploitation of girls and women through enforced prostitution in the culture of Bangladesh: Denial of Islamic moral principles. In *Muslim Women Seeking Power, Muslim Youth Seeking Justice: Studies from Europe, Middle East and Asia* (212-228). Cambridge Scholars Publishing, 2019.

Adam-Bagley, Chris and Wesam Abubaker. Child marriage as traumatic rape: A cause of PTSD in women in Bangladesh and Pakistan? In *Muslim Women Seeking Power, Muslim Youth Seeking Justice: Studies from Europe, Middle East and Asia* (255-262). Cambridge Scholars Publishing, 2019.

Adam-Bagley, Chris, Alice Sawyerr and Mahmoud Abubaker, M. Psychological profiles of successful career nurses: Implications for managerial psychology in an era of Covid challenge. *European Journal of Business and Management Research* 6 (2021): 168-175.

Adam-Bagley, Chris, Alice Sawyerr, Mahmoud Abubaker, and Afroze Shahnaz. Resilient nurses coping with covid care: A longitudinal study of psychology, values, resilience, stress and burnout. *Journal of Human Resource & Leadership* 5 (2021): 125-145.

Allport, Gordon. *The Nature of Prejudice*. New York: Doubleday; and Addison-Wesley, 1954 & 1979.

Allport, Gordon. *The Person in Psychology*. Beacon Press, 1968.

Archer, Margaret S. *Realist Social Theory: The Morphogenetic Approach*. Cambridge: Cambridge University Press, 1995.

Archer, Margaret S. *Being Human: The Problematic Agency*. Cambridge: Cambridge University Press, 2000.

Archer, Margaret S. *Structure, Agency and the Internal Conversation*. Cambridge University Press, 2003.

Archer, Margaret S. *Making Our Way through the World: Human Reflexivity and Social Mobility*. Routledge, 2007.

Archer, Margaret S. *Conversations about Reflexivity*. Routledge, 2010.

Archer, Margaret. S. Morphogenesis: Realism's explanatory framework. Margaret S. Archer (Ed.). *Sociological Realism* (66-101). Routledge, 2011.

Archer, Margaret S. *The Reflexive Imperative in Late Modernity*. Cambridge University Press, 2012.

Archer, Margaret S. *Social Origins of Educational Systems*. Routledge, 2013.

Archer, Margaret S. *Late Modernity: Trajectories Towards Morphogenetic Society*. Springer, 2014.

Archer, Margaret S. *Morphogenesis and Human Flourishing*. Springer, 2017.

Archer, Margaret. S. The story of a small charity for resettlement of trafficked people. In *Pope Francis*, Edited by Barbara E Wall and Massimo Faggioli, (199–217). Orbis Books, 2019.

Archer, Margaret S. and Jamie Morgan. Contributions to realist social theory: An interview with Margaret S. Archer. *Journal of Critical Realism* 19 (2020): 179-200.

Archer, Margaret S., Andrew Collier and Douglas V. Porpora. *Transcendence: Critical Realism and God*. Psychology Press, 2004.

Afridi, Mehnaz. *Shoah through Muslim Eyes*. Academic Studies Press, 2017.

Afridi, Mehnaz M. and Stephen D. Smith. Muslim and Christian perspectives on the Holocaust and genocide. In *The Routledge Handbook of Religion, Mass Atrocity, and Genocide* (430-442). Routledge, 2021.

Ahmed, Sara. *The Cultural Politics of Emotion*. Edinburgh University Press, 2014.

Akram, Sadiya and Anthony Hogan. On reflexivity and the conduct of the self in everyday life: reflections on Bourdieu and Archer. *The British Journal of Sociology* 66 (2015): 605-625.

Allen, Douglas. Mahatma Gandhi on violence and peace education. *Philosophy East and West* July (2007): 290-310.

Akyol, Mustafa. *The Islamic Jesus: How the King of the Jews Became a Prophet of the Muslims*. St. Martins Griffin, 2017.

Alderson, Priscilla. *Childhoods Real and Imagined: An Introduction to Critical Realism and Childhood Studies*. Routledge, 2013.

Alderson, Priscilla. *The Politics of Childhoods Real and Imagined: Practical Application of Critical Realism and Childhood Studies*. Routledge, 2016.

Alderson, Priscilla. *Critical Realism for Health and Illness Research: A Practical Introduction*. Policy Press, 2021.

Allport, Gordon W. *Becoming: Basic Considerations for a Psychology of Personality*. Yale University Press, 1955.

Allport, Gordon W. *The Person in Psychology: Selected Essays*. Beacon Press, 1968.

Allport, Gordon W. *Waiting for the Lord: 33 meditations on God and man*. MacMillan Publishing, 1978.

Allport, Gordon W. and J. Michael Ross. Personal religious orientation and prejudice. *Journal of Personality and Social Psychology* 5 (1967): 432-442.

Aruri, Naseer Hasan and Muhammad A. Shuraydi, Eds. *Revising Culture, Reinventing Peace: The Influence of Edward W. Said*. Olive Branch Press, 2001.

Austin, Ian. *Canada settles $2 billion suit over 'cultural genocide' at residential schools*. New York Times, January 21st, 2023.

Banfield, Grant. *Critical Realism for Marxist Sociology of Education*. Routledge, 2016.

Baron-Cohen, Simon. *Zero Degrees of Empathy*. Penguin, 2011.

Bai, Yang, Laura A. Maruskin, Serena Chen, Amie M. Gordon, Jennifer E. Stellar, Galen D. McNeil, Kaiping Peng and Dacher Keltner. Awe, the diminished self, and collective engagement: Universals and cultural variations in the small self. *Journal of Personality and Social Psychology* 113 (2017): 185-195.

Baron-Cohen, Simon. *Zero Degrees of Empathy. On Empathy and the Origins of Cruelty*. Penguin Books, 2011.

Basso, Frederick and Darro Krpan. The WISER framework of behavioural change interventions for mindful human flourishing. *Lancet Planetary Health* 7 (2023): e106-e108.

Bellis, Mark A., Karen Hughes, K., Alyson Jones, Clare Perkins and Philip McHale. Childhood happiness and violence: a study of their impacts on adult well-being. *BMJ Open* 2013-063427.

Benedict, Ruth. *Ruth Benedict Fulton Papers*. [Personal correspondence between Benedict, Mead, and Maslow]. Special Collections. Vassar College Libraries, Poughkeepsie, New York, 1940.

Benson, Suzanne G, and Stephen P. Dundis. Understanding and motivating health care employees: integrating Maslow's hierarchy of needs, training and technology. *Journal of Nursing Management* 11 (2003): 315-320.

Berman, Sophie. Human free will in Anselm and Descartes. *The Saint Anselm Journal* 2 (2004), 1-10.

Bernstein, Richard J. *Radical Evil: A Philosophical Interrogation*. Polity Press, 2002.

Beauregard, Mario and Denyse O'Leary. *The Spiritual Brain: A Neuroscientist's Case for the Existence of the Soul*. Harper Collins, 2007.

Beveridge, William. *Social Insurance and Allied Services, 1942*. Her Majesty's Stationery Office, 1968 (original issued in 1942).

Bhaskar, Roy. *Scientific Realism and Human Emancipation*. Verso, 1986.

Bhaskar, Roy. Dialectic: *The Pulse of Freedom*. Routledge. 2008.

Bhaskar, Roy. *The Philosophy of Metareality: Creativity, Love and Freedom*. Routledge, 2012a.

Bhaskar, Roy. *From Science to Emancipation: Alienation and Enlightenment*. Routledge, 2012b.

Bhaskar, Roy. *From East to West: The Odyssey of a Soul*. Routledge, 2015.

Bhaskar, Roy. *Enlightened Common Sense: The Philosophy of Critical Realism*. Routledge, 2016.

Bhaskar, Roy and Berth Danermark. Metatheory, interdisciplinarity and disability research: a critical realist perspective. *Scandinavian Journal of Disability Research* 8 (2006): 278-297.

Bland, Andrew M. The personal hero technique: A therapeutic strategy that promotes self-transformation and interdependence. *Journal of Humanistic Psychology* 59 (2019): 634-657.

Bland, Andrew M. and Eugene M. DeRobertis. *Humanistic perspective.* Encyclopedia of Personality and Individual Differences (2020a): 2061-2079.

Bland, Andrew M. and Eugene M. DeRobertis. Maslow's unacknowledged contributions to developmental psychology. *Journal of Humanistic Psychology* 60 (2020b): 934-958.

Bleidorn, W., Hopwood, C.J., Ackerman, R.A., Witt, E.A., Kandler, C., Riemann, R., Samuel, D.B. and Donnellan, M.B., 2019. The healthy personality from a basic trait perspective. *Journal of Personality and Social Psychology* 118 (2019): 1207-1225.

Boldt, M. *Surviving as Indians: The Challenge of Self-Government.* University of Toronto Press, 1993.

Bonicalzi, S. and Haggard, P. From 'freedom from' to 'freedom to': New perspectives on intentional action. *Frontiers in psychology* 10 (2019: 1193 online.

Bourdieu, Pierre. Social space and symbolic power. *Sociological Theory* 7 (1989): 14-25.

Boucher, David and Andrew Vincent. T.H. Green: citizenship as political and metaphysical. In D. Boucher & A. Vincent *British Idealism*. London: Continuum, 2006.

Boucher, David. *British Idealism*. Oxford University Press, 2014.

Bowlby, John. Attachment and loss: retrospect and prospect. *American journal of Orthopsychiatry* 52 (1982): 664-680.

Bridgman, Todd, Stephen Cummings and John Ballard. Who built Maslow's pyramid? A history of the creation of management studies' most famous symbol and its implications for management education. *Academy of Management Learning and Education* 18 (2019): 81-98.

Bronfenbrenner, Urie and Stephen J. Ceci. Nature-nurture reconceptualized in developmental perspective: A bioecological model. *Psychological Review* 101 (1994): 568-578.

Brooks, Thom. *Ethical Citizenship: British Idealism and the Politics of Recognition*. Springer, 2014.

Brown, Alyson and David Barrett. *Knowledge of Evil: Child Prostitution and Child Sexual Abuse in Twentieth Century England*. Willan Publishing, 2002.

Bruner, Jerome S. *Acts of Meaning*. Harvard University Press, 1990.

Bruner, Jerome S. The autobiographical process. *Current Sociology* 43 (1995): 161-177.

Bugental, James FT, J. Fraser Pierson and Kirk J. Schneider, eds. *The Handbook of Humanistic Psychology: Leading Edges in Theory, Research, and Practice*. Sage Publications, 2001.

Bukowska, Monika. Critical realism: one of the main theoretical orientations of the social sciences in the twentieth and twenty-first centuries. *Journal of Critical Realism* 20 (2021): 441-447.

Burnell, George M, and Mary Ann Norfleet. Evaluating psychosocial stress: Preliminary report on a brief and convenient instrument for health professionals. *International Journal of Psychiatry in Medicine* 12 (1983): 141-151.

Butler, Judith. *The Force of Nonviolence: An Ethico-Political Bind*. Springer, 2020.

Butler-Bowdon, Tom. *50 Spiritual Classics: Great Books of Inner Discover, Enlightenment and Purpose*. Nicholas Brealey, 2005.

Case, A. and Deaton, A. *Deaths of Despair and the Future of Capitalism*. Princeton University Press, 2020.

Castro-Molina, F.J. Abraham Maslow, human needs and their relationship with professional caregivers. *Cultura de los Cuidados* 22 (2018): 102-108.

Chamorro-Premuzic, Tomas, and Adrian Furnham. *Personality and Intellectual Competence*. Psychology Press, 2014.

Chess, Stella, Alexander Thomas and Herbert George Birch. *Your Child is a Person*. Penguin Books, 1976.

Chess, Stella and Alexander Thomas. *Goodness of Fit: Clinical Applications, from Infancy Through Adult Life*. Routledge, 2013.

Coard, Bernard. How the West Indian child is made educationally subnormal in the British school system: the scandal of the Black child in schools in Britain. In B. Richardson (Ed.). *Tell it Like It Is: How Our Schools Fail Black Children.* Stoke: Trentham Books (first published in 1971 by New Beacon), 2005.

Collier, Andrew. *Critical Realism: An Introduction to Roy Bhaskar's Philosophy.* Verso, 1994.

Collier, Andrew. *Being and Worth.* Routledge, 1999.

Collier, Andrew. Dialectic in Marxism and critical realism. In A. Brown, S. Fleetwood and J.M. Roberts (Eds.) *Critical Realism and Marxism* (168-186). Routledge, 2002.

Connolly, Brian. Introduction: Psychoanalysis and history. *History of the Present* 12 (2022): 1-3.

Coopersmith, Stanley. *The Antecedents of Self-Esteem.* Freeman & Co., 1967.

Coopersmith, Stanley. Self-concept, race and education. In G.K. Verma and C. Adam-Bagley (Eds.) *Race and Education Across Cultures.* Heinemann, 1975.

CRAE *State of Children's Rights in England.* London: Children's Rights Alliance for England, 1967.

Creaven, Sean. *Emergentist Marxism: Dialectical Philosophy and Social Theory.* Routledge, 2007.

Creaven, Sean. The 'Two Marxisms' revisited: humanism, structuralism and realism in Marxist social theory. *Journal of Critical Realism* 14 (2015): 7-53.

Crowe, David. *Oskar Schindler: The Untold Account of His Life, Wartime Activities, and the True Story Behind the List.* Basic Books, 2007.

Dąbrowski, Kazimierz and Michael Marian Piechowski. *Theory of Levels of Emotional Development: Multi-Levelness and Positive Disintegration.* Dabor Science Publications, 1977.

Dahlsgaard, Katherine, Christopher Peterson, and Martin E.P. Seligman. Shared virtue: The convergence of valued human strengths across culture and history." *Review of General Psychology* 9 (2005): 203-213.

Davidson, Larry. Philosophical foundations of humanistic psychology. *The Humanistic Psychologist* 28 (2000): 7-31.

DeCarvalho, Roy José. Contributions to the history of psychology: Carl Rogers' naturalistic system of ethics. *Psychological Reports* 65 (1989): 1155-1162.

DeCarvalho, Roy José. A history of the" third force" in psychology. *Journal of Humanistic psychology* 30 (1990): 22-44.

DeCarvalho, Roy José. *The Founders of Humanistic Psychology*. Praeger Publishers. 1991a.

DeCarvalho, Roy José. The humanistic paradigm in education. *The Humanistic Psychologist* 19 (1991b): 88-104.

DeCarvalho, Roy José. Gordon Allport and humanistic psychology. *Journal of Humanistic Psychology* 31 (1991c): 8-13. i

DeCarvalho, Roy José. The humanistic ethics of Rollo May. *Journal of Humanistic Psychology,* 32 (1992): 7-18.

deMause, Lloyd. *Foundations of Psychohistory.* New York, Creative Roots Press, 1982.

deMause, Lloyd. *The Emotional Life of Nations.* New York, Other Press, 2002.

DeRobertis, Eugene M. On framing the future of humanistic psychology. *The Humanistic Psychologist* 44 (2016): 18-26.

DeRobertis, Eugene M. and Andrew M. Bland. Tapping the humanistic potential of self-determination theory: Awakening to paradox. *The Humanistic Psychologist* 46 (2018): 105-120.

DeRobertis, Eugene M. and Andrew M. Bland. Lifespan human development and "the humanistic perspective": A contribution toward inclusion. *The Humanistic Psychologist,* 47 (2019): 1-25.

DeRobertis, Eugene M. and Andrew M. Bland. Humanistic and positive psychologies: the continuing narrative after two decades. *Journal of Humanistic Psychology* (2021): 00221678211008353.

De Waal, Frans. *The Age of Empathy: Nature's Lessons for a Kinder Society.* Broadway Books, 2010.

Dillon, James J. Humanistic psychology and the good: A forgotten link. *The Humanistic Psychologist* 48 (2020): 244-254.

Dovemark, Marianne and Dennis Beach. From learning to labour to learning for precarity. *Ethnography and Education* 11 (2016): 174-188.

Dovidio, John F., Jane Allyn Piliavin, David A. Schroeder and Louis A. Penner. *The Social Psychology of Prosocial Behavior.* Routledge and Psychology Press, 2017.

D'Souza, Jeevan and Michael Gurin. The universal significance of Maslow's concept of self-actualization. *The Humanistic Psychologist* 44 (2016): 210-220.

Easwaran, Eknath. *Nonviolent Soldier of Islam: Badshah Khan, a Man to Match his Mountains.* Nilgiri Press, 1999.

Easton, Geoff. *Critical realism in case study research. Industrial Marketing and Management,* 39 (2010): 118-128.

Eccles, John C. and Karl Popper. *The Self and its Brain: An Argument for Interactionism.* Routledge, 2014.

Eccles, John C. and Daniel N. Robinson. *The Wonder of Being Human: Our Brain and our Mind.* The Free Press, 1984.

Edwards, David J.A. Systematic case study research in clinical and counselling psychology. *Research Methods in the Social Sciences* (151-171). WITS University Press, 2019.

Edwards, Paul K., Joe O'Mahoney, and Steve Vincent, Eds. *Studying Organizations using Critical Realism: A Practical Guide.* Oxford University Press, 2014.

Ellis, A. and Ellis, D.J. Rational emotive behavioral therapy. *Current psychotherapy.* Washington, DC: American Psychological Association, 2011.

Engels, Friedrich. *The Condition of the Working Class in England.* Penguin Books, (1845/1978).

Erikson, Erik H. *Life history and the Historical Moment: Diverse Presentations.* Norton, 1977.

Erikson, Erik H. *Gandhi's Truth: On the Origins of Militant Nonviolence.* Norton, 1993a.

Erikson, Erik. H. *Childhood and Society.* Norton, 1993b.

Erikson, Erik H. and Joan M. Erikson, *The Life Cycle Completed: Extended Version.* Norton, 1998.

Ewen, Robert B. *An Introduction to Theories of Personality.* Psychology Press, 2014.

Farrington, David. The development of offending and anti-social behaviour from childhood: key findings from the Cambridge Study on Delinquency Behaviour. *Journal of Child Psychology and Psychiatry* 36 (1995): 929-964.

Fasching, Darrell J. *The Ethical Challenge of Auschwitz and Hiroshima: Apocalypse or Utopia?* SUNY Press, 1993.

Feigenbaum, Kenneth D. and Rene Anne Smith. Historical narratives: Abraham Maslow and Blackfoot interpretations. *The Humanistic Psychologist* 48 (2020): 232-245.

Finkelhor, David, Anne Shattuck, Heather A. Turner, Richard Ormrod, and Sherry L. Hamby. Poly-victimization in developmental context. *Journal of Child & Adolescent Trauma* 4 (2011): 291-300.

Finkelhor, David, and Corinna Jenkins Tucker. A holistic approach to child maltreatment. *The Lancet Psychiatry* 2 (2015): 480-481.

Flaschel, Peter. *The Macrodynamics of Capitalism: Elements for a Synthesis of Marx, Keynes and Schumpeter.* Springer Media, 2008.

Flood, Alison. How to be happy: interview with Robert Waldinger. *New Scientist*, January 14th 46-49 (2023).

Foucault, M. The ethics of the concern of the self as a practice of freedom. In P. Rabinow (Ed.), *Michel Foucault: Ethics Subjectivity and Truth. Essential Works of Foucault 1954–1984.* New York, Free Press, 1997.

Foucault, M. *Power: The Essential Works of Michel Foucault 1954-1984.* Penguin, 2019.

Focquaert, Farah, A. Glenn, and Adrian Raine. Psychopathy and free will from a philosophical and cognitive neuroscience perspective. *Free Will and the Brain* (2015): 103-124.

Fowler, James H. and Nicholas A. Christakis. Dynamic spread of happiness in a large social network: longitudinal analysis over 20 years in the Framingham Heart Study. *British Medical Journal* 337 (2008): online.

Franco, Zeno, Harris Friedman, and Mike Arons. Are qualitative methods always best for humanistic psychology research? A conversation on the epistemological divide between humanistic and positive psychology. *The Humanistic Psychologist* 36 (2008): 159-203.

Frank, Arthur W. *Letting Stories Breathe: A Socio-Narratology*. University of Chicago Press, 2010.

Frank, Anne. *The Diary of a Young Girl*. Eastern Publishing Company, 1995.

Frankl, Viktor. *The Unconscious God*. Simon and Schuster, 1975.

Frankl, Viktor. *The Doctor and the Soul*. Vantage Books, 1986.

Frankl, Viktor. *The Will to Meaning*. Penguin Books, 1988.

Frankl, Viktor. *Recollections: An Autobiography*. Perseus Books, 2000.

Freud, Sigmund. *Civilization and Its Discontents*. Penguin Book, 2002.

Friedman, Harris. Humanistic and positive psychology: The methodological and epistemological divide. *The Humanistic Psychologist* 36 (2008): 113-126.

Fromm, E. *Man for Himself: An Inquiry into the Psychology of Ethics*. Routledge, 2013.

Galvez, Cesar Augusto, Chirlynor Calbayan, Kepha Pondi and Maria Vallejos. Influence of knowledge and attitude on lifestyle practices among Seventh-Day Adventists in Metro Manila, Philippines. *Journal of Religion and Health* 60 (2021): 1248-1260.

Gelvin, James L. *The Israel–Palestine Conflict: A History*. Cambridge University Press, 2021.

George, Rosalyn, and John Clay. Challenging pedagogy: Emotional disruptions, young girls, parents and schools. *Sociological Research Online* 18, (2013): 214-222.

Giarretto. Henry. A comprehensive child sexual abuse treatment program. In C. Mrazek & P. Kempe (Eds.) *Sexually Abused Children and their Families* (179-198). Pergamon Press, 1981.

Gergen, Kenneth. J. The acculturated brain. *Theory & Psychology*, 20 (2010): 795-816.

Gergen, Kenneth J. Toward a visionary psychology. *The Humanistic Psychologist*, 44 (2016): 3 online.

Giarretto, Henry. A comprehensive child sexual abuse treatment program. *Child Abuse & Neglect* 6 (1982): 263-278.

Gibson, A. Boyce. *The Philosophy of Descartes*. Routledge, 2016.

Giddens, Anthony. *Modernity and Self-Identity: Self and Society in the Late Modern Age*. Sage, 1992.

Gilbert, Paul. *Mindful Compassion*. Hachette UK, 2013.

Gilbert, Paul. The origins and nature of compassion focused therapy. *British Journal of Clinical Psychology* 53 (2014): 6-41.

Gillespie, Alex. GH Mead: Theorist of the social act. *Journal for the Theory of Social Behaviour* 35 (2005): 19-39.

Gorski, Phillip S. What is Critical Realism? And why should you care? *Contemporary Sociology* 42: (2013): 658-670.

Gorsuch, Richard L. Toward motivational theories of intrinsic religious commitment. In *The Psychology of Religion* (11-24), Routledge, 2019.

Green, Thomas. *Lectures on the Principles of Political Obligation and Other Writings*. Cambridge University Press, 1986.

Greengarten, Ian M. *Thomas Hill Green and the Development of Liberal-Democratic Thought*. University of Toronto Press, 1981.

Haddad, Yvonne Yazbeck and John L. Esposito, Eds. *Daughters of Abraham: Feminist Thought in Judaism, Christianity, and Islam*. University Press of Florida, 2001.

Hammond, Claudia. *The Keys to Kindness: How to be Kinder to Yourself, Others and The World.* Canongate Books, 2022.

Hanley, Adam W. The mindful personality: Associations between dispositional mindfulness and the Five Factor Model of personality. *Personality and Individual Differences* 91 (2016): 154-158.

Healy, Kevin. A theory of human motivation by Abraham H. Maslow. *The British Journal of Psychiatry* 208 (2016): 313-313.

Heavy Head, R. Report on Blackfoot concepts and practices in exploring Maslow's concept of synergy. *Abraham Maslow and the Blackfoot experience & Influence of Blackfoot images and culture on the work of Abraham Maslow.* Symposium conducted at the Archives of History of American Psychology, University of Akron, Akron, Ohio, 2006.

Heavy Head, R. Blackfoot world view and influence on Abraham Maslow. Presentation to *Symposium on Abraham Maslow* at Center for Cross-Cultural Research, Western Washington University, 2011.

Heimler, Eugene. *Mental Illness and Social Work.* Penguin, 1967.

Heimler, Eugene. *Night of the Mist.* Gefen Publishing House, 1997.

Heimler, Eugene. *Survival in Society.* Weidenfeld; and Eugene Heimler Literary Trust, 2014.

Hoffman, Edward. The life and legacy of Abraham Maslow: Why Abraham Maslow still matters. *Psychology Today* 44 (2011): 551-563.

Hoffman, Edward. The social world of self-actualizing people: reflections by Maslow's biographer. *Journal of Humanistic Psychology* 60 (2020): 908-933.

Hillesum, Etty. *Etty: A Diary 1941-1943.* Triad Books, 1985.

Hillesum, Etty. *The Letters and Diaries of Etty Hillesum 1941-1943, Unabridged.* (Arnold Pomerans, translator). Eerdmans Publishing, 2002.

Hoffman, Louis. Multiculturalism and humanistic psychology: From neglect to epistemological and ontological diversity. *The Humanistic Psychologist* 44 (2016): 56-65.

Howe, David. *Attachment Theory for Social Work Practice*. Bloomsbury Publishing, 1995.

Huxley, Francis. *The Way of the Sacred*. Aldous Books, 1974.

Hy, Le Xuan and Jane Loevinger. *Measuring Ego Development*. Lawrence Erlbaum, 1996.

Irfan, Lamia and Matthew Wilkinson. The ontology of the Muslim male offender: a critical realist framework. *Journal of Critical Realism* 19 (2020): 481-499.

Irvine, William B. *A Guide to the Good Life: The Ancient Art of Stoic Joy*. Oxford University Press, 2008.

Jackson, Michael R. *Self-Esteem and Meaning: A Life Historical Investigation*. SUNY Press, 1984.

Jakobsen, Ove. *Transformative Ecological Economics: Process Philosophy, Ideology and Utopia*. Routledge, 2017.

Jamal, Mahmood (Ed.). *Islamic Mystical Poetry: Sufi Verse from Early Mystics to Rumi*. Penguin Classics, 2015.

James, William. *The Principles of Psychology*. Harvard University Press, 1983.

James, William. *The Varieties of Religious Experience*. Longmans, 1982.

Joas, H. *GH Mead: A Contemporary Re-Examination of his Thought*. Boston, Mass: MIT Press, 1997.

Joseph, Stephen. *Positive Therapy: Building Bridges between Positive Psychology and Person-Centred Psychotherapy*. Routledge, 2015.

Jung, Carl Gustav. *The Undiscovered Self*. Little Brown, 1958.

Kaufman, Scott Barry. There is no one way to live a good life. *Scientific American Mind*, 15552284, Jan/Feb (2018a): 29, Issue 1.

Kaufman, Scott Barry. Self-actualizing people in the 21st century: Integration with contemporary theory and research on personality and well-being. *Journal of Humanistic Psychology* (2018b): 0022167818809187.

Kaufman, Scott Barry. The Light Triad versus Dark Triad of personality. *Scientific American*, (March 19th, 2019): online.

Kaufman, Scott Barry. *Transcend: The New Science of Self-Actualization.* Penguin, 2020.

Kaufman, Scott Barry. *Choose Growth: A Workbook for Transcending Trauma, Fear, and Self-Doubt.* Tarcher-Perigee, 2022.

Kaufman, Scott Barry, David Bryce Yaden, Elizabeth Hyde, and Eli Tsukayama. The light vs. dark triad of personality: Contrasting two very different profiles of human nature. *Frontiers in Psychology* 10 (2019): 467, online.

Kelland, Mark. *Personality Theory: A Multicultural Perspective.* OpenText Library, 2017.

Keltner, Dacher. *Born to be Good: The Science of a Meaningful Life.* WW Norton, 2009.

Keltner, Dacher, Jason Marsh, and Jeremy Adam Smith, Editors, *The Compassionate Instinct: The Science of Human Goodness.* Norton & Co., 2010.

Keltner, Dacher and Yang Bai. *Awe: The Transformative Power of Everyday Wonder.* Allen Lane, 2022.

Keltner, Dacher and Paul K. Piff. Self-transcendent awe as a moral grounding of wisdom. *Psychological Inquiry* 31 (2020): 160-163.

Kemple, Thomas. *Intellectual Work and the Spirit of Capitalism: Weber's Calling.* Springer, 2014.

Kirschenbaum, Howard (Ed.) *The Carl Rogers Reader Constable,* 1990.

Kirschenbaum, Howard and April Jourdan. The current status of Carl Rogers and the person-centered approach. *Psychotherapy: Theory, Research, Practice, Training* 42, (2005): 37-51.

Koltko-Rivera, Mark E. Rediscovering the later version of Maslow's hierarchy of needs: Self-transcendence and opportunities for theory, research, and unification. *Review of General Psychology* 10 (2006): 302-317.

Kwok, Chun Shing, Saadia Umar, Phyo K. Myint, Mamas and Yoon K. Loke. Vegetarian diet, Seventh Day Adventists and risk of cardiovascular mortality: A systematic review and meta-analysis. *International Journal of Cardiology* 176 (2014): 680-686.

Lambert, Michael J. and David M. Erekson. Positive psychology and the humanistic tradition. *Journal of Psychotherapy Integration* 18 (2008): 222-232.

Lampen, John. The Quaker peace testimony in twentieth-century education. *Quaker Studies (Quaker Studies Research Association)* 19 (2015): 295-315.

Lantz, James and Karen Harper. Stories and tales in logotherapy with urban-Appalachian families. *Contemporary family therapy* 14 (1992): 455-466.

Layard, Richard and Judy Dunn. *The Good Childhood Inquiry: Searching for Values in a Competitive Age*. Penguin, UK, 2009.

Layard, Richard. *Happiness: Lessons from a New Science*. Penguin UK, 2011.

Layard, Richard, Andrew E. Clark, Francesca Cornaglia, Nattavudh Powdthavee and James Vernoit. What predicts a successful life? A life-course model of well-being. *The Economic Journal* 124 (2014): F720-F738.

Layard, Richard and David M. Clark. *Thrive: The Power of Evidence-Based Psychological Therapies*. Penguin UK, 2014.

Layous, Kristin, S. Katherine Nelson, Eva Oberle, Kimberly A. Schonert-Reichl and Sonja Lyubomirsky. Kindness counts: Prompting prosocial behavior in preadolescents boosts peer acceptance and well-being. *PloS One* 7 (2012): e51380.

Leland, Abby Porter. *The Educational Theory and Practice of TH Green*. Leopold Classic Library, online resource, 2011.

Lester, David. Measuring Maslow's hierarchy of needs. *Psychological Reports* 113 (2013): 15-17.

Lester, David, Judith Hvezda, Shannon Sullivan and Roger Plourde. Maslow's hierarchy of needs and psychological health. *The Journal of General Psychology* 109 (1983): 83-85.

Lewis, Bernard. *The Jews of Islam*. Routledge, 2013.

Linley, P. Alex. and Stephen Joseph, S. *Positive Psychology in Practice*. John Wiley, 2004.

Linley, P. Alex, Stephen Joseph, Susan Harrington, and Alex M. Wood. Positive psychology: Past, present, and (possible) future. *The Journal of Positive Psychology* 1 (2006): 3-16.

Linley, P. Alex, Susan Harrington, and Nicola Garcea, Eds. *Oxford Handbook of Positive Psychology and Work*. Oxford University Press, 2012.

Little, Daniel. *Varieties of Social Explanation: An Introduction to the Philosophy of Social Science*. Westview Press, 2012a.

Little, Daniel. Analytical sociology and the rest of sociology. *Sociologica* 6 (2012b): 1-10.

Llanos, Luis Felipe and L. Verduzco Martínez. From self-transcendence to collective transcendence: In search of the order of hierarchies in Maslow's transcendence. *Frontiers in Psychology* 13 (2022): 787591.

Loevinger, Jane. On ego development and the structure of personality. *Developmental Review* 3 (1983): 339-350.

Lomas, Tim. Positive social psychology: A multilevel inquiry into sociocultural well-being initiatives. *Psychology, Public Policy, and Law* 21 (2015): 338-350.

Lovelock, James. Gaia: *A New Look at Life on Earth*. Oxford University Press, 2016.

Luobbad, Mousa and Chris Adam-Bagley. Work-life balance policies and traditional culture in a competitive market: Three Jordanian case studies. *Journal of Human Resource & Leadership* 5 (2021): 25-45.

Lyubomirsky, Sonja. *The How of Happiness: A Scientific Approach to Getting What You Want*. Penguin, 2008.

Lyubomirsky, Sonja, Laura King and Ed Diener. The benefits of frequent positive affect: Does happiness lead to success? *Psychological Bulletin* 131 (2005): 803-835.

Lyubomirsky, Sonja, and Kristin Layous. How do simple positive activities increase well-being? *Current Directions in Psychological Science* 22 (2013): 57-62.

Mackes, Nuria K., Dennis Golm, Sagari Sarkar, Robert Kumsta, Michael Rutter, Graeme Fairchild, Mitul A. Mehta, Edmund JS Sonuga-Barke and ERA Young Adult Follow-up team. Early childhood deprivation is associated with alterations in adult brain structure despite subsequent environmental enrichment. *Proceedings of the National Academy of Sciences* 117 (2020): 641-649.

Malone, Johanna C., Sabrina R. Liu, George E. Vaillant, Dorene M. Rentz, and Robert J. Waldinger. "Midlife" Eriksonian psychosocial development: Setting the stage for late-life cognitive and emotional health. *Developmental Psychology* 52 (2016): 496-508.

Margolin, Leslie. Rogerian psychotherapy and the problem of power: A Foucauldian interpretation." *Journal of Humanistic Psychology* 60 (2020): 130-143.

Markham, Ian S. *Engaging with Bediuzzaman Said Nursi: A Model of Interfaith Dialogue*. Routledge, 2016.

Maslow, Abraham H. The role of dominance in the social and sexual behavior of infra-human primates: I. Observations at Vilas Park Zoo. *Journal of Genetic Psychology* 17 (1936): 261-277.

Maslow, Abraham H. Personality and patterns of culture. In R. Stagner (Ed.), *Psychology of Personality* (408-428). McGraw-Hill, 1937.

Maslow, Abraham H. A theory of human motivation. *Psychological Review* 50 (1943): 370-396.

Maslow, Abraham, H. Resistance to acculturation. *Journal of Social Issues* 7 (1951): 26-29.

Maslow, Abraham H. Toward a humanistic psychology. *ETC: A Review of General Semantics* (1956a): 10-22.

Maslow, Abraham H. *Self-Actualizing People: A Study of Psychological Health*. Harper, 1956b.

Maslow, Abraham H. Further notes on the psychology of being. *Journal of Humanistic Psychology* 4 (1964a): 45-58.

Maslow, Abraham H. Synergy in the society and in the individual. *Journal of Individual Psychology* 20 (1964b): 153-164.

Maslow, Abraham H. *Self-Actualization and Beyond*. Center for Study of Liberal Education, University of Boston, 1965.

Maslow, Abraham H. *The Psychology of Science: A Renaissance*. Harper & Row, 1966.

Maslow, Abraham H. *The Farther Reaches of Human Nature*. The Viking Press, 1971.

Maslow, Abraham H. *Motivation and Personality*. 3rd Edition. HarperCollins, 1987.

Maslow, Abraham H. The farther reaches of human nature. *Journal of Transpersonal Psychology* 1 (1996a): 1-9.

Maslow, Abraham H. Toward a humanistic biology. *American Psychologist*, 24 (1996b): 724-735.

Maslow, Abraham. H. *Future Visions: The Unpublished Papers of Abraham Maslow*. Sage Publications, 1996c.

Maslow, Abraham H. *Religions Values and Peak-Experiences*. Rare Treasure Editions, 2021.

Maslow, Abraham H. *Toward a Psychology of Being*. General Press, 2022.

Maslow, Abraham H. and John J. Honigmann. *Northern Blackfoot Culture and Personality*. In Abraham Maslow papers (M416). Archives of the History of Psychology, University of Akron, Akron, OH, 1970.

Maslow, Abraham H., John J. Honigmann and Margaret Mead. Synergy: Some notes of Ruth Benedict. *American Anthropologist* 72 (1970): 320-333.

Maslow, Abraham H., Deborah C. Stephen, and Gary Heil. *Maslow on Management*. John Wiley, 1998.

Maslow, Abraham H. and I. Szilagyi-Kessler. Security and breastfeeding. *The Journal of Abnormal and Social Psychology* 41 (1946): 83-93.

Maulawi, Faysal. *The Muslim as a European Citizen*. Dublin: Islamic Cultural Centre of Ireland, 2012.

May, Rollo. *Love and Will*. Norton, 2007.

May, Rollo. *The Discovery of Being*. Norton, 2015.

Mayall, Berry. *A History of the Sociology of Childhood*. London University Institute of Education, 2013.

McAdams, Dan P. The psychology of life stories. *Review of General Psychology*, 5 (2001): 100-122.

McAdams, Dan P. Narrative identity. In *Handbook of Identity Theory and Research*, 99-115. Springer, 2011.

McAlmont, David. *The Question of Evil Remains Unanswered*. Washington, DC: The American Humanist Association, 2020. I

McCarraher, Eugene. *The Enchantments of Mammon: How Capitalism Became the Religion of Modernity*. Harvard University Press, 2019.

McKenzie, Kwame, Rob Whitley and Scott Weich. Social capital and mental health. *The British Journal of Psychiatry* 181 (2002): 280-283.

McCrae, Robert R, and Paul T. Costa. Openness to experience and ego level in Loevinger's Sentence Completion Test: Dispositional contributions to developmental models of personality. *Journal of Personality and Social Psychology* 39 (1980): 1179-1190.

McCrae, Robert R., and Oliver P. John. An introduction to the five-factor model and its applications. *Journal of Personality* 60 (1992): 175-215.

Mea, William J. and Ronald R. Sims. Human dignity-centered business ethics: A conceptual framework for business leaders. *Journal of Business Ethics* 160, (2019): 53-69.

Mead, George H. *Mind, Self and Society*. University of Chicago Press, 1964.

Mehlman, Jeffrey. *Legacies of Anti-Semitism in France*. University of Minnesota Press, 1983.

Mehta, Mitul A., Nicole I. Golembo, Chiara Nosarti, Emma Colvert, Ashley Mota, Steven CR Williams, Michael Rutter and Edmund JS Sonuga-Barke. Amygdala, hippocampal and corpus callosum size following severe early institutional deprivation: the English and Romanian Adoptees study pilot. *Journal of Child Psychology and Psychiatry* 50 (2009): 943-951.

Mendaglio, Sal. *Dabrowski's Theory of Positive Disintegration: A Personality Theory for the 21st Century*. Great Potential Press, 2008.

Midgley, David. *The Essential Mary Midgley*. Routledge, 2004.

Midgley, Mary. *Wickedness*. Routledge, 2003a.

Midgley, Mary. *Heart and Mind: The Varieties of Moral Experience*. Routledge, 2003b.

Midgley, Mary. *The Myths We Live By*. Routledge, 2003c.

Midgley, Mary. *The Solitary Self*. Durham: Acumen, 2010.

Midgley, Mary. *Are You an Illusion?* Routledge, 2015.

Miller, Madeline. *Circe*. Bloomsbury, 2019.

Montag, Christian, Cornelia Sindermann, David Lester, and Kenneth L. Davis. Linking individual differences in satisfaction with each of Maslow's needs to the Big Five personality traits and Panksepp's primary emotional systems. *Heliyon* 6 (2020): e04325.

Morin, Edgar. *Rumour in Orleans*. Pantheon Books, 1971.

Mruk, Chris J. *Self-Esteem Research, Theory, and Practice: Toward a Positive Psychology of Self-Esteem*. Springer, 2006.

Mruk, Chris J. *Self-Esteem and Positive Psychology: Research, theory, and practice*. Springer, 2013.

Mruk, Christopher J., and Travis Skelly. Is self-esteem absolute, relative, or functional? Implications for cross-cultural and humanistic psychology. *The Humanistic Psychologist* 45 (2017): 313-325.

John Henry Muirhead. *The Service of the State: Four Lectures on the Political Teaching of TH Green*. J. Murray Publishers, University of Toronto, 1908.

Neff, Kristin. D., Kristin L. Kirkpatrick, and Stephanie S. Rude. Self-compassion and adaptive psychological functioning. *Journal of Research in Personality* 41 (2007: 139-154.

Neff, Kristin D., Stephanie S. Rude, and Kristin L. Kirkpatrick. An examination of self-compassion in relation to positive psychological functioning and personality traits. *Journal of Research in Personality* 41 (2007): 908-916.

Neff, Kristin D. The role of self-compassion in development: A healthier way to relate to oneself. *Human Development*, 52 (2009): 211.

Newton, Neill. *Summary Report of Quaker Schools Research Project.* University of Bristol School of Education, 2016.

Neff, Kirsten D. Self-compassion, self-esteem, and well-being. *Social and Personality Psychology Compass* 5 (2011): 1-12.

Norrie, Alan. *Dialectic and Difference: Dialectical Critical Realism and the Grounds of Justice.* Routledge, 2010.

Nye, Robert D. *Three Psychologies: Perspectives from Freud, Skinner and Rogers.* Wadsworth Thomson Learning, 2000.

Obuchowski, Karl. Alfred Adler: precursor of humanistic psychology. *Individual Psychology* 44 (1988): 263-269.

Olssen, Mark and Will Mace. British idealism, complexity theory and society: The political usefulness of TH Green in a revised conception of social democracy. *Linguistic & Philosophical Investigations* 20 (2021): 1-10.

Parekh, Bhikhu, Anthony Parel, Vinit Haksar, Richard L. Johnson, Nicholas F. Gier, Fred Dallmayr, and Joseph Prabhu. *The Philosophy of Mahatma Gandhi for the Twenty-First Century.* Lexington Books, 2008.

Parvizian, Saja. Al-Ghazālī and Descartes on defeating skepticism. *Journal of Philosophical Research* 45 (2020): 133-148.

Parry, Ken W. Viewing the leadership narrative through alternate lenses: An autoethnographic investigation. *Management Revue* 19 (2008): 126-147.

Peat, F. David. *Blackfoot Physics: A New Journey into the Native American Universe.* Weiser Books, 2002.

Peet, Christopher. *Karl Jaspers and the Axial Age. In Practicing Transcendence: Axial Age Spiritualities for a World in Crisis.* Springer, 2019.

Perrin, Paul B. Humanistic psychology's social justice philosophy: Systemically treating the psychosocial and health effects of racism. *Journal of Humanistic Psychology* 53 (2013): 52-69.

Peterson, Christopher and Martin Seligman. *Character Strengths and Virtues: A Handbook and Classification.* Oxford University Press, 2004.

Piechowski, Michael. M. Etty Hillesum: "The thinking heart of the barracks." *Advanced Development* 4 (1992): 105-118.

Piechowski, Michael M. From William James to Maslow and Dabrowski: Excitability of character and self-actualization. In D. Ambrose (Ed.) *Creative Intelligence: Toward a Theoretic Integration* (283-322). Hampton Press, 2003.

Piechowski, Michael M. Discovering Dabrowski's theory. In S. Mendaglio (Ed.) *Dabrowski's Theory of Positive Disintegration: A Personality Theory for the 21st Century* (41-77). Great Potent Press, 2008.

Pilgrim, David. *Critical Realism for Psychologists*. Routledge, 2019.

Plummer, Ken. *Telling Sexual Stories: Power, Change and Social Worlds*. Routledge, 1995.

Plummer, Ken. *Narrative Power: The Struggle for Human Value*. John Wiley, 2019.

Plummer, Ken. *Critical Humanism: A Manifesto for the 21st Century*. John Wiley, 2021.

Popper, Karl. *Unended Quest: An Intellectual Autobiography*. Routledge, 2005.

Porpora, Douglas V. *Reconstructing Sociology: The Critical Realist Approach*. Cambridge University Press, 2015.

Porpora, Douglas V. Dehumanization in theory: anti-humanism, non-humanism, post-humanism, and trans-humanism. *Journal of Critical Realism* 16 (2017) 353-367.

Pritchard, Colin and Chris Adam-Bagley. Multi-criminal and violent groups among child sex offenders: a heuristic typology in a 2-year cohort of men in two English counties. *Child Abuse and Neglect* 24 (2000): 579-586.

Pritchard, Colin and Chris Adam-Bagley. Suicide and murder in child murderers and child sexual abusers. *Journal of Forensic Psychiatry* 12 (2001): 269-286.

Pujo, Bernard. *Vincent de Paul, the Trailblazer*. University of Notre Dame Press, 2003.

Ridley, Matthew. *Rational Optimism: How Prosperity Evolves*. Fourth Estate, 2010.

Ridley, Matthew. *Foreword to Simon Baron-Cohen: Zero Degrees of Empathy.* Penguin, 2011.

Rashid, Tayyab, and Martin P. Seligman. *Positive Psychotherapy: Clinician Manual.* Oxford University Press, 2018.

Rifkin, Jeremy. *The Empathic Civilization: The Race to Global Consciousness in a World in Crisis.* Penguin, 2009.

Robson, David. *The Expectation Effect: How Your Mindset Can Transform Your Life.* Canongate 2022.

Rogers, Carl R. *Client-Centered Therapy.* Houghton Mifflin, 1951.

Rogers, Carl, R. The necessary and sufficient conditions of therapeutic personality change. *Journal of Consulting Psychology*, 21 (1957): 95-103.

Rogers, Carl, R. *A Way of Being.* Houghton Mifflin Harcourt, 1995.

Rogers, Carl R. and H. J. Freiberg. *Freedom to Learn.* Macmillan, 1994.

Rosling, Hans, Ola Rosling and Anna Rosling Rönnlund. *Factfulness: Ten Reasons We're Wrong About the World--and Why Things are Better than You Think.* Flatiron books, 2018.

Roth, John K. *The Failures of Ethics: Confronting the Holocaust, Genocide, and Other Mass Atrocities.* Oxford University Press, 2015.

Rousseau, Jean Jacques. *Emile or On Education* (Translated by A. Bloom). Basic Books, 1979.

Russell, P. *Hume on free will. Stanford Encyclopedia of Philosophy.* Stanford, CA: Stanford University Press, 2008.

Rutter, Michael. *Fifteen Thousand hours: Secondary Schools and their Effects on Children.* Harvard University Press, 1979.

Rutter, Michael. Developmental catch-up, and deficit, following adoption after severe global early privation. *The Journal of Child Psychology and Psychiatry and Allied Disciplines* 39 (1998): 465-476.

Rutter, Michael and Thomas G. O'Connor. Are there biological programming effects for psychological development? Findings from a study of Romanian adoptees. *Developmental Psychology* 40 (2004): 81-89.

Rutter, Michael, Celia Beckett, Jenny Castle, Emma Colvert, Jana Kreppner, Mitul Mehta, Suzanne Stevens, and Edmund Sonuga-Barke. Effects of profound early institutional deprivation: An overview of findings from a UK longitudinal study of Romanian adoptees. *European Journal of Developmental Psychology* 4 (2007): 332-350.

Rutter, Michael, Edmund J Sonuga-Barke and Jennifer Castle. I. Investigating the impact of early institutional deprivation on development: Background and research strategy of the English and Romanian Adoptees (ERA) study. *Monographs of the Society for Research in Child Development* 75 (2010): 1-100.

Saeednia, Yadolla, and Mariani M. Measuring hierarchy of basic needs among adults. *Procedia-Social and Behavioral Sciences* 82 (2013): 417-420.

Said, Edward W. *The Question of Palestine*. Vintage, 1992.

Said, Edward W. *After the Last Sky: Palestinian Lives*. Columbia University Press, 1999.

Said, Edward W. *The Edward Said Reader*. Granta Books, 2001.

Said, Edward W. *Culture and Imperialism*. Vintage, 2012a.

Said, Edward W. *Out of Place: A Memoir*. Vintage, 2012b.

Said, Edward W. Orientalism. In *Social Theory Re-Wired*, (402-417). Routledge, 2016.

Sandmel, Samuel. *Anti-Semitism in the New Testament?* Philadelphia, Fortress Press, 1978.

Saroglou, Vassilis. Religiousness as a cultural adaptation of basic traits: A five-factor model perspective. *Personality and Social Psychology Review* 14: (2010): 108-125.

Savage, Mike. *Social Class in the Twenty First Century*. Pelican, 2015.

Sawyerr, Alice and Chris Adam-Bagley. *Equality and Ethnic Identities: Studies of Self-Concept, Child Abuse and Education in a Changing English Culture*. Leiden, Brill, 2017a.

Sawyerr, Alice, and Chris Adam-Bagley. England's Sure Start pre-school childcare centres: Public policy, progress and political change." *Open Journal of Political Science* 7: (2017b): 116-128.

Sawyerr, Alice and Chris Adam-Bagley, C. Can prior sexual abuse explain global differences in measured self-esteem in male and female adolescents? *Children* 10 (2023): 276-290.

Scambler, Graham. Resistance in unjust times: Archer, structured agency and the sociology of health inequalities. *Sociology* 33 (2012): 275-296.

Scambler, Graham. Archer and 'vulnerable fractured reflexivity': A neglected social determinant of health? *Social Theory & Health* 11 (2013): 302-315.

Scambler, Graham. *Sociology, Health and the Fractured Society: A Critical Realist Account.* Routledge, 2018.

Scambler, Graham. The fractured society: Structures, mechanisms, tendencies. *Journal of Critical Realism* 19 (2020): 1-13.

Schatzman, Morton. *Soul Murder: Persecution in the Family.* Allen Lane, 1973.

Schneider, Kirk J., J. Fraser Pierson and James FT Bugental, Eds. *The Handbook of Humanistic Psychology: Theory, Research, and Practice.* Sage Publications, 2014.

Schneider, Kirk J. *The Spirituality of Awe: Challenges to the Robotic Revolution.* Waterfront Press, 2017.

Schott, Richard L. and Abraham Maslow. Humanistic psychology, and organization leadership: A Jungian perspective. *Journal of Humanistic Psychology* 32 (1992): 106-120.

Schueller, Stephen M. and Martin EP Seligman. Pursuit of pleasure, engagement, and meaning: Relationships to subjective and objective measures of well-being. *The Journal of Positive Psychology* 5 (2010): 253-263.

Sedikides, Constantine and Marilynn B. Brewer. *Individual Self, Relational Self, Collective Self.* Psychology Press, 2015.

Seligman, Martin. *Helplessness: On Depression, Development, and Death.* Freeman,1975.

Seligman, Martin and Garber, Judy. *Human Helplessness: Theory and Applications.* Academic Press, 1980.

Seligman, Martin. *Authentic Happiness: Using the New Positive Psychology to Realize your Potential for Lasting Fulfillment.* Free Press, 2002.

Seligman, Martin, Tracy A. Steen, Nansook Park, and Christopher Peterson. Positive psychology progress: empirical validation of interventions. *American Psychologist* 60, (2005): 410-415.

Seligman, Martin. *Learned Optimism: How to Change Your Mind and Your Life.* Vintage, 2006.

Seligman, Martin. *The Optimistic Child: A Proven Program to Safeguard Children Against Depression and Build Lifelong Resilience.* Houghton Mifflin Harcourt, 2007.

Seligman, Martin. *Flourish: A Visionary New Understanding of Happiness and Well-Being.* Atria Books, 2012.

Seligman, Martin EP, Randal M. Ernst, Jane Gillham, Karen Reivich, and Mark Linkins. Positive education: Positive psychology and classroom interventions. *Oxford Review of Education* 35 (2009): 293-311.

Seligman, Martin. *The Hope Circuit: A Psychologist's Journey from Helplessness to Optimism.* Hachette UK, 2018.

Shahnaz, Afroze., Chris Adam-Bagley, Padam Simkhada, and Sadia Kadri. Suicidal behaviour in Bangladesh: A scoping literature review and a proposed public health prevention model. *Open Journal of Social Sciences* 5 (2017): 254-266.

Shalin, Dmitri N. GH Mead, socialism, and the progressive agenda. *American Journal of Sociology* 93 (1988): 913-951.

Shengold, Leonard. *Soul Murder Revisited: Therapy, Hate, Love, and Memory.* Yale University Press, 2000.

Shipway, Brad. *A Critical Realist Perspective of Education.* Routledge, 2013.

Shipway, Brad. The theological application of Bhaskar's Stratified Realty. *Journal of Critical Realism*, 3 (2003): 191-203.

Smith, Adrian. The power of Bayesian statistics. *BBC Radio 4 "Life of Science" Interview*, February 7th, 2023.

Smith, Anne. *The Possibilities and Limitations of Using Drama to Facilitate a Sense of Belonging for Adult Refugees, Asylum Seekers and Migrants in East*

London (Doctoral dissertation, Queen Mary University of London), 2013.

Smith, Christian. *What is a Person? Rethinking Humanity, Social Life, and the Moral Good from the Person Up.* University of Chicago Press, 2011.

Sonuga-Barke, Edmund JS, Mark Kennedy, Robert Kumsta, Nicky Knights, Dennis Golm, Michael Rutter, Barbara Maughan, Wolff Schlotz, and Jana Kreppner. Child-to-adult neurodevelopmental and mental health trajectories after early life deprivation: the young adult follow-up of the longitudinal English and Romanian Adoptees study. *The Lancet* 389 (2017): 1539-1548.

Stahl, Garth. *Identity, Neoliberalism and Aspiration: Educating White Working-Class Boys.* Routledge, 2015.

Steinhauer, Paul D. The foster care research project. *American journal of orthopsychiatry* 59 (1989): 430-441.

Steinhauer, Paul D. *The Least Detrimental Alternative.* University of Toronto Press, 2016.

Sternberg, Robert J. Wisdom, *Intelligence, and Creativity Synthesized.* Cambridge University Press, 2003.

Straus, Murray A. and Denise A. Donnelly. *Beating the Devil out of Them: Corporal Punishment in American Families and its Effects on Children.* Routledge, 2017.

Stretton, Simon. Maslow and the modern public servant: A lateral approach to performance and integrity in the public sector work environment. *Australian Journal of Public Administration* 53 (1994): 144-151.

Takaki, Jiro, Toshiyo Taniguch, and Yasuhito Fujii. Confirmation of Maslow's hypothesis of synergy: Developing an acceptance of selfishness at the workplace scale. *International Journal of Environmental Research and Public Health* 13 (2016): 462, online.

Tawney, Richard Henry. *The Radical Tradition: Twelve Essays on Politics, Education, and Literature.* Allen & Unwin, 1964.

Taylor, Eugene. William James and the humanistic implications of the neuroscience revolution. *Journal of Humanistic Psychology,* 50 (2010): 410-429.

Templer, Klaus J. Five-factor model of personality and job satisfaction: The importance of agreeableness in a tight and collectivistic Asian society. *Applied Psychology* 61 (2012): 114-129.

Thompson, Allan. *Media and the Rwanda Genocide*. Pluto Press, 2007.

Timmins, Nicholas. *The Five Giants: A Biography of the Welfare State*. HarperCollins, 2017.

Todorov, Tsvetan. *Memory as a Remedy for Evil* (translated by Gila Walker). Seagull Books, 2010.

Truth and Reconciliation Commission. *Honouring the Truth, Reconciling for the Future. Manitoba*: Manitoba, TRC of Canada, 2015.

Valdesolo, Piercarlo, Andrew Shtulman and Andrew S. Baron. Science is awe-some: The emotional antecedents of science learning. *Emotion Review* 9 (2017): 215-221.

Vincent, Andrew and David Boucher. *T.H. Green, Citizenship as Political and Metaphysical. British Idealism and Political Theory*. Edinburgh University Press, 2006.

Voltaire. *Candide, or Optimism*. Simon and Schuster, 1758/2005.

Waldinger, Robert and Marc S. Schulz. *What Makes a Good Life. Lessons from the Longest Study on Happiness*. Penguin Books, 2015.

Waldinger, Robert and Marc S. Schulz. The long reach of nurturing family environments: Links with midlife emotion-regulatory styles and late-life security in intimate relationships. *Psychological Science* 27 (2016): 1443-1450.

Waldinger, Robert. *The Good Life*. Random House UK, 2023.

Ward, Colin. *The Child in the City*. Bedford Square Press, 1990.

Webb, James T. Dabrowski's theory and existential depression in gifted children and adults. In *Eighth International Congress of the Institute for Positive Disintegration in Human Development*, August, 7-9. 2008.

Wellik, Jerry J. and John H. Hoover. Authentic happiness. *Reclaiming Children and Youth* 13 (2004) 59-60.

Wempe, Ben. *TH Green's Theory of Positive Freedom: From Metaphysics to Political Theory*. Imprint Academic, 2004.

White, Mathew A. and Lea E. Waters. A case study of 'The Good School: Examples of the use of Peterson's strengths-based approach with students. *The Journal of Positive Psychology* 10 (2015): 69-76.

Whitman, Walt. *Walt Whitman's "Song of Myself": A Sourcebook and Critical Edition*. Psychology Press, 2005.

Wiesel, Elie. *Night; Dawn; Day*. Jason Aronson, 1985.

Wiesel, Elie and Eugene Heimler. Beyond survival. European Judaism: A *Journal for the New Europe* 6 (1971): 4-10.

Wilkinson, Matthew L. N. Introducing Islamic critical realism: A philosophy for underlabouring contemporary Islam. *Journal of Critical Realism* 12 (2013): 419-442.

Wilkinson, Matthew L. N. *A Fresh Look at Islam in a Multi-Faith World: A Philosophy for Success Through Education*. Routledge, 2015a.

Wilkinson, Matthew L. N. The metaphysics of a contemporary Islamic Shari'a: A meta-realist perspective. *Journal of Critical Realism* 14 (2015b): 350–365.

Wilkinson, Matthew L.N., Lamia Irfan, Muzammil Quraishi and Mallory Schneuwly Purdie. Prison as a site of intense religious change: The example of conversion to Islam. *Religions* 12 (2021): 162-180.

Wilkinson, Matthew L.N., Muzammil Quraishi, Lamia Irfan and Mallory Schneuwly Purdie. Building on the shoulders of Bhaskar and Matthews: a critical realist criminology. *Journal of Critical Realism* 21 (2022): 123-144.

Willis, Paul. *Learning to Labour: How Working-Class Kids Get Working Class Jobs*. Routledge, 2017.

Wilson, Catherine, Seyyed Hossein Nasr and Oliver Leaman. *History of Islamic Philosophy*. Routledge, 1996.

Wilson, Tom. *His Blood be Upon Us: Completion and Condemnation in Matthew's Gospel*. Ethics International Press, 2022.

Wong, Paul T.P. Meaning-seeking, self-transcendence, and well-being. In *Logotherapy and Existential Analysis*, (311-321). Springer, 2016.

Wong, Paul T.P. Meaning-centered approach to research and therapy, second wave positive psychology, and the future of humanistic psychology. *The Humanistic Psychologist*, 45 (2017): 207, online.

Woodhouse, Patrick. Etty Hillesum: *A Life Transformed*. Continuum Books, 2009

Xyst, Kurt. Constructivism, Dewey, and academic advising. *NACADA Journal* 36 (2016): 11-19.

Yaden, David B. and Andrew Nuberg. *The Varieties of Spiritual Experience: 21st Century Research and Perspectives*. Oxford University Press, 2022.

Young, Loretta and Chris Adam-Bagley, C. Self-esteem, self-concept and the development of black identity: a theoretical overview. In Gajendra Verma & Chris Adam-Bagley (Eds.) *Self-Concept, Achievement and Multicultural Education* (41-59). London: MacMillan, 1982.

Yousafzai, Malala. *We are Displaced: My Journey and Stories from Refugee Girls Around the World*. Weidenfeld and Nicholson, 2019.

Yu, Timothy TF. Sailing away from the Pyramid: A revised visual representation of Maslow's theory Z. *Journal of Humanistic Psychology* (2022): 00221678221074755.

Zachariadis, Markos, Susan V. Scott and Michael I. Barrett. *Exploring Critical Realism as the Theoretical Foundation of Mixed-Method Research*. Cambridge Judge Business School, 2010.

Zakaria, Maheran, and Nur Ain Abdul Malek. Effects of human needs based on the integration of needs as stipulated in Maqasid Syariah and Maslow's hierarchy of needs on zakah distribution efficiency of asnaf assistance business program. *Jurnal Pengurusan (UKM Journal of Management)* 40 (2014): 41-52.

Zamir, Syed Rizwan. Descartes and Al-Ghazālī: Doubt, certitude and light. *Islamic Studies* (2010): 219-251.

Ziller, Robert C. *The Social Self*. Elsevier, 2013.

Ziller, Conrad. Ethnic diversity, economic and cultural contexts, and social trust: Cross-sectional and longitudinal evidence from European regions, 2002–2010. *Social Forces* 93 (2015): 1211-1125.

Index

Absence, in Critical Realism: 37-8, 42-48

Adam, first Prophet: 5, 48, 74, 89-90, 106

Adler, Alfred: 8, 146-7

Adoption of children: 11, 136 (see also Romanian adoptees)

Al-Ghazali, Abu Hamla: 6

Alienation: 24, 34, 36, 38-9, 42-4, 55-7, 66-7, 127, 140

Alderson, Priscilla: 24, 38, 40, 41-6, 52, 57-8, 60-5, 133

Allport, Gordon: 12, 24-5, 29, 31, 184

Anti-Semitism: 74, 76, 117-8, 146, 154

Archer, Margaret: 9, 17-18, 39, 42, 50, 54, 66-7, 133, 158, 165

Arabic language: 78

Armstrong, Karen: 74, 105-5, 116-7, 122, 129

Assimilation of minorities: 101, 103

Autoethnography: 33-70

Awe: 17-18, 39, 42, 50, 54, 60, 66-7, 133. 158, 165

Balbi, Mohammed: 113

Banfield, Grant: 58-60

Bangladesh: 11, 71, 107-110, 131, 134, 142

Baron-Cohen, Simon: 165

Bhaskar, Roy: 14, 17-18, 21. 24, 29, 33-49, 56-59, 66, 114, 132

Behaviourist psychology: 12, 25, 28

Blackfoot Nation: 3, 170-172, 195

Bourdieu: 23, 51-54

Bowlby, John: 30, 136, 149, 185

Bronfenbrenner, Urie: 157, 187

Brothels in Bangladesh: 110

Bruner, Jerome: 2, 9

Buddhism: 27, 56, 49, 104, 184-5

Business: see Management & Organisations

Butler, Judith: 3, 142

Calvinism: 92, 122

Canada, studies: 108, 131, 170, 172

Catholics, theology and ritual: 34, 113, 116, 189

Child abuse, emotional, physical & sexual: 11, 23, 29, 114, 127, 135-138, 142

Child abuse, personality & adjustment: 108, 134, 142

Child adoption: 11, 136 (see also Romanian adoptees)

Child-Centred Humanism: 10-19, 22, 24, 32, 64-70

Child in Islam, prayer at birth: 89-90

Child marriage, Bangladesh & Pakistan: 111-2, 131

Child murder & infanticide in Pakistan: 111

Children, disadvantaged: 185

Children's health: 21, 24, 32, 43, 61, 66, 68-9, 131-3, 137, 141, 159, 175-6, 185-190

Childhood charter: 68

Childhood's history: 24

Children in cities: 11

Children's Rights: 11, 13, 43, 63, 68-70, 150, 171

Christian Gospels, verity: 94, 96, 107, 116, 121, 121, 136

Citizens & Citizenship Education: 2, 9, 13-23, 29, 58-9, 63, 72, 88, 99-107, 119, 126, 139, 143, 150, 161, 169, 174, 176

Coard, Bernard: 58

Cognition & cognitive psychology: 2, 15, 28, 35, 55. 98, 121, 161, 174, 177

Corruption of values: 4, 20-21, 84, 91.105, 108, 110, 140, 142

Creation of the world: 74, 81, 83

Creation of Adam & Hawwa: 97

Creaven, Sean: 36, 60

Cross as symbol: 83, 94-5, 105, 107, 114, 115, 123, 130

Criminal justice: 161-2

Critical Humanism: 155

Critical Realism: 4, 33-70 (see also Dialectical Critical Realism):

Crusades: 75, 118

Dabrowski, Kazimierz: 180-6, 194

Dalits: 112, 131

Daoism: 15, 27, 184

Dawood, N.J. & Qur'an: 87

DeCarvalho, Roy: 9, 12

deMause, Lloyd: 142-3

DeRobartis, Eugene: 15, 29, 173

De Waal, Frans: 150

Descartes, Renee: 5-7, 12, 14, 167

Developmental psychology: 13-5, 69, 137, 140, 173, 181-7, 194

Dialectical Critical Realism: 34-7, 47-9, 52, 56, 61

Dutch: see Netherlands

Ebionites: 84-5, 121-2

Economic inequality: 140 (see also Social class; Socialism; & Marx)

Economic issues: 1, 8, 16, 30-1, 51, 57-8, 67, 108, 111, 140, 157-9, 190-1

Educational issues: 15, 21-27, 43, 46, 51, 58, 61, 65, 73, 97, 131, 149, 151, 174

Educational policies: 22, 60, 98-100

Empathy: 21, 70, 139, 148-150, 153, 155, 181

Engels, Friedrich: 60-1, 67

Erikson, Erik: 14, 24-26, 31, 143, 180-1, 186-7, 194

Esack, Farid: 103, 113, 129

Esposito, John: 11, 113, 123-4

Ethnicity & ethnic minorities: 3, 16, 29-30, 76, 78, 102, 119, 127, 155, 168, 194, 196

Ethnography: 33-4

Eu-Psychia: 21, 30

Eve, first woman: see Hawwa

Evil: 12-14, 18, 32, 63, 89-93, 105. 122-3, 134-1488. 157-162, 170, 193-5

Exegesis of religious texts: 72, 75, 78, 87

Exordium, opening prayer: 81, 89-90

Fiqh of Minorities: 72, 100

Finkelhor, David: 137

Flourishment, of children, humans & nations: 43-7, 68, 107-8, 133-140, 146, 157-160, 196

Forgiveness: 5, 8. 72, 79, 82, 86, 93, 95, 104-6, 186-8

Fox, George: 12, 72-3, 122

Frank, Anne: 145, 155, 165

Frank, Arthur: 12

Frankl, Viktor: 12, 144, 147, 165, 176-7, 188

Free will: 10, 20, 81-3

Freud, Sigmund: 12, 24, 142-3, 149, 186

Gandhi, Mahatma: 162-3

Gates, Bill: 141

Gaza: See Palestine

Gay identity: 73, 79-80, 119

Genocide: 144, 154, 194 (see also Holocaust)

Gergen, Kenneth: 9, 29, 16

Giarretto, Henry: 186

Gibreel (Gabriel), angel: 3, 78

Glass ceiling: 109

Gnostics: 84

Good deeds in Islam & Christianity: 56, 64-5, 74, 81-2, 86, 93, 99, 107, 160, 184-5

Goodness, innate: 4-5, 23, 69, 73, 89-90, 106, 134-152, 160, 194-5

Gramsci: 59

Green, Thomas: 5, 9-10, 16-22, 32, 66-7, 140

Habitus: 51-2, 54, 56

Hadith, sayings of Muhammad: 65, 69, 82, 86-93, 96-100, 106, 120

Happiness studies: 10, 13, 25-32, 181, 190

Harvard longitudinal studies: 181-2

Hawwa (Eve), first woman: 5, 48, 74, 89, 90, 106

Hegel: 17-9, 36, 39, 44, 47, 49. 56, 59

Helping behaviour: 31, 88, 93, 101, 159

Heimler, Eugene: 12, 144-7, 165, 188

Hillesum, Etty: 144-5, 165

Hinduism: 27, 49, 63, 104, 112, 127, 132, 163, 185

Hitler, Adolf: 73, 142, 162

Hobbes, Thomas: 10, 32, 60, 64

Holocaust against Jews: 71, 76, 83, 118, 148-158

Index

Homosexuality: see Gay identity

Hume, David: 10, 120

Human goodness: 141-2, 157, 167, 187

Humanism, principles: 22-7, 31-2, 64-6. 114, 118, 144, 165, 185, 188, 193-5

Humanist psychology: 9, 24, 26-9, 31. 50, 145, 184, 186, 194

Humanist treatment of abuse victims: 11, 186

Huxley, Francis: 32-34

Identity: 7, 10, 35, 42, 45, 47, 54, 71-2, 119, 156, 176, 180-1, 184, 192, 194 (see also Self-Concept)

Intrinsic religiosity: 184-5

Incest taboo: 186

India: 75, 110-2, 131, 142, 153

Indonesia: 78

Integration of minorities: 99, 101-2, 119, 127 (see also Pluralism)

Isa (Jesus), Prophet: 4-5, 46, 73, 84-5, 59, 91, 94-6, 106, 121-4.

Islam & education: 98-100

Islam & tolerance: 85

Islamophobia: 72, 88, 103-6, 122-3, 126-8, 165

Israel: 11, 55, 72. 75, 83, 108, 104, 118, 129-130, 145, 150-4, 165, 195

James, William: 7, 9, 40, 166-7, 189-190

Jesus: see Isa

Jewish ethics & values: 81, 89, 104, 118, 129 (see also Judaism)

Jewish experience of prejudice, pogroms and holocaust: 71, 76, 83, 118, 148-158

Jewish refugees: 72-3, 75, 101, 121, 148

Jewish scholarship: 1, 3, 169

Jews as a minority group: 29, 67, 75, 78, 92, 100-104, 119, 127, 185

Jihad, Muslim: 72, 87-8, 103

Jihad, Quaker: 72, 88

Joseph, Prophet: see Yousef

Judaism: 10-11, 27, 75, 76, 97, 124

Jung, Carl: 8, 143-4, 145

Justice, in Christianity: 1, 19, 27, 45, 118, 143, 154, 178

Justice, in Islam: 1, 19, 27, 124, 126, 178

Justice, in Judaism: 1, 19, 27, 45 115, 143, 178

Kaufman, Scott Barry: 169, 172, 174, 179, 187-190, 194-5

Khan, Badshah: 105, 113, 129, 163

Layard, David: 30

Learned helplessness: 25-29

Lester, David: 179

Light, as spiritual metaphor: 9-13, 45, 52, 72, 88, 92-5,106-7, 114, 132, 134, 152, 162, 167, 187-8, 190

Loevinger, Jane: 180, 186, 194

Long term studies of children & adults: 30, 137, 181-2, 192

Lovelock, James: 48

Marriage, in Bangladesh: 109-112

Marriage, in Pakistan: 112, 131

Marriage, same sex: 73

Malaysia: 78, 119, 183, 185

Management & Organisations: 25, 29, 61, 69, 73, 89, 97, 109-11-, 126, 131, 169-170, 173, 183, 190-191

Marx, Karl: 10, 21, 36, 38-9, 44, 49, 54, 65-7, 132, 191 (see also Engels)

Maryam: 85, 95

Maslow, Abraham: 1, 3, 7, 12-14, 19, 164-195

May, Rollo: 8-10

Media, mass & electronic: 62-63, 69, 155-6

Midgley, Mary: 65, 141, 143

Minority groups: 24, 29, 67, 72, 75-6, 78, 92, 100-104, 126-8, 184-5, 196

Mixed marriages: 102

Morphogenesis & Critical Realism: 4, 17, 21, 32, 42, 52, 65, 68, 133, 140, 158, 165, 184, 193

Mosques, life: 76-100, 111, 132, 168, 195

Muhamad, Prophet: 10, 19, 46, 65, 67, 71, 76,78, 82, 84-91, 95-6, 120-3, 129

Multiculturalism: 78 (see also Minority groups; & Pluralism)

Murder: 4, 108-9, 110

Murder of children: 143, 152, 162

Murder of Jews: 135, 141 (see also Holocaust)

Murder of women: 135, 141

Muslims as minority groups: 29, 67, 69, 72

Muslim tolerance of non-Muslims: 75, 117, 153, 155

Muslim states' tolerance of Jews: 118

Neoliberalism: 23, 57

Netherlands: 71, 76, 128, 138, 144

Non-violence: 27, 72-3.,103, 105, 129, 135, 105 (see also Pacifism)

Norrie, Andrew: 17, 39, 48

Nurses, self-actualization: 192-3

Ontology & Critical Realism: 11, 36, 40, 45-7, 59, 61, 66, 114

Openness-to-Experience personality: 182-3

Optimistic child: 31

Optimism & humanistic psychology: 8, 10, 25-9, 135, 156, 159, 165, 189, 191

Original Sin: 10, 31, 89-90, 94-7, 106, 122-3

Paulite faction: 84-5. 94

Pacifism & peace-making: 5, 36, 74, 105, 138, 153, 157 (see also Non-violence)

Pakistan: 11, 71, 78, 92, 105-8,110-112, 131-4,142, 153, 157, 163

Palestine: 35, 53, 57, 71-2, 97, 107-9, 115, 130, 151-3

Parents & parental care: 2, 12, 19, 22, 28, 31, 69, 74, 127, 135-140, 144, 148-9

Peak Experiences (Maslow): 1, 7, 12, 176-180, 189

Penn, William: 71, 73, 107, 114-5, 130

Personality dis-integration: 181-3

Personality (OCEAN) profiles & Maslow: 179, 182-4

Phenomenology: 14, 24, 58, 182

Physical health in Maslow's schema: 192-3

Play & playfulness, 11-12, 22, 70, 179

Prison policies: 161-2

Prostitution of children & adolescents: 111, 131

Plummer, Ken: 66, 155-7, 162, 165

Pluralism, ideological: 15, 72, 123

Pluralism, social: 76, 86, 102, 123, 126 (see also Minority groups)

Pogroms against Jews: 71, 76, 83, 118, 148-158 (see also Holocaust)

Positive Psychology: 12, 26-32, 157-9,194

Poverty: 21-3 (see also Social Class)

Prophets of Islam, Christianity & Judaism: 76, 83-4, 88-92, 95-6

Psychohistory: 142, 147

Quakerism: 13, 17, 20-25, 45, 69, 71-133

Quakers & business: 73

Quakers & humanism: 24

Quaker Universalism: 77, 82, 116, 122

Qur'an: 85-87

Ramadan, Muslim fasting: 76, 78-9, 82

Ramadan, Tariq: 102-3, 113, 123-4, 126, 129

Rape in Bangladesh & Pakistan: 108-9, 111, 112, 131

Refugees: 67, 100, 108, 129, 149, 151, 171, 182

Reflexive ethnography: 33-4

Reflexivity, of self & others: 10, 17-89, 33-4. 37, 42, 50-56, 66-8, 155

Religious journeys: 113, 184

Rogers, Carl: 7-9, 12-13, 15, 18-25, 31

Romanian adoptees: 136, 147

Rousseau, Jean: 15, 32

Rumi: 107

Rutter, Michael: 126, 136, 147, 149, 174, 186

Said, Edward: 164-5

Scambler, Graham: 10, 34, 43, 51, 66-7

Secular humanism: 14, 195

Secularism: 1, 2, 4, 10-11, 16, 27, 31, 92, 99, 141, 160, 164-5,168, 189, 194-5

Self-actualization: 12, 14-5, 30, 40, 140, 169, 172-6, 179-185, 187-192

Self-compassion: 140, 151

Self-concept: 52, 127, 149, 176 (see also Identity)

Self-esteem: 21, 128, 136-9, 149, 158, 176, 185, 188

Self-narration: 7, 10 (see also Stories)

Self-transcendence: 12-13, 27, 30, 36, 40, 46-50, 56, 64, 72, 105-6, 140-149, 160-1, 169-190, 178-181, 187-185

Seligman, Martin: 9-13, 25-32, 156, 187, 194

Seventh Day Adventists: 102, 168

Shaitan (Satan): 89-90, 115, 134-5

Shari'a law: 71, 92, 109-10, 123. 132

Shipway, Brad: 46-7, 60

Social bonds: 30-31, 159

Social class: 36, 52, 58, 65, 67, 112, 115, 140, 160 (see also Economic issues; Socialism; & Marx)

Social contract: 13, 15-17, 20-21, 32, 68, 100, 104, 126, 150, 159, 166, 169, 194

Social science studies: 5, 10-11, 35-6. 41, 44-5, 56, 61, 107-119, 127, 133, 160, 167., 180, 188

Social structures, value base: 17, 35-7, 42-5, 51, 56, 60, 62, 109, 114, 131, 142, 158, 172, 185

Socialism: 17, 20, 22, 47, 58-9, 64, 191 (see also Economic issues; Marx; & Social class)

Stoning of women, Pakistan: 108, 110, 132

Soul or Spirit: 6, 10, 27, 46, 49, 60, 67-9, 71, 81, 90. 93, 105-6, 114, 122, 132, 135, 162, 165, 180, 187-195

Soul murder: 135

Steinhauer, Paul: 135, 139

Stewardship of nature by Adam & Hawwa: 90, 134

Stories, telling of: 32, 54, 66, 95, 124, 129, 147, 150-1, 154-7, 164-195

Straight Path, in Islam: 10, 67, 81, 83, 86, 89, 107, 117, 123, 134, 165, 183

Sufism: 105-7, 130, 154, 195

Suicide & suicidal behaviour: 94, 111, 131-2, 168, 173, 197, 199

Sunnah of Islam: 19, 65, 82, 92

Terrorism: 104-5, 127

Todorov, Tsvetan: 134, 166

Transcendence of self: 7, 12, 14, 27, 30, 36, 49, 140, 149, 164, 166, 169, 174-9, 193-5

Ubuntu: 29, 64

Under-labouring: 10, 16, 64-5

Ummah of Islam: 77, 80, 97-8, 125

Uniqueness of children: 13

Vincent-de-Paul: 13, 17, 21-2, 66, 162

Wahhabism: 72, 92, 123

Weber, Max: 38

Welfare of citizens: 20-21

Whitman, Walt: 11-12

Wiesel, Elie: 12, 146-7, 165

Willis, Paul: 58

Wilkinson, Matthew: 10, 39-43, 47-9, 60-68, 132

Women's equality: 15, 18, 72, 90, 96-8, 111, 118, 125-6

Work-life balance: 109, 130, 131, 192-3

Yousafzai, Malala: 105, 129, 153

Yousef, Prophet: 95

Zakat, Muslim charity: 64, 76, 79, 109, 161, 183